EVERTON

SUMMER

A Football
Diary

EVERTON WINTER MEXICAN SUMMER

A Football Diary

PETER REID
with Peter Ball

Macdonald
Queen Anne Press

A Queen Anne Press BOOK

© Peter Reid 1987

First published in Great Britain in 1987 by
Queen Anne Press, a division of
Macdonald & Co (Publishers) Ltd
3rd Floor
Greater London House
Hampstead Road
London NW1 7QX

A BPCC plc Company

All photographs courtesy of Bob
Thomas unless otherwise credited.

British Library Cataloguing in Publication Data

Reid, Peter
  Everton Winter Mexican Summer
  1. Reid, Peter   2. Soccer players—Great
  Britain—Biography
  I. Title   II. Ball, Peter, 1943–
  796.334'092'4   GV942.7.R/

  ISBN 0-356-12245-X

Typeset by Acorn Bookwork, Salisbury, Wiltshire
Printed and bound in Great Britain by
Hazell, Watson & Viney,
Aylesbury, Bucks
A Member of the BPCC Group

The first half of 1985 was the most exciting and rewarding of my football career: it was almost one long story of success, as Everton won the Football League Championship and the European Cup Winners Cup, and only just failed to do a historic treble by ending as beaten finalists in the F.A. Cup. I was proud to be a part of that great team, and personally delighted and honoured to be picked as PFA player of the year for my part in it, while at almost 29 I at last achieved my ambition of an England cap. With the World Cup ahead it was a good moment to be chosen. The only cloud on our horizon was the Heysel tragedy in Brussels, which, when we got back from the England trip to Mexico that summer, we discovered meant that Everton were to be denied the opportunity of playing in the European Cup. That was a blow, but after going to see Bruce Springsteen at Wembley and Elland Road – a high-light to almost match winning the League – the season ahead held promise enough. There was the World Cup to look forward to and before that, another exciting season chasing honours with Everton. This diary is the story of that season.

Thursday 11 July

Back to work. Actually we're not reporting back until Monday, but I went in today to do a few laps and ease myself back into things gently. The younger lads say that at my age I probably need to. A few of the others were in – Alan Harper, Ratters (Kevin Ratcliffe), Kevin Sheedy and Gary Stevens. It was good to see them, but it was a sad day too, because it was the day Andy Gray left us. He has signed for Villa, but he is training with us for the moment. We will miss him. As a personality in the dressing-room his contribution to the rise of Everton was enormous. He has got a little bit of magic about him, a great, bubbly, very popular personality, with a great determination as well. He is one of the best players I've ever played with because, allied to his ability, he has this fierce will to win. I shudder to think what he was like when he came down from Scotland at 19 or 20, because even now, when he has got problems with his knees, he is a tremendous asset to have in your side and at your club. Everyone respects and likes him. I get on very well with him off the park, as I think everyone does, and, as I said, he gave the club a tremendous lift when he arrived at a time when we were in the doldrums and only 8,000 people were turning up at Goodison to watch us.

It is a big risk letting him go because Andy had a tremendous influence on the lads on the field as well as off it. I'm a great believer in the adage that 'If you've got a good dressing-room off the field, you've got a chance on the field' and it is a risk the boss has taken; by deciding that Andy is the one to make way for Gary Lineker. I can see his point of view, because there are some great characters at the club anyhow, like John Bailey, but it is a risk and we will just have to see how it works.

5

And it is not the first time he has changed a winning team. After we got things together and reached the League Cup Final and then beat Watford in the F.A. Cup Final in 1984, he bought Paul Bracewell during the summer and then Pat van den Hauwe soon after the beginning of last season. At the time I was a bit surprised, but both worked out brilliantly. I think he was influenced by his own experience at Everton when he was a player, playing in that 1970 championship side, which then won nothing else. That was a terrible let-down for all Everton fans, and I think he is determined to see that it doesn't happen this time. And you look at Liverpool, which everyone has to do because they've had so much success for so long, but which is an even stronger influence for us, because they are our neighbours, and what they've done is to keep on strengthening the squad. And that is what Howard is doing. He's spent £800,000 on Gary Lineker, £250,000 on Paul Wilkinson, £100,000 on Bobby Mimms, the England Under-21 keeper from Rotherham, so he is trying to continue the success now that we've got something to build on. You always need to improve areas if you think they can be improved, because that is the only way to stay ahead of the game, and that is what a manager has to do. He has to be ruthless and say, 'Thanks very much for all you've done for us, but now we want to try something else, so that's it. Good luck'.

And I can see the point of changing the side a little. Andy did do a great job for us, and you could never criticise his contribution, but in the F.A. Cup Final, I thought we actually needed a bit more pace at the front, so that we could play the ball over the top. It hadn't really been exposed through the season, but I felt that that match, where they pushed up on us, did show that we were a bit lacking in that area. That was a personal opinion, and possibly the boss had the same idea and so has brought in Gary, who certainly has the pace.

If Andy's departure was sad, the sight of Adrian Heath back running provided a silver lining. I told him he'd got a limp, but he really looked very good after the knee injury which kept him out most of last season.

On Mondays during the season we have two laps warming up. The slowest laps imaginable, but Andy and I were always at the back, 20–30 yards behind, and Inchy used to give us terrible stick. 'What's up with you two old men?' that sort of stuff. And we always used to say, 'You wait until you get a serious injury, then you'll know what it's like'. Then he did, so when we went to see him in hospital, he laughed and said, 'You two wished this on me'. Now he's back, and Andy's going.

Monday 15 July

The first day back. Well, for all of us except Gary Lineker! Our new signing is missing the first two days because he's still on holiday. So he'll get some stick when he does show up!

6

It was a typical first day, catching up with all the summer gossip, all the holidays we'd had, and things we'd done. Those of us who went on the England trip to Mexico had missed the club tour to Magaluf and the celebrations there for winning the League and the European Cup Winners Cup last season, so the rest were winding us up about that and all the fun they'd had while we were being put through it in Mexico. By the end I almost felt jealous – almost, because I wouldn't have swapped the trip to Mexico for anything. I fulfilled my greatest personal ambition, which was to play for England, when I went on as substitute against Mexico and then played the game against West Germany, and I want more of it. I think I appreciated it all the more because the honours, like our club successes, have come late in my career, but I enjoyed every minute of it, and I'm still hungry for more. It really gave me a target for this season, to keep my place so I can play in the World Cup. To pull on an England shirt and go out and play for your country is just the best thing that has ever happened to me. Everything about it was tremendous, and knowing that I've only got a short time left in my career, I'm determined I'm going to make the most of it.

It was an interesting trip as well. I thought that it was very successful as a fact-finding mission, which was the object of the exercise. I felt it was very informative, but it did not do anything to shake my conviction that the England team must play the English way. Obviously you have to modify things a bit in Mexico to take account of the conditions, but I still believe that we can apply the basics of our game, even if we do have to play in bursts out there, rather than flat out all the time. We are always too ready to knock the English game, and not recognise the qualities we have. We have had great success in Europe at club level playing our way, and I don't think that playing international football is that different. Personally I know the only way for me to play is my natural game, which I play for Everton. When I got my first cap I was determined to enjoy it, and I'd always said that the best way to ensure that I enjoyed it was to play like I do for my club, which was what I did. My job at Everton is to tidy up, and play simple balls, and that was what I tried to do for England. And playing with Glenn Hoddle and Bryan Robson in midfield I just sat in the hole, so that if those two got caught out I could hold things up if the other side tried to break on us, so it gave them the freedom to go forward and to get on the ball and play. I thought it worked quite well, although I'm not sure about the balance with only three in midfield.

I'm sure that if it's right for me personally to play the way I do for the club, it's also right for the team to play the way we do at club level. One of the great fallacies in international football to my mind is keeping possession as the main target. Of course you don't give the ball away, but we've won loads of trophies in international club football by keeping defences under pressure, and by pressurising teams when they're in possession. Of course Liverpool are great when they are in possession, but they aren't bad when they haven't got the ball either. They pressure teams constantly as a group, they win the ball back in the other team's half a lot by doing that, and it works well for them.

People say you can't do that against top international players, but I think you can. Against Tottenham last season, which was a really important match, because they were still pressing us really closely at that stage, I remember one instance clearly. Ossie Ardiles got the ball on the edge of their box. And we closed in on him. And he turned, and he turned again, and at the end he had five of us breathing down his neck. And you can't find anyone with better control than him, he has brilliant ability, and he ended up trying to hit it back to Ray Clemence and put it out for a corner. There was this World Cup footballer, one of the brilliant players of his generation, panicked into giving away a corner, because we put him under so much pressure. It's a great asset if you can do that without the ball, and I think all the good sides, the sides that win things, have that ability.

In the European Cup Winners Cup semi-final last season, we played Bayern Munich. They've got some technically brilliant players. People like Augentheiler and Matthaus are brilliant if you give them time on the ball, but if you don't give them time, they are vulnerable like everybody else. And that was what we did at Goodison and in Munich, and in the end our football came out on top, we were able to play and they weren't. I think everyone would concede that we are a good team and play good football, but physical endeavour and shutting people down is as important as the other side of it, and that is what we are brought up on because of the nature of the English game and the English winter.

People say that you can't do that in Mexico, because of the altitude and the heat. You have to pace it and do it in bursts, but I think you can do it if you do it as a team, and drop off and let them come at you, and then all go in together, and I think an England team that does its own thing together can be successful.

The other thing though is that we are now getting to the stage where we ought to have a settled team. I was delighted to get in to the squad, delighted, but I think that we've reached the point where Mr Robson has got to say 'This is my best side' and play it together as often as possible. I do believe that it is settled sides which win things.

A great gesture by the Supporters' Club. When we went in for training, we discovered it was their Player of the Year do in the evening, so we all went off to that. And they had given the award to everyone, which is a novel idea, and a very good one, because we had our success as a team, and the award recognised that. We had a really good evening.

If anything, our success last season meant even more to our supporters than it did to us, because they have lived with Liverpool's constant victories even longer than most of us have. I think the rivalry in Liverpool is one reason why we won't be just a one season wonder like some of the other teams who've won the championship, because having Liverpool across the park is a permanent reminder that we have to keep on doing it, we can't just rest on our laurels. To be a great team we have to forget about what we've done and go and do it again. My dad still lives in Liverpool, and if I go and have a drink with him, the Liverpool supporters in the pub will all say, 'You've only got to win everything for the next fourteen years to catch up with us' and things like that, which really brings you down to earth, so I don't think there's much danger of us being complacent. We know we will have them breathing down our necks, because they don't like us beating them, while we do like it, and the knowledge that they will be all out to get back on top in the city is a great motivator. We've been denied the chance of winning the European Cup, so we'll just have to try and win everything at home.

Our pre-season at Everton is different class. We hardly do any running – no long running or strenuous running. Basically everything is done with the ball, and you get your running in that way. Of course these days you only get four–six weeks off, not like in the past when they got nearly three months, so you don't have time to get out of condition, so you don't need so much physical slog. Ian Greaves at Bolton was pretty good about doing most of the work with the ball, but the thing which distinguishes our training at Everton is that we enjoy it so much we don't notice just how much work we are doing.

The heart of it is competition. We're split into groups of five, each with a captain – Richo's Raiders, Ratcliffe's Rheumatics, Bertie's Body-builders (Alan Harper's team), Bailey's Bootleggers, Southall's Softies, and my team Reid's Ragmen. All the senior players put in a fiver, with the young lads paying £2.50, and the team which wins gets the pot. You compete against one another in a range of exercises and skills keeping the ball up between the team, heading to one another, things like that. We were against Bertie's Bodybuilders today, working with Mick Heaton. All his exercises are to do with the ball, quite ingenious, so you are working without realising it, but the thing is you aren't stiff the next day, you come in eager to start training again.

It's also pretty good for the young lads, although they would probably disagree because the tests are quite demanding. While you are doing your tests the other team are watching, and if you do anything wrong you get slaughtered. And of course for a young lad it can be quite a pressure to have people taking the mickey, and so they made more mistakes, but that is part of football, and it breaks them in nicely. It's an initiation into the group, and a preparation for the rigours to come.

After the games, we have a cup of tea and then do some running – about 20 minutes at three-quarter pace, so it doesn't kill you. Again you go off with one of the other teams, while the rest are playing head-tennis or passing a ball in a circle. And that's it for the day. One hears horror stories about the training they do at some clubs. I've been lucky, in that throughout my career I've never been really killed during pre-season, but I must say that the training at Everton is tremendous. And it certainly works for us too – we've never been found wanting for stamina, or fitness.

Tuesday 16 July

The competition is hotting up. The Bodybuilders and the Ragmen were on 'The Running Order' today with Graham Smith, the youth team coach; running with the ball under close control through a series of beacons and other such exercises against the clock. You actually do quite a lot of hard work, but because you are so involved in trying to beat the record time and trying to beat the times of the other team, you don't realise it, it just drifts by without you noticing.

After that, and our cup of tea, we played five-a-sides interspersed with the 15 minute lap round Bellefield, again nothing flat out, just something to get your lungs going. The five-a-sides are restricted, with strictly no tackling and no long balls, just something to start your kicking muscles working.

Andy Gray rang while I was out. He told Barbara he was absolutely shattered, he couldn't believe the training they were doing – he said it was one of the hardest pre-seasons he had ever had.

Shoot rang up offering a contract to do a weekly column. It's not the same rewards as doing one for a national daily, but I think the idea of doing things for a kids' magazine is always interesting, so we are in the process of sorting something out.

Wednesday 17 July

The last day of our competition. I've got a sneaking feeling that Bertie's Bodybuilders might be the team to beat. They've had the better of us over the last couple of days, and they did well again today. We were with Colin Harvey and Terry Darracott on another skill test; the ball is thrown in and you have to volley it 20 yards to a partner who hits it back, rotating positions.

Mark Higgins is one of the Bodybuilders along with Trevor Steven, Adrian Heath and their young lad, Mike Brookes. Mark was Club Captain, and he was told he had to finish through injury just when we

10

started to get things together. He'd been at Everton all his career. I was out for over a year with an injury when I was at Bolton, so I can imagine what he has been going through. He was a good, strong player, and it makes you aware of how lucky you are when you see someone like that cut down at what should have been the height of his career. He has stood up to it remarkably well, and I just hope that his testimonial year proves a success. We had 17 000 to watch a Manchester v Merseyside game, and the lads have really rallied round and given all the help they can, as you would expect, so hopefully he will get a few bob.

For the moment I think he is just trying to keep up his general fitness, doing a wee bit of training with us. Funnily enough he looks quite good, as if he could still play.

After training the lads went off to our annual cricket match over in Wallasey. I love cricket, but I didn't play because I was feeling a bit stiff, a few twinges in my achilles tendon and in the groin. Nothing serious, I think it's just a reaction to the hard grounds at this time of year.

Gary Lineker turned up today! Nice of him, we thought. John Bailey went up to him, shook hands, and said 'I'll bet you're well pleased aren't you, meeting me? One of the high-lights of your career'. Typical Bails, and Gary didn't know whether to take him seriously or start laughing. He'll get used to it.

Coming into a new dressing-room can be difficult at some clubs, but if you've got a happy dressing-room it makes it much easier, new players just fit in immediately. I think Paul Wilkinson and Mimmsy found they just blended in straightaway, and it seems it will be like that for Gary. He had a head-start, because he knew Paul Bracewell, Trevor Steven, Gary Stevens and me from the Mexico trip, and we obviously started talking about that, and it quickly seemed as if he'd been there for ages instead of just arrived.

He couldn't believe the training. When we were getting dressed afterwards he could not believe that we had finished. He said that at Leicester they would still be running round, so I think he quite enjoyed that.

Obviously I've played against him a few times, but I got a better chance to appreciate him on the tour playing with him. I'd always known that he had pace, but what impressed me about him is that he has got tremendous power as well. He can hold the ball up under pressure, and he is one of those players whom nothing can get down. He'll always keep trying to do the right thing, so he will keep scoring goals. People say he misses chances, but he is always there to get them. I think one of his greatest assets is that he doesn't worry about missing chances.

As I suspected, Alan Harper's team were the winners when the results were published. Reid's Ragmen (Ian Atkins, Garry Marshall, Colin Walsh and Nick Lunden) came third, which was quite respectable. I didn't really fancy our chances at the start. We were a bit disappointed of course . . .

Instead of the competition, we're having games. Nothing stupid, no tackling, just a question of getting your legs working and getting a feel of the ball. But, as always happens every year, as soon as you see a ball in an eleven-a-side, the lads want to try and take people on. The gaffer and Colin Harvey are there shouting 'just play it', 'take it easy' as everyone gets caught up in it.

I had a discussion with the boss and my solicitor about the possibility of my signing a new contract. My old one has a year to run, so we were just having some initial talks. Then I went down to Goodison and met Andy. He wouldn't tell me what he was doing but I think he must have been picking up some money. I'm not sure, but he had a big smile on his face and a big briefcase with him. Then we went into Liverpool and had an Italian meal – Italian food is my passion. I love pasta, and used to eat it constantly – now, of course, it's become part of an athletes' diet, which is no hardship for me.

We swapped stories about pre-season. He said his was proving a little bit harder than ours. Their only light day had been today, when they'd gone for a swim and then been told they could have the rest of the day off. I told him we were doing the usual – Nothing! Then we got on to last season's exploits. I think we both got a few goose pimples thinking about the games we'd had over the last year and the experiences we had shared and of course the trophies. The only thing wrong was the F.A. Cup Final. The defeat in that still rankles for both of us. We're quite similar in character – not the best of losers. I don't think I shall ever get over that, having the treble so close, and I don't think he will either. That apart we had a great time.

Friday 19 July
I'm still feeling my groin and achilles tendon, so I didn't train, I finished early. We are now on a five-a-sides competition, again on a fiver a head, and I had to miss the last game. We were doing quite well in the competition until then – won three, drawn one. It would be nice to win it, because I've a feeling I shall be skint by the end of pre-season at the rate we're chucking fivers in.

The contract with *Shoot* was confirmed. I'm doing alternate weeks with Ian Rush.

We've got the weekend off. The gaffer said we'd all worked hard.

12

He also told us that we are going to Canada for two games on the 29th. We were supposed to go there at the end of last season, but with our build up of matches, we still had league matches to play after the Cup Final, we couldn't fit it in. I thought it was a long way to go for a pre-season tour, but with Europe out because of the ban there's not much else available. And the gaffer is usually right, so we'll see.

Saturday 20 July
I spent the day with my feet up, taking it easy, and watching the Benson & Hedges final on TV. Leicestershire won.

Sunday 21 July
Slightly more active, as I had a squash match, although as I was resting my groin and achilles I had to take it easy. Ken Heathcote, who comes from Bolton, does a lot of charity work. It was his fiftieth birthday, so he ran 50 miles, lifted 50lb weights for 50 minutes and then played five games of squash all for a children's charity. He had Des Drummond, the Leigh rugby player, Ann Hobbs, the tennis player and Jill Warwick from badminton to play him. Des is struggling a bit with his ankle, so I said I'd take him to see our physio, John Clinkard, who is excellent. I talked to Ann about the difference between playing individual sports and team ones, which was quite interesting. She said tennis is a lonely occupation sometimes and she'd quite like to be involved in a team.

I think Ken doing that was really fantastic. I was also pleased when I got home to see Sandy Lyle win the Open.

Monday 22 July
Louise's birthday. We had a quiet day with her – she's having a party tomorrow.

The usual training: five-a-sides. I'm pleased to say we won the competition, so I got some money back: a nice little bonus.

There was the usual transfer speculation in the papers this morning, which we chatted about. One story was that Villa want Paul Walsh to link up with Andy in exchange for Stevie McMahon. I certainly wouldn't be surprised to see Stevie Mc go to Anfield, because I know Kenny is a great admirer of him, and he might help fill the gap Liverpool have had since Graeme Souness left.

Tuesday 23 July
Training was a bit hectic – we had a progressive lap as well as five-a-sides. You run a length, then jog the rest of the lap, then two lengths and jog the rest, then three and so on until at the finish you run the whole lap.

13

I'm still feeling my achilles and the groin. I always feel my achilles in pre-season – I think it's the hard ground, so I'm not too concerned about it. I did the groin against Rapid Vienna in the European Cup Winners Cup Final, so I felt it in the F.A. Cup Final, and all the time in Mexico. So it's hung over me for some time, and it is actually concerning me more than the achilles at the moment. So my training is just a question of me ticking over, and giving my achilles as much protection as possible.

It was Louise's party today. Thousands of kids around, so I stayed out of the way for most of the day.

Wednesday 24 July
A game of possession, shooting practice and then a run in the afternoon.

A fun evening. Met up with Gary Bailey and Paul Walsh to do our bit on 'Play The Game' – a record asking the fans to do just that. Having heard it when it was played back, I don't think we've got the three best voices in the world, but it's amazing what they can do with their equipment in recording studios, so perhaps they'll be able to make us sound like George Michael or Rod Stewart by the time they've finished with it. We're only part of it – I think Andy Gray is involved in London, along with Steve Perryman, Graham Rix and John Hollins. It's got a good, catchy tune – it was written by the people who wrote 'Matchstalk men' – so I hope it goes well. Peter Reid Pop Star!

Thursday 25 July
A full-scale game for the first time – half an hour each way, and no tackling. Just a game for ticking over really. On Saturday we've got a friendly with Wigan, which will be a bit more serious. Gary Lineker played up front with Graeme Sharp, which was the only change from last season. We looked quite sharp, so did Inchy for the opposition. He is buzzing a bit. At the moment he is just happy to be back running about and feeling part of things again. It was a bad injury, and some people thought it might finish him. Knowing his determination, I knew he would be back. Knowing his determination, he is going to get back in the side at some stage, and then he will take some shifting. Sharpy and Gary know they will be under pressure from him, and it is always good to have players like that in the club. But for the moment after eight months out, he is just enjoying playing, training and getting involved in things.

When Paul Wilkinson is fit again there will be more pressure on the strikers' positions. He's got a back injury at the moment, so we haven't seen much of him. In fact Colin Harvey says he is Lord Lucan in disguise, because no one sees anything of him, but we're sure he's still around.

My groin stood up to the game quite well. It's still a wee bit stiff, and so is my achilles tendon. It's just a matter of keeping going and hoping it will just drift away.

Spoke to Frank Worthington, who I played with at Bolton – he's just become player-manager of Tranmere Rovers. Delighted he's got a job. I keep trying to imagine him in boardrooms up and down the country in his Elvis Presley jackets.

I think it will be good for the game, because he is an entertainer, and I'm sure his side will play entertaining football. I was very fortunate to play with him at Bolton. He and players like Tony Dunne, Willie Morgan and Peter Thompson had a big influence on me as a young player. I think I benefited a lot from playing with them – very talented, good pros who looked after themselves and provided some good early examples. Tony Dunne was very quiet, but he helped me a lot, pulling me into positions, teaching me things on the field.

I was pleased to hear Frank has taken George Mulhall with him to Tranmere. He was Ian Greaves's assistant manager at Bolton, a tremendous thinker about the game. He had great knowledge of the game, he helped me a lot, and I have a lot of respect for him. It means Frank has someone experienced with him, and I think it's a very good appointment. I hope they do well.

Saturday 27 July
I went in in the morning to have a bath and loosen myself up a bit, then watched the reserves play Tranmere. We won 4-2. Adrian Heath scored a great goal – he brought it down with his back to goal on the right-hand side of the box, turned one feller, beat another and bent it in off the post, which is his trademark. He is looking quite good – it'll take him a couple of games to be ready, but he is definitely on his way.

Frank and George were there with Tranmere. I called Frank 'boss', which gave him a laugh. He must be the best-dressed manager in the Football League with all his modern clothes.

Then on to Wigan. They had had some success with a good run at the end of last season, culminating in winning the Freight Rover Trophy at Wembley, so they were buoyant; there was a crowd of 4500, and so they had a go and it was a tough game. We won 4-1, and played some good stuff considering it was our first competitive game. I just got through it. I was still feeling my groin and my achilles, and I can't say I really enjoyed it. I enjoyed watching the lads though, because they were doing most of the work and knocking it about a bit. The passing was tremendous, and we did have Wigan chasing shadows a bit with the quality of our football. Gary Lineker scored one goal and set up Paul Bracewell for another, but funnily enough he missed the best chance of the lot, a tap-in from about a yard. He took a bit of stick afterwards, but he said, 'Well, it wasn't the first I've missed, and it won't be the last', which was the end of story. He doesn't worry about missing, which is the perfect attitude for a striker.

I had a drink in the evening with Adrian Heath and Paul Walsh.

Sunday 27 July
Getting ready to go to Canada tomorrow, so I took Barbara and Louise out for an early Italian meal, and had an early night.

Spoke to Terry Curran on the phone. He is now at Huddersfield. I think he'll do quite well for them. He was a bit unlucky with injuries at Everton. He is a great character, with tremendous ability, but I don't think he has fulfilled his dreams even though he has played under some of the great managers.

Toronto. Monday 28 July
We had to be at Manchester Airport by 6.30 for the shuttle to London to connect with a nice eight hour flight to Toronto. I'm not a great traveller – the nice was used ironically. We've come for a week, so we will only be back for four days before we go down to London to play the Charity Shield, and I'm not sure how we'll cope with the jet lag.

It was a typical flight – tedious. Hanging around hotels, waiting in airports, all the normal part of travelling. And one abnormal hold up – John Bailey was stopped at Customs in Toronto, which delayed things longer. We were stuck at the airport for an hour, then we went without him. Of course we slaughtered him when he turned up.

You are asked if you have any convictions coming through customs. Bails said 'Yes, drinking and driving' and was promptly whisked aside for interrogation. Of course anyone else would have said 'No' as we told him afterwards, but John is that type of character. He likes talking to people and was probably just being friendly – and they stopped him. He said he panicked a wee bit. The boss stayed on with him.

It was a bit of light relief. The lads were all flying around calling him 'jailbird' and generally taking the mickey when he turned up.

There's a five hour time difference, but we were a bit tired, so it was just a question of having a meal and going to bed.

Tuesday 29 July
I'm still feeling both my injuries a wee bit, so I don't expect to play on Wednesday. That's disappointing, but that's the way it goes, I suppose.

The lads trained quite hard – a session of 'keep ball' with two teams.

16

I had a light session with John Clinkard the physio. I've been seeing quite a bit of him over the last few days! He is a good physio – I think the job he's done on Adrian Heath is tremendous. Obviously Inchy had good surgery, but I think the physio deserves a pat on the back as well.

Bails had to pull out of training. He's got a groin strain. That just about sums up his trip. I told him it was psychological – he is really afraid of going to jail.

Still felt a bit tired after the flight, but it was interesting to have a walk round Toronto. It is a bustling city. Our hotel is just off Young Street, which looks a bit like Soho in parts, so it felt like an end of season tour rather than a serious pre-season trip at one stage.

Dave Byrne, the son of Budgie Byrne, came up to watch us train. He had a trial with Everton earlier in the year, now he's playing over here and said he would be playing against the lads tomorrow.

Ionics 1 Everton 1   **Wednesday 31 July**
I think it was their Cup Final. It was a tough game. They were bombing a bit, a tough side to play against. Nev had to make a couple of good saves, because they had a couple of good chances. We weren't bombing like they were, weren't bombing into the tackles they were going into. The boss said we had to get our running in but not to do anything daft, and that was essentially how we played it. It was a good training game for us, a good physical workout. The pitch was on the heavy side, which didn't help our passing movements, but Sharpy looked sharp up front – Gary Lineker and Gary Stevens didn't play – and the pre-season is coming on well.

I still have reservations about Canada though. It is a bit of a long way to come for a training game. I assume that the club was guaranteed some money to come, and with the UEFA ban on games in Europe they thought it was better than nothing. And I was amazed at how many Britons there were watching.

It was Nev's first game since he had a knock on his elbow. He was as brilliant as ever, he clearly hasn't lost anything. His importance to us is vital. There were times last season when he was the difference between us getting three points and one or none. If you look at any successful side, they always have a good keeper – Peter Shilton for Nottingham Forest when they were winning things, Ray Clemence for Liverpool.

I didn't play, obviously. I just did a little light training in the morning. Nothing strenuous.

17

Thursday 1 August

The lads had the day off. Those of us who didn't play just had a light session. I had a massage – my groin is still a bit sore.

Then we went to see Niagara Falls. A good experience. I think all the lads enjoyed it. It makes you appreciate being a footballer, knowing you get to visit sights like that all over the world as part of the job, while other people have to pay a lot of money to get to them. It's not a bad life.

Friday 2 August

It can be a frustrating one though. My groin felt a lot easier, but I was feeling my achilles a bit more. So it is a matter of taking it easy again, which is beginning to get to me. This morning I was doing light running, while the lads were working hard with the ball – everything at Everton is done with the ball – and I was a wee bit envious watching them train. Coming to Canada and not being able to play or even to train properly is frustrating, because it is an important part of the season. What you do in pre-season is very important, and I'm not being able to prepare properly. I'm beginning to get bored with it – in fact it's driving me mad, but there is nothing you can do but be patient, as I keep telling myself.

We had a 12 o'clock curfew tonight. The gaffer is great on tours like this. He doesn't regiment you, he treats you like adults, and trusts you not to let him down. And because he puts his faith in us, we respond. We will have a few drinks, but it is all very low key. We do look after ourselves.

Saturday 3 August

Again I had to take it easy in training, which is very frustrating, but it is just something I have to put up with, however reluctantly. I'm itching to play, but if you try and push it, it can set you back even further.

There's a game tomorrow so the curfew was brought forward to 11 p.m. For a change I went out for a Chinese meal with Paul Bracewell, Adrian Heath, Ian Atkins and Kevin Ratcliffe.

Canada 0 Everton 1   Sunday 4 August

The lads trained in the morning and then went on to the game. The pitch had long grass again, which makes a lot more difference than you might think, and the game was similar to the previous one – a fitness exercise. Gary Lineker got the goal. He got on the end of a flick-on by Graeme Sharp, and as usual his pace took him clear and he tucked it away very well.

Afterwards we went to a function with the Canadian team. The Ionics

18

team, our opponents from Wednesday, were there too, and it was quite enjoyable, spoilt only by the thought of the flight home tomorrow. I'm not looking forward to that, especially with the Charity Shield less than a week away.

Before that, there's a game at Crewe on Wednesday night, which I'm hoping to play in, to see if I'm fit for Wembley. In fact I'm desperately keen to play in it. I need all the preparation I can get with the new season approaching fast. I do think it is important to be ready when the season starts, and that means being properly prepared.

Tuesday 6 August

We travelled home through the night, and I actually got home at lunchtime. I always find flying very tiring, and this time was no exception. It's always good to get home though and have a good cup of tea and see Barbara and Louise – these are always the plus sides of coming home from a trip away. I spent the rest of the day sleeping. I'm still hoping to be able to play at Crewe tomorrow – it says something about a footballer's life that three months ago I was looking forward to playing two Cup Finals in a week. Now playing at Crewe tomorrow is my current ambition.

Wednesday 7 August

I played for an hour, and it went all right. I went to the training ground and had a loosener, and although my achilles was still a bit sore, my groin felt all right, so I was able to play. And I survived OK. My achilles still felt sore, but there was no reaction from my groin, which was positive.

I'm still a bit worried about not having played a proper full match. I took it easy against Wigan, and again tonight. This is hardly the ideal preparation for going into the Charity Shield. I don't feel at my fittest.

It was quite a powerful reserve side we fielded in this match: Ian Atkins, John Bailey, Bobby Mimms, Alan Harper and Adrian Heath all played. Ian Marshall played up front with Inchy. I think he's got a chance of becoming a good player. He's tall and gangly, but he's got tremendous pace and he uses it well. He can play up front or at the back. He's definitely got a chance.

Inchy scored with another bender. He took it up to a defender and curled it past him into the top corner. A great goal.

He is playing really well at the moment, and it is really pleasing to see him doing so well. I was also pleased for his Dad and his Uncle Tony, who were there. His Dad watches him everywhere, and they were really worried when he got injured, so it is good to see them watching again and knowing that he is going to be back without any problems.

19

He's now got three goals in four games, so he is progressing all the time. I think it will take him 10 games, maybe 20, to get his real sharpness back, but he's looking good.

I went in for a bath and a bit of treatment on the achilles. We ran through all our dead-ball routines, which we were very successful with last year. Obviously they will change a little with Gary Lineker replacing Andy, but they will still be based on Kevin Sheedy's left foot, which is deadly at dead-ball kicks. I'm involved in them with him, but I'm just the dummy while he does what he wants with his left foot. I can't argue with that. I haven't seen many better left foots than his. You can compare it with Brady's and Rixy's. Muhren's is brilliant, he chips balls onto a sixpence at any angle, but I think Kevin has more power in his than any of the other three, he hits great long shots as well as having the ability to dink it in.

I'm still sleeping at funny times through the jet lag. I'll fall asleep at 5.30 p.m. and wake up at 11.30 p.m., and then find it difficult to get back off to sleep. It's just a matter of time before it settles down, but it always seems worse coming from America than going out there. Perhaps because when you come home, you are trying to fit back into your normal settled routine and can't seem to, while going the other way the routine is not established, so you adapt that to your body clock more.

Overall the lads are looking sharp. We're all looking forward to Wembley again. You never become blasé about playing there, and it's always a great experience to start the season off with the Charity Shield.

Last year against Liverpool was really memorable, and quite important. Obviously we had come there with a good record behind us. We had won the Cup, and from January had been possibly the most consistent side in the country. But Liverpool were there as Champions, and to go to Wembley and beat them 1-0, and deserve to, gave the lads a lot of confidence for the season. Mind you, we then went and lost our first two league matches, so you wonder how significant it was – perhaps it just gave us over-confidence!

I've only ever been on the losing side against Liverpool once – that was in the Milk Cup Final in 1984, which was the first sign that we were emerging as a power. And we were a bit unlucky in that game. I think the signs were that we had been catching them up all the time, and in the Charity Shield I think we showed what a good side we were, not just by beating them, which we deserved to, but by the way we played. It was Paul Bracewell's debut, and I think we fitted in well together. And psychologically the result was important for us, because Liverpool obviously had been the number one team, and we had gone there and done the business against them. This game might be less significant, but it will be interesting, because Manchester United are the team who stopped us doing the treble. Most of the lads were disappointed at the way we played in the Final. It will give us a bit of revenge if we beat them on Saturday, although it won't compensate for not winning the Final. I think that was something which took a lot of getting over for most of the lads.

We had played Rapid Vienna in the final of the European Cup Winners Cup on the Wednesday, so we got home in the early hours of Thursday morning. We were confident. We had two legs of the treble under our belts with the League and the Cup Winners Cup already won, and we had played United three times that year without seeing anything really to fear. We had beaten them twice and drawn the other, and looked the better side on all three occasions.

But on the day we didn't do it. We weren't at our sharpest. I would have liked to have had a week's rest before the game. And, if we had kept it to 0-0, which looked likely, and had to go back for a replay on the Thursday I'd have fancied us. But that's history. On the day they were the better side in the end, and deserved to win it. It was a great goal by Norman Whiteside. I've watched it a few times, and I'm not sure that Nev had quite the right position, but how can you criticise a keeper who has been the best in the country throughout the season? You just have to hold up your hand and say we were beaten by a great goal.

Funnily enough, it felt as if we were the better side until the unfortunate incident with Kevin Moran. Unsurprisingly, having been involved in what was the first ever sending off in an F.A. Cup Final, that is something I get asked about rather a lot. I know Kevin, I've had a drink with him occasionally, he isn't the malicious type, and I don't think he meant to do me. So I don't think he deserved to get sent off, but I thought the referee was unfortunate to get pilloried for it in the way he was. He was there, he had to make an instant decision on what he saw without benefit of slow motion play-backs from several angles. It is easy for managers and players and people in TV boxes to say he is wrong, but he is the man who has to make the decision. But I suppose one of the beauties of our football is that everyone has got an opinion. As I saw it, I intercepted the ball from Paul McGrath and was going for goal. I got a touch on it, and Kevin was coming in. I saw Andy to my left and Graeme Sharp to my right, so I knew if I got to it we were through. I did get there first and touched it on before Kevin, but then he arrived and hit me. And the next thing I knew he had been sent off.

But it seemed the spur they needed, because when he went off they got into it. And there were a lot of tired legs on our side. I felt OK personally, but I think it affected quite a few of the lads, because as well as playing in another final on the Wednesday, we'd played four league matches in seven days before that, which is not the ideal preparation. That's the price of success in English football; you have to live with it.

They had decided to play us as tight as possible at the back, to really squeeze us in that area. And with the greatest respect to Andy and Sharpy, we didn't have the pace to play the ball over the top and stretch them. To do that we had to rely on our wide men, Trevor Steven and Kevin Sheedy, and on the day we didn't get much joy there. So it was just a case of plugging away. I might have scored early on. Bailey came to punch a long throw or a corner, I forget which, and it fell to me. I hit it, saw it go past him, and from my angle it was going in, but John Gidman just stretched to get a touch on it and deflect it onto a post. The merest of touches on his studs! But they are the sort of things which win games, and that probably did win it for United. And it was good defending by a full-back in the right position.

I thought we were the more likely to score off a dead-ball kick, but it didn't come.

After the game Paul Bracewell and I were driven from Wembley to join the England party at Luton. We got to the hotel, and to our surprise there was a party in full swing – for United fans! They enjoyed it! We had a few drinks and tried to forget about it. It's not nice losing in Cup Finals, but if you play any sport you have got to learn how to lose. Providing you can say you have given everything you can still hold your head up, and it didn't cloud a great season.

Friday 9 August

We travelled down to the Bell House, where we always stay. That sounds as if we are at Wembley the whole time, and it is beginning to feel a bit like that. We have stayed there a few times now. I spent the journey down with ice on my achilles as a last-minute precaution.

The phone in my room, which I share with Paul Bracewell, my regular room-mate these days, wasn't working. So I used Inchy's. I hadn't any money to pay for them, and he was going mad as the calls kept mounting up.

Afterwards I popped into the room shared by Kevin Ratcliffe and Kevin Sheedy. Ratters was winding Sheeds up about his performance in the Cup Final. He said that Gidman was bringing an alarm clock to Wembley tomorrow set to wake him up at 4.40 after another easy afternoon. Sheeds just smiled and told Ratters to get his own house in order.

I'm not sure that the preparations have been right for this game. We'll find out tomorrow.

Everton 2 Manchester United 0   **Saturday 10 August**
Woke up to that lovely feeling you get when you are playing at

Wembley. We really want to do ourselves justice, because we didn't in the Final.

We had our usual morning. We always go for a ten-minute walk about 11.30, then we have a pre-match meal about 11.45. Nowadays they are eggs and beans or omelettes. We used to have fish or steak, but the gaffer changed it about 18 months ago, which was when our run of success started, so there are no deviations. Gary Lineker was used to having fish at Leicester, so it was, 'He'll have to have a fish omelette. No, he'll have to have an omelette'. I said to him, 'I used to have fish as well, but there you go'.

As I said, Wembley is becoming quite familiar to us, but it is always an occasion to be enjoyed, for the fans as well as the players. And our fans certainly enjoyed it.

We were in control in the first half all the time. In the second half they had a spell on top, but we deserved to win.

Trevor Steven got a great goal. Paul McGrath was caught trying to play too much football by Sheeds, who dispossessed him and whipped in a great cross, and Trevor just got in there.

And it was great news for Adrian Heath again. He is scoring goals left, right and centre at the moment. It has obviously been a very successful operation – in fact I think they've put a goal-scoring aid in his knee. Goal-scoring ligaments perhaps. He came on as sub, for Gary Lineker, and got his first Wembley goal. He was absolutely delighted.

Gary played well himself, stretching United on occasions, so it is all looking quite good. It's reassuring to know that we played well in last year's Charity Shield before all our success, and this year we've started off in the same vein.

There was no alcohol allowed at Wembley this year – part of the new measures to try and cut down on hooliganism after the Brussels disaster – so the boss pulled the coach off the motorway at Coventry, and we had a couple of beers at the Post House to celebrate. A very pleasing day. A bit of revenge for the Cup Final, and a good curtain-raiser to the new season.

I had more treatment on my achilles. It is a bit stiff again. Obviously I'm not 100 per cent fit, but it's just a question of keeping me ticking over.

John Bailey brought his pet monkey on the trip with him. He got it in Toronto. It's a puppet, but I think he thinks it's real to hear him talking to it.

Sunday 11 August

Open Day at Bellefield. All the Junior Blues, the club for our young supporters, come, and we are all there to sign autographs and chat to

23

them. It's usually a great day for the kids, but I don't think anyone could have enjoyed it this time, because it tipped down all day. Everything was sodden, so we had to have it indoors. We still signed autographs and chatted of course – there were about 3,000 of them, so it was a bit hectic.

Phil Neal Testimonial: **Monday 12 August**
Liverpool 2 Everton 3

Another day, another match. Except that games against Liverpool are never just another match. Derby games are Derby games on Merseyside, even if it's only a testimonial. I went in for treatment in the morning, and spent the afternoon at my Mum's, lounging on the couch. But then my Dad came in, and he was excited about the game. He used to be a Liverpudlian, but he's changed now! And as soon as he came in, it was, 'How are you doing? You fit?' really getting excited about it, and he started getting me excited as well.

There was a good crowd, 20 000 plus, so there was a bit of atmosphere. The Everton fans had come because they were still bubbling from the Charity Shield, and obviously Liverpool fans came to pay tribute to someone who had done a tremendous job for them, and for England.

The game was a bit competitive. We went 2-0 down. George Courtenay gave them a penalty – the ball was blasted against Derek Mountfield's hand – which Phil Neal tucked away. Then we were caught out thinking Craig Johnston was off-side, so we went two down. We had to lift ourselves to get back at them. Gary and Inchy were playing together up front, and looking quite good, and then Derek Mountfield scored, so we were only 2-1 down at half-time.

Colin Harvey had a go at us in the interval. He's a great personality, a winner all the time. He hates getting beaten, especially by Liverpool; it was like a league game to him, so he wound us up a bit. 'Come on. Get into them!'

So we went out and we did. Gary was causing them problems, and Inchy was doing well, and he ended up getting another two goals, which is quite incredible. He hit one in low from inside the box, and then he got a header from a Kevin Sheedy free-kick for his second. So in the end we beat them 3-2, and looked quite good.

I've still got problems with my achilles and groin, but I managed to last the 90 minutes, which was what I basically wanted to do, to try and get some fitness back.

Kevin Richardson has got thigh problems, which is a blow for him. Lord Lucan – I mean Paul Wilkinson – however has started training again. The specialist told him to push on and see how it stood up, which is good news for him. It's the first time he has really trained since pre-season started, so he's got quite a task on if he wants to be fit for Saturday!

Liverpool will always be a threat. They were experimenting a bit. Jim Beglin was playing midfield, and Kenny didn't play. Walsh played up front. He's a tricky customer, but we had Ian Marshall playing because Derek got a bit of a knock in the Charity Shield, and Ian did well. But Liverpool looked the same as ever, with very, very good passing. They've got too many good players not to be involved; you can't draw too many conclusions from a testimonial, even one as competitive as this, but we were just pleased to have won.

Tuesday 13 August

A typical day off. I just lounged about, and had a couple of hot baths to help the injuries and stiffness.

Wednesday 14 August

Photo-call. It was nice to see all the trophies on show. There were quite a few: as well as the League Championship, European Cup Winners Cup and Charity Shield, the gaffer had got his Manager of the Year Award, and he had asked Nev and I to take in our PFA and football writers' Player of the Year awards, which made quite a collection.

After the photo-call, the lads did a bit of training on the pitch. I just went to Bellefield and had a bath – I told the trainer the Doc had had a look at me and told me to take it easy.

Then we made a team appearance to promote our LP 'Everton the Champions' – another of Eric Hall's masterpieces – at a Merseyside record shop. The response was staggering. There were queues stretching right down the road. They sold out of both the LP and cassette – 300 of them I think – so we were there about two and a half hours. In the end we just had to disappoint people and leave – obviously we couldn't hang around so long.

The reception Inchy got was like the second coming of one of the Beatles. All the young girls love him – it's that cute little baby face as we tell him. Sitting next to him while he was signing autographs was like being in the midst of an onset of Beatlemania: although they didn't tear his clothes off him, so perhaps it wasn't quite like that.

Thursday 15 August

Again I didn't train because of my achilles. I took plenty of stick from the lads, which wasn't surprising as I haven't really trained since we reported back. They think I'm a part-timer. But you can't do anything in case it gets worse. I'm just hoping it will mend.

Otherwise most of the lads are looking really sharp. Kevin Sheedy pulled out of training with a thigh strain; it might keep him out of Saturday. Richo is still having treatment, but Wilko is working hard and looking quite strong.

I went in early for treatment, the lads had a game of head-tennis. I'm having a fitness test tomorrow, as is Kevin Sheedy. If we're fit I think he's going to play Gary and Sharpy up front with Inchy as sub, but it will depend on who is fit. We travelled down by coach, me with what is beginning to seem the regular thing for coach journeys, an ice pack on my achilles. We're staying at the Holiday Inn.

John Bailey is playing in the A team, and just before we left, Terry Darracott was asking him about free-kicks. 'Oh well,' Bails said, 'we've so many experienced players in the team we'll just play it off the collar.' That's typical of Bails, you wouldn't believe some of the things he comes out with. You could say he likes playing things off the collar.

Leicester City 3 Everton 1   **Saturday 17 August**
Another good start to the season – but it's a wee bit better than last year. We got beaten 4-1 at home by Tottenham then, so this is a bit of an improvement.

Kevin and I both passed our fitness tests and so we played. My achilles is not right, but I thought if I gritted my teeth it would get me through the game. The pitch looked in good nick, we had our usual 11.30 walk and I had my usual mushroom omelette.
   We started quite well too. We missed a couple of early chances, but we were knocking the ball around very confidently, and Derek Mountfield gave us the lead. And that is normally it. When we get in front we don't usually lose games. But then the left-back got through for the equaliser just before half-time, and we lost our grip. We had a goal disallowed for off side, and Mark Bright picked up two for them.

The gaffer was obviously not very pleased. He had a go at all the back four except Gary Stevens, who had a great game. He had a go at Brace and me for not being as tight as usual. I had to agree with him – we'd let ourselves get stretched out. I think to be fair to him that everything he said was absolutely right.

Looking back at the game, we had a lot of the ball, and we kept going forward, and I think we left ourselves too open at the back as a result. And all credit to Leicester, they came back well, and deserved to win.
   It was a great contrast to our game there last year, when we were under a lot of pressure and won 2-1. That was a very important result for us in the Championship, because it was at the end of February when Tottenham were right on our heels. They got a good away win at West Brom the same day, and they must have been sickened when they saw our game on Match of the Day, because Leicester had a few chances that

day, and we just had to hang in there. In typical fashion we did so and won a game which possibly could have gone the other way. Gary Lineker got through for a couple of one-on-ones against Nev, which he might have put away. But the beauty about Nev is that in that situation he stays big, so he is a keeper which the forward has to actually beat, he doesn't sell himself or give it away as some keepers might in that situation. It is all very well saying strikers should put those chances away, but I think it must be a hell of an experience for a striker going one-on-one with him, because he really comes into his own in that situation. He is a big keeper when he is coming out and he is very difficult to beat, and he did ever so well for us.

And then Andy got his first goal since September, so after being under the cosh, he had sparked us off. And although they got back near the end with a goal which we thought was off side, we went straight back and Andy got this second great goal and we had got away with it. Of course at that stage we were in the habit of winning. No matter what happened, we believed we were going to win, we didn't let them get a lot of chances to stop us trying to do the right things, and once you get in the habit of winning things do roll along, and that's what happened at Leicester last season. And it possibly set us up for the title. I'm a great believer in scraping 1-0 and 2-1 wins. I think that's what wins you the title, not beating Manchester United 5-0. And if you look over the years, Liverpool have been great exponents of that.

So Leicester is one place where we got three points last year which we haven't got this. But funnily enough we lost our first two games last year, to Tottenham and then West Brom, so there's no pressing the panic buttons, it's just a matter of getting it right, which we will.

When we got back I went out for a drink, and met up with Bryan Robson, Sam Allardyce and Ashley Grimes. Sam is back at Bolton. We played together in the promotion team; he was a big favourite with the Bolton fans, so I'm sure they are delighted he is back; I think he is what the team need. He was suspended today though, so he didn't play and neither did Ashley. United beat Villa 4-0, and Robbo said he was pleased with the way it went. It was a bit tight up to half-time, but he said that once they got a goal they steam-rollered Villa.

Sunday 18 August
A quiet day – I just had a bath and tried to take it easy. My achilles is still a problem, and I am now getting a bit worried about it. I shall train properly tomorrow and then see what we are going to do about it, because I can't go on this way.

I trained. I got through it alright, but I'm not 100 per cent fit. Afterwards the boss pulled me aside and asked if I was ready to play tomorrow. I said 'Yes, I'm ready to play, but I'm not 100 per cent'. So we decided to talk to the physio and the doctor, because it has now been hanging on for so long without getting any better, and by playing with it I'm not doing myself or the team any favours, because I'm clearly restricted by it. So we talked to them and it was decided that I should have a painkiller, which is what I've done. It means I'm missing three games – against West Brom, Coventry and Tottenham – which is disappointing at the beginning of the season. But there is no way I would take a jab to play. I think that just defeats the object, because it just masks the pain, and you end up doing yourself more harm.

Hopefully this will get me fit and then I can bomb on from there. I think it was a decision which had to be made. I'm a bit sick about it, but it was inevitable.

The thing which really worries me is that the England–Romania game is coming up early next month, and having just got into the squad I don't want to miss out on that. I've got to have a complete rest for a week or so, and Bobby Robson will be naming the squad in two weeks, so if I can get back for the Birmingham match I should have a chance.

Derek Mountfield is out, and so is Graeme Sharp, so we have got a few problems for tomorrow. But it means Adrian Heath will get his first game.

Everton 2 West Bromwich Albion 0   **Tuesday 20 August**
I went in and had a bath and did some weights to keep the rest of myself in trim and then got ready to watch the game. The lads played well and won deservedly. Adrian Heath scored another couple of goals, which is tremendous. He and Gary Lineker looked great together up front.

Ian Marshall played in place of Derek Mountfield and came through with flying colours. It's always good to see a young lad come through the ranks, especially at bigger clubs where it is harder for them to break through, so I was very pleased for him. He was up against Varadi, who is a flyer, and he was able to stay with him. I think it is important to have pace at the back, and like Derek, Kevin Ratcliffe and the two full-backs, Ian Marshall has got it. Alan Harper, who played in my place, was possibly the best player on the field. It just goes to show the importance of having a good squad. Alan Harper is one of those valuable players who will come in and always do a great job for you. He'd do a good job in most first division sides.

West Brom made it a bit easy for us, because they never really stretched us at the back. If I'd been the West Brom manager, I'd have said 'Here's a young lad, Marshall, making his debut, so get the ball over the top of him and let's test him', and I was surprised they never really attempted that. They had Stevie Hunt, Steve McKenzie and Derek Statham playing in midfield, and they played some lovely touch football, but they never stretched us; it was all taking place in front of us. If anything they played too much football. I know John Giles, their manager, likes the passing game. Obviously he does, because he was one of the best passers of the ball in the country, but I think he's got them playing too much football if that is possible, because you have got to get at people, especially in the first division. It is all very well playing the ball about, knocking it square, knocking it forward, but you've got to hit people where it hurts, and that's over the back of the back four. I wondered if they didn't do it because they were scared of our pace at the back, but Terry Darracott had scouted them on the Saturday and that had revealed the same fault. I talked to Gerry Armstrong and Garth Crooks, who weren't playing, Gerry because his registration hadn't come through from Spain, and Garth because he had picked up an injury on Saturday, and when I said that to them, Garth said, 'I've just said that to Johnny Giles in the dressing-room'.

Someone suggested they hadn't done it because we had played a lot of off side in the Charity Shield, and they were wary of being caught that way. But we aren't playing off side more this season. We don't play off side basically, we just hold the line and squeeze people into certain areas and make it difficult for them. The thing that surprised me in the Charity Shield was how many times United went off side. They were trying to sneak things on us, possibly because they thought our back four were quicker than their strikers. But if you play good football, you can beat the off side trap. Of course you are going to get caught sometimes, but you can beat it with deep runs and good runs from front men who have got pace. With Varadi, West Brom have someone who is a great exponent of those runs, so I was a bit surprised they didn't try to use him. Of course they'd get caught sometimes, but you've got to risk that to beat it, because if you don't take risks you'll never score goals.

United had a good win at Ipswich which I think makes it their best start to a season. It's early days yet, but you have to expect them, Tottenham and Liverpool to be our main threats. I think it is going to be a good League though. I don't like Sheffield Wednesday's style particularly, but it is effective for them, and I think they will be there or thereabouts. I think Nottingham Forest will be, because I rate Brian Clough very highly, and he has got quality players there. And they don't concede goals, which I am a great believer in – not conceding, that is. I think in the end last year Tottenham let themselves down because the back four gave away goals too often. Funnily enough I was talking to Arthur Albiston when there were about 16 games left, and he said Tottenham had to be favourites because they had 10 home games left out of 16, while we had 7 or 8 out of 15. But I said 'But they've got to win those home games.' It's all right saying you've got home games, but sometimes they can be hard to win when the pressure is on in front of your fans.

I quite fancy Chelsea as outsiders too – they've got a few good players there. And I wouldn't discount Arsenal. So I think it is going to be a very difficult league to win, but if I was pushed I'd pick the big four, Liverpool, Everton, Manchester United and Tottenham as my tips. But I wouldn't be surprised if one of the other four came out of the pack, because if one of them gets in and starts winning, the momentum builds up.

I've said before that winning gets to be a habit, and our game against West Brom last year was an example. It was one of the games near the end of the season when we were just getting the last few points we needed to end Tottenham's theoretical chance of overtaking us. Ian Atkins scored after about two minutes, and the crowd were singing 'Here We Go', and we got a bit lax, and they got on top for a bit, and Nev had to make two or three great saves. But I thought on the day that if they had scored, we could always have stepped up a gear and got back at them. And that is not the way to win championships, but I think by then the smell of the title was at Goodison, and we were being carried towards it on the crest of an unstoppable wave. In certain games on that run, when the other team had chances I always thought that if they had scored, we'd have got it back somehow, it was just the way things were going, and that was why we won the Championship. We had got into the habit of winning, and when you are doing that, it is amazing how often you come out of tight games with a win.

It works the other way round too. I've been down at the bottom with Bolton once or twice, and once you get used to getting beaten, it goes on happening. You can play well in games and not get chances, or fail to put one or two away, and then the other team will go and snatch one, and it gets into a vicious circle.

It's a lot better to be at the top. I remember Jimmy Armfield, who was my first manager at Bolton and now works for Radio Two, asking me in an interview as we were getting near to the end of last season how the lads were reacting to the pressure, and I just said to him there is no such thing as pressure at the top of the league. I said 'You want to ask the lads at the bottom of the league, because that's real pressure; it's just quite exciting at the top.'

We, the Reid family, aren't having much luck with injuries at the moment. My young brother Shaun broke his leg playing for Rochdale last night. It looks like it runs in the family – at least that's what my mother says – because he had a cartilage out last year, and now this. I went to see him to try and buck him up a bit, but he seemed to be coping quite well. He is only 19, so he has time on his side. We are a close family, and I try to go and watch Rochdale play whenever I can, but with such a big age gap between us I haven't played with him. When he first went to Rochdale, on the YTS scheme, he stayed with me for the first year, I tried to help him with little tips, but basically I've tended to leave him to it. In the end it's up to you whether you make it or not, and I've not interfered. He prefers it that way too. My Mum and Dad go and watch him and me on alternate weeks, and my Dad says he's better than me.

Ian Marshall and Alan Harper doing so well for us last night shows how important the squad system is, but it also brings out the difficulties of keeping a squad together. Ian Marshall coming through means he has gone ahead of Ian Atkins, who has gone to see the boss, and I understand he's been made available. Ian Atkins is a very good player, he's a winner, and I think he could do a good job as a defender for most sides. His only handicap is that he perhaps lacks a couple of inches to be a first-class centre-half who's going to win the ball. In the game against West Brom last season Garry Thompson gave us problems in the air when he was playing, instead of Derek Mountfield, but he is a good defender and a good user of the ball and hates getting beaten. But it is a difficult situation. Alan Harper wants to go as well – he's on a week to week contract at the moment, so it will be interesting to see if anyone comes in for him.

Yet I think it is imperative the boss tries to keep him. A squad system is vital. Without players like him, Richo, Bailes, Ian Atkins and Inchy to come in, you can't succeed, and at the moment Ian Atkins wants to go, Harper wants to go and Richo wants to go, because they want regular first team football. I can understand that. I wouldn't like to be a 'squad' player, and I don't think I could be one. I think I'm a player who needs to play every week – I'm certainly a player who wants to play every week. So I can understand why they get frustrated and want to go; I can also understand why the gaffer wants them to stay. It will be interesting to see how we deal with it, because it is a situation Liverpool have managed very successfully for years, and that has been one of the bases of their success. You don't hear tales of unrest from players who are out of the team there; they've held it together over the years.

Another problem the gaffer is going to have is who plays up front, between Gary Lineker, Inchy and Sharpy. Gary and Inchy looked very good together on Tuesday. The speed of Inchy's recovery might have taken him by surprise I think, but he is obviously ready, and has been looking very good. Obviously, having spent all that money on Gary, he is going to play, but whoever is left out is going to be unhappy. If he does play Gary and Inchy it will be quite a change from last season, going from two orthodox centre-forwards to none.

Thursday 22 August

The same routine. Treatment and, for variation, a bit of swimming. Boring.

Went to see Shaun again. He is bearing up. There is nothing worse for a footballer than being seriously injured but things could always be worse. It might sound ridiculous, but I thought he could have been going off on holiday on the aeroplane which caught fire at Manchester, so by comparison with that a broken leg at his age, which should mend fairly easily, isn't so bad compared with such a tragedy.

Friday 23 August

I just did bodywork and working on the bike. The lads were wondering what the gaffer is going to do; some people thought he would leave Sharpy out. I think people think that Inchy linked up well enough with Gary to stay in, so we'll see what happens.

Ratters has got a toe injury, although we think he'll play. He is a very strong influence on the side. He's possibly the quickest back-four-player in the country, which is what people always talk about, but his positional sense is good too, which doesn't get noticed so much because people think it is just his pace which has got him there. He has tremendous determination, so he is a great influence on the lads around him.

Everton 1 Coventry 1   **Saturday 24 August**

Ratters didn't make it, which meant the gaffer didn't have to make a straight choice between the front lads. Alan Harper moved into the back-four, with Inchy playing in midfield so that Sharpy and Gary played at the front.

We played quite well in the first half, but then at the end of the half little Gibson stuck one in. It was very frustrating, because we had had all the ball. And in the end Sharpy got one from a corner, which we obviously needed because Manchester United won again.

We're playing Spurs on Bank Holiday Monday, so we could really have done with three points from this game. Things aren't too clever at the moment, because with all respect to Coventry and Leicester, they are two of the weakest teams in the division, and we've only got one

32

point from the two games. Of course it is early days and there's no need to panic, but it is a bit disappointing.

I'm just feeling frustrated at being out. I'm not happy just doing body work. Ratters was in doing some too. He's hoping that he'll be fit for tomorrow. If so, the boss will have to make a decision on the strike force. Three into two won't go. A decision does need taking, because chopping and changing is unsettling for the side.

We travelled down to London for the Tottenham game. I'm really disappointed not to be playing in this game. It's always been a very, very good ground for me. Without going back through records, which aren't really my thing, I can't be certain, but I think I've only been on a losing side there once. I've played there twice for Everton and we won both times, but even going there with Bolton we always did well, drawing or winning. It's one of those grounds where I always seem to play well, and the team always seems to play well.

They are a team I always fancy us to get a goal against, which means that they have to score two to win, so I just hope the lads go there and do a job.

Our win there last year was very important, because they had started to slip a bit at home, but they played well that day and I think our win told them it wasn't to be their year after all.

That game will probably be remembered for Nev's save from Falco five minutes from time which stopped them getting a point. Falco got his head to a corner five minutes from time, and I was watching and I thought, 'It's in' but Nev came from nowhere to make this terrific save. It was a great save – one or two papers afterwards compared it to Gordon Banks' famous save from Pele – but I thought he made even better ones throughout the season. It was just that it was at a vital stage of a vital match, with 50 000 people watching, and in London too, so it was high-lighted; but I thought his saves from Gary Lineker against Leicester and from Imre Varadi, when he was going the wrong way and seemed to change course in full flight to turn it round the post against Sheffield Wednesday, were as good if not better. But you get a bit blasé about Nev and start regarding extraordinary saves as just being the norm for him.

That save though gave Ratters an opening. He's got a very quick wit, always got a quip, and he looked at Nev and said, 'Can't you grab hold of it instead of giving corners away?' When you play in our team you get a few quips out of the lads – we are quite a humorous team. If I play a forty yard pass and it gets cut out, Ratters jumps in, 'You've never been able to play anything like that in your life, just play it short, you can do

33

that.' And of course you aren't very happy with the ball you've played anyway, so you turn round to have a go back, and he's laughing.

The funniest thing I remember in football though was a game for Bolton against West Brom. I was playing in midfield with Len Cantello. We were struggling at the time, but we were winning this game 2-1, a miracle for us, when this ball was played into our box and there was Peter Barnes suddenly in acres of space, and he controlled it and chipped it over Jim McDonagh. And Len and I were running back desperately and Mike Walsh was trying to get across to him, but it's in the net. So Len's run back and he's fuming, because it's against his old club, and he says to Walshy accusingly, 'Where the hell did he come from?' and Walshy just turned and said 'Manchester City, wasn't it?' And I looked at Len, and we both just burst out laughing. We'd had a goal scored against us, but he was so quick. I mean, how can you think of a reply like that in that situation?

Tottenham 0 Everton 1   **Monday 26 August**
A good day. I started running in the morning. Nothing too strenuous, and I only did a little, but hopefully it is a start and I can get going.

Then we came to the game, and it was a terrific result. To go there and win again is tremendous. It was typical of games we had last year, where they had a lot of the ball but we were together and kept it tight, and then we nicked one. Gary Lineker got it, his first. Like last year too, Neville made two fabulous saves. Mark Falco must be sick to death of him. He headed one in the bottom corner, and Nev somehow got down there and clawed it out – that was similar to Banks' save. It was a great save, and although Gary's goal actually won the game for us, the goalkeeper saved us at least two points, which just goes to show what a goalkeeper is worth. He is, in my opinion, the best in the country. I've played with Peter Shilton for England, and with Neville, and I think Nev just edges the verdict, which is the highest compliment you can pay him. He deserves it though, because he works very very hard for everything he gets.

Ratty was fit, so it was decision time, and the boss dropped Sharpy, playing Inchy and Gary together. Sharpy obviously was not happy, particularly as he'd got the goal on Saturday, so there could be something coming to a head there.

It means though that we haven't got a settled side at the moment. We did last year until Inchy got injured, but then Andy came in for him. Later on there was a lot of chopping and changing because of injuries, but we overcame the problems because we were so together as a group and because we had such a momentum going. And it was something like that at Tottenham with the way we played and the result.

Tottenham get good support, but I always feel there is a lot of pressure on Tottenham sides at White Hart Lane. Whether the days of the double team still haunts them I don't know, but there is a lot of pressure for Tottenham teams to come out and entertain, and to do well, and if you can hold them at 0-0 for a time I think they get anxious and then become vulnerable, because they are pressing too much and trying too hard, because they are conscious that the crowd can get critical. And we found we could use that at Bolton, set out to hold them for a time and then hit them afterwards, and that was how it worked out again this time.

I thought Glenn Hoddle played a wee bit too deep. With his ability to chip and bend the ball, and for that matter to hammer it from 25 yards, he scares me to death when he is on the edge of the box. But he never really got into those positions – and from an opponent's point of view you are delighted to see him playing deep. He was playing in midfield with Ossie, who has been playing really well, and they had had a couple of good results with the pair, but on the day it didn't really work.

Tuesday 27 August

Joined in the training. I felt good running, there was no pain from the achilles, so hopefully I might be fit for Saturday. Hopefully. Mind you, after the Spurs result and the form of Alan Harper, I might not get in.

A few of the lads have got minor knocks: Alan Harper, Kevin Sheedy, Paul Bracewell and Kevin Richardson, but except for Richo and Paul Wilkinson, who is still doing his pre-season stuff and trying to get fit, I think they'll all be fit for Saturday.

Wednesday 28 August

Joined in with the lads again. It is great to be back in training. I enjoyed it very much. Training just involved a game with the emphasis on shooting. I must have a chance for Saturday now, because I feel pretty sharp.

There's a lot of speculation in the papers that Sharpy will be leaving. He obviously is very unhappy, and with the result on Monday I can see the boss playing the same two up front.

Thursday 29 August

Training is going quite well – there's no pain now. Then I travelled down to London with Paul Walsh to do a promotion for this record 'Play The Game'. We picked up Andy in Birmingham on the way down. It was at Spurs, and we met up with Steve Perryman, Graham Rix, and Gary Bailey there. We had to wait for Johnny Hollins – typical, a manager being late. All the players were there on time!

Charlie Nicholas had come along with Rixy, so we had a chat about how the season was going so far. It seems that Arsenal are changing their approach now that John Cartwright has come in as trainer, so it will be interesting to see how that works out. Had the normal laugh with Andy.

The boss named his team: I'm picked, and Derek Mountfield is back in as well. This is very unfortunate for both Alan Harper and Ian Marshall, who played in the game at Tottenham, have done great jobs for the team and seen us get a tremendous result, and then find themselves left out. That is the way football is, and you need a squad where you have people like them who can come in and do jobs for you, but it is hard on them.

And Graeme Sharp is sub again. I don't envy the boss his job. It must be difficult when a team does ever so well down at Tottenham, and he has to make changes. But I have always thought that if I were a manager I would have my best team in my mind, and I would always stick by it. If they are fit, I would always play my best team. I know there is an adage about not changing a winning team, but I'm a great believer in playing your best 11.

It was quite unusual this morning, because we don't usually worry about what other teams do, but we had a little routine to defend against their free-kicks. We had had them watched and evidently Billy Wright, who is an ex-Everton player, is a free-kick specialist anywhere near the 18 yard box. He puts his head down and drills them in. He scored in their last game against Oxford, and obviously the boss thinks it is a danger, so we are having a four-man-wall anywhere around the area, even if the free-kick is from a narrow angle.

I'm really looking forward to playing, and obviously against Birmingham we expect to win.

Everton 4 Birmingham 1   **Saturday 31 August**
Gary Lineker got a great hat-trick, so having broken his duck at Tottenham, he's starting to show what the boss bought him for. It was tremendous.

It was a funny game in a way. We were coasting at 2-0, and then Derek made a mistake and Andy Kennedy, who has been getting a few goals for them, nipped in. He'd come and trained with us for a week after leaving Rangers, but the boss didn't fancy him, so I think he enjoyed his goal.

And then it became a battle. Birmingham have always been a hard side to play against, and with the results against Leicester and Coventry, these are the type of teams we are having most problems with at the moment, because we haven't quite got it together, and it makes it hard. They stuck at their task well until the big lad at the back, Armstrong, got sent off, then we took over again. The Birmingham players were a bit surprised when he was sent off. I wasn't. It wasn't a bone crunching tackle or anything, just a push in the back, but the lad had already been booked and he had just gone on fouling Gary persistently. He had been warned three times while I was around him, and the ref had also told their skipper Billy Wright to cool him down, so I thought he had to go.

I was delighted with the way it went. My groin was a wee bit stiff towards the end, but that is no problem, and I didn't feel my achilles at all. And that's two wins on the trot now, so we've got something to build on.

Sunday 1 September

No stiffness when I woke up, so it looks as if I'm in the clear. I went up to Blackpool to do a promotion for Courage, the England team sponsors, so I took Barbara and Louise, and spent a couple of hours on the South Pier signing autographs.

Monday 2 September

A day for team announcements. We are playing Sheffield Wednesday at Hillsborough tomorrow, so after our usual Monday morning – just a game – the team went up. And the boss has made another decision. In spite of our 4-1 win on Saturday, Inchy's been dropped and this time Sharpy is in. It seems he is not sure who to play up front. Whether he has decided this for this game because Sheffield have so many big men and they play in lines so he wanted more height, I don't know.

Then the England squad was announced and I'm in, along with Gary Lineker, Gary Stevens, Trevor Steven and Paul Bracewell, which is a great boost for the club and for us. I'm delighted, because I've only been back for the one game after injury, and I was wondering if I would be picked.

I'm really looking forward to tomorrow's game. I don't like Wednesday's style to watch, and I don't think I could play in a team with a style like that, but you can't criticise it because it works for them, and they get a lot of goals. But I love playing at Hillsborough. It's a great atmosphere.

We had two hard games with them last year. We drew 1-1 at Goodison, when they were very strong, and we beat them 1-0 at the end of the season.

The draw at Goodison was the end of Inchy's season. Marwood went in a bit late and a bit high on him, and he was off with damaged ligaments about 20 minutes into the game. Inchy is a big pal of mine, and just before half-time I went very late and caught Marwood; and he went off too. There was some criticism afterwards, and I was quoted as saying, 'It was an eye for an eye'. I didn't say that. All I said to the press was that it was a late tackle and I deserved to be booked. It was as simple as that.

I certainly hadn't gone in to injure him – I've had a few injuries myself, so there is no way I would ever do that. But I did go in to rattle him up. One of our lads had gone down, the tackle on him was late and high, we were having a bad time, and something had to be done. I'm a great believer in team mates sticking together on the park. Sometimes games can get physical, and if teams think they can intimidate you they will do, so you have to be strong and stand up for yourselves. You don't win anything if you don't. And at Everton I think we won the championship last year through team work and looking after one another. And long may it continue.

The return at Hillsborough was an epic. They were on a good run, and if we won we only needed one more point to win the Championship, and the atmosphere was terrific. We won 1-0, Andy getting the goal, but it was another of those games which Nev won for us. I've already mentioned that great save he made from Varadi, when he changed direction and turned it round the post – it was an unbelievable save because Varadi had struck it well. But he made two or three that day, because they really battered us for a time. And those are the games which win you championships, the 1-0 wins when you've been under the collar and you've had to fight for it and the keeper has managed to keep you in the game. I'm a great believer in the 1-0 wins; the 4-0s and 5-1s are just icing on the cake when you are in a good run, but it is the 1-0 wins which are decisive. And I think everyone who saw that game thought it was a great match.

It was a good time for us then, because although we knew that Manchester United were on a great run and could catch us if we faltered, we were playing so many games that there wasn't time to think about it, and we didn't really feel any pressure. There was so much happening, what with reaching two Cup Finals and the League Championship, that it was just a case of going from one game on to the next and thinking let's try to enjoy it. Possibly in the Cup Final we paid for it a bit, but up until then I think we were lucky because we didn't have time between games; there was a league game, then a European game or a Cup match, and they were all coming round so quickly we didn't feel the pressures, just here's another game to win. We won on the Saturday at Sheffield and then on the Monday beat QPR 2-0 to win the League.

Sheffield Wednesday 1 Everton 5   **Tuesday 3 September**
No one seeing the scoreline will believe this, but it looked a bit grim for us at one stage! They bombarded us for 25 minutes. It's always difficult against them. They were so strong and powerful, and they were getting in behind us. We went in front when Derek Mountfield went up and got one, but then Gary Thompson equalised for them from a ball knocked

into the box and we were under a lot of pressure until half-time. But once we got it sorted out at the back we were all right, because we started getting the ball down and not entering into the hurry-scurry but playing to our strengths, and we played some really good stuff. And suddenly we started scoring from all over the place. Trevor Steven got one. Gary got another two, he can't stop scoring now. Then I came off ten minutes from the end, I was feeling my groin a wee bit, so I came off as a precautionary measure, and Inchy went on and stuck one in.

Gary's goals are almost all headers. Two of the three on Saturday; another two tonight. Incredible, because he isn't exactly renowned for being the best header of the ball in the game.

A real laugh at the end of the game. At Wembley in the Charity Shield, Nev had taken his jersey off as he was leaving the field to reveal a tee-shirt with 'I love my wife' printed on the front. It got spotted, and one or two of the papers ran it the next day. So at the end of tonight's game Martin Hodge, who is a really good, funny lad, ran off the field and pulled his shirt off, and underneath was a tee-shirt proclaiming 'I love Nev's wife too'. He came into our dressing-room and gave it to Nev, and everyone was falling about.

I found out afterwards that Bobby Robson had been at the game, which I was quite pleased to hear. I thought I'd had a good game, so him being there won't have done me any harm.

Wednesday 4 September
I went in for treatment again, because my groin was a bit sorer than I expected.

United won again tonight – that's six out of six now. They are looking very strong. Obviously they and Liverpool are going to be the threats – I remember saying that last year, and it looks as if it is going to be similar this time.

Thursday 5 September
Training and treatment this morning. I'm still a little stiff in the groin. It should be alright for Saturday, although the fact that it is at QPR doesn't help. It's not one of my favourite grounds, and especially on the Saturday before an international it's not the best place for me to be playing. I've had a few knee injuries from playing there in my time, the artificial pitch is pretty hard on the knees and ankles.

I won't say I'm not looking forward to it, but to make matters worse, it isn't a very successful ground for me either. I don't think I've played in a side which has scored a goal there – the best result I've ever had was a 0-0. With Bolton we got beaten 7-0; it was like bingo!

Personally I think it is a terrible surface, and I think most players would say the same if you asked them. It's like playing on ice, you can't trust your footing, so you just have to get the ball forward and support. You can't play football on it, and you can't even make a tackle on it either, that's how bad it is. A game in which you can't make a tackle is not football. But you've just got to go out and try and do your best.

After training I went on a hospital visit with Adrian Heath to see a youngster who had been in a coma for three weeks. I enjoy hospital visits, because they really make you appreciate your own good fortune and buck you up when you are feeling sorry for yourself. The lad looked quite good, we were glad to see.

The ward of course was full of Liverpool and Everton supporters, full of typical scouse humour. We got a lot of ribbing from the Reds, but everyone gets slaughtered by the other side.

Friday 6 September

Training went quite well. I went in early at 10 a.m. to have some treatment. The lads started at 1.30, and we had a head-tennis competition. We had the usual Friday £1 a man, and my team won, so I had a few bob to buy sweets for the journey down to London while I told everyone about the 7-0 defeat there with Bolton and what I thought about the pitch.

We really need to win there though to stay in touch with the top, because obviously there's a really hot pace being set.

Kevin Sheedy is injured, so Inchy is playing. The boss wants him to play in behind the front two, with three of us across the middle instead of four. It's a bit of a change of style for us.

QPR 3 Everton 0   **Saturday 7 September**

It was a real drubbing in the end. Funnily enough though it could have been different. I'm not making excuses, but Trevor had a good shot disallowed because someone else had gone off side, and it was one of those which could go either way depending on the referee, because some would have said he wasn't interfering with play. Sharpy had a great chance from a header which he missed. But from the moment they scored their first goal, we were always chasing and always getting caught by their counters.

Bobby Robson was there again. I found it a bit strange that he should watch anyone playing on that surface, especially after seeing us on Tuesday, but as Terry Butcher is injured, perhaps he wanted to check on Terry Fenwick. He had a word with me afterwards, and said 'Have a quiet night'. Doesn't he know I don't drink? I think it means I might have a change of playing on Wednesday, which would be great, but a surprise.

We did have a night out anyway. Kevin Sheedy was staying down because he is flying out to Switzerland with Eire tomorrow, so we met up with some of the other England lads and went out for a meal at Langans.

I was given the Man of the Match award by the sponsors, my second of the week, so I got something out of it. At Sheffield it was a bottle of Scotch. Today it was a carriage clock. I'd sooner have had the three points, especially as Manchester United won again, which was more good news! Even at this early stage we don't want to get too far behind.

They claim that they've sorted out the problems with the QPR pitch this year. I didn't see any sign of it. They've just lobbed more sand on, but it seemed just as bad as ever to me. It is not a pitch you can have a proper game of football on in my opinion.

Sunday 8 September
I had a stroll round London in the afternoon, then we all met at The Crest hotel in High Wycombe, had a meal, with the normal discussions over what's going on, which you get when players from different clubs get together, and then we had an early night.

Monday 9 September
Trained at Bisham Abbey. I pulled out after about 20 minutes because my groin felt stiff again. It was just a precaution, if I'm selected I will be fit.

Glenn Hoddle and Alvin Martin were also injured, so we all had treatment from Fred Street. I always enjoy seeing him, he is a great personality, with a fund of stories from his career which I love hearing.

Ray Wilkins and the other two lads from Italy, Mark Hateley and Trevor Francis joined us today after playing yesterday. Ray's presence just illustrates how strong the competition is in midfield. Bryan Robson, Glenn, Brace and Trevor Steven, Ray and me. It will be interesting to see what he does.

Tuesday 10 September
I trained full today and then came the moment we'd all been waiting for – the team. It was great news. My first cap at Wembley. Obviously I'm absolutely delighted. Being picked for your country is always a great personal honour, and to be picked for such an important match, a World Cup qualifying match, ahead of Ray Wilkins is, I feel, a great compliment. I think Ray and I play a similar type of game, but he is such a good player, and has so much experience – I think he's played 72 internationals – to be picked in preference to him means that Mr Robson has shown great confidence in me, and it's up to me now to go out and do the job.

41

Of course I'm also delighted for my mother and father, who supported me through the bad times, and it's a nice reward for their faith in me. So I've just got to go out and do the business.

When you have time to yourself, lying on the bed thinking about things as I am now, you start to think about the people who have helped you, and the person I was thinking about was Jimmy Hedridge, the Bolton physio. I don't think I'd be where I am today without the help he gave me through some really bad times there, when I was out for long spells with injuries. I can't put into words what I feel for him and what he did for me.

In the evening we watched the Wales–Scotland game on TV, a 1-1 draw which decided that Scotland are going to Mexico (assuming they beat Australia) and Wales aren't. I thought the Welsh were a little unlucky. Scotland's equaliser came from a penalty, which was a harsh decision. Scotland had had the better of the second half, but, especially after the way Wales went out four years ago when Joe Jordan handled and the referee gave Scotland a penalty, it seemed like rough justice. It was a hard cross, which I thought hit the boy's hand, rather than him handling it. Those things do happen in football, and you have to put up with them, but I thought it was harsh.

The game though was overshadowed by the death of Jock Stein. Obviously that is a tragedy for his family and for Scottish football – he will be missed. But they've at least got the result, and hopefully he would have been quite pleased with that. I mean, I hope to live to a ripe old age, but when I go I'd love it to be at a football match.

The Under-21s also played tonight, and had a great result. They beat Romania 3-0, so we'll be quite happy to repeat that. The excitement about tomorrow is beginning to build up. I'm really looking forward to the game now.

I thought about my parents and Jimmy Hedridge, because there have been some bad times. After things had been so promising in my early years I had to wait a long time for better times. The Bolton team when I got into it was a very good one, we just missed out on promotion a couple of times, and then we got it, and because I was the sort of player who got involved, I got some international recognition. I played with Glenn, Steve Williams and Gary Owen in the England Under-21s midfield, I skippered the side eventually, and everything seemed rosy.

Then at the beginning of our first season in the first division, we played Sheffield United in a pre-season Anglo-Scottish Cup match. Tony Kenworthy caught me on the left knee. I thought it would mean missing the start of the season, which was only a week away, because my knee blew up and was very painful. But I went to see a specialist, who said there was a lot of fluid on my knee, drained it out and said I would be fit. So I had a couple of days rest and started training again. It still wasn't right, I was still in pain, so Jimmy Hedridge took me to see another specialist. He X rayed it, and found that I'd broken my knee cap, so it was straight into plaster for a month. That meant missing the start of the season, our first in division one, so naturally I was very disappointed. And that was the start.

I got fit again and got back into the side, and had been playing for a couple of months when we played Everton, ironically, on New Year's Day 1979. It was in a blizzard on ice, at Burnden Park. They didn't want to play, because they were joint top at the time, and it was going to be a lottery, and we shouldn't have played. When we were kicking in before hand, we couldn't see one another in the snow because we had our white shirts on, and the referee made us go and change into red shirts. It was ridiculous, a total farce. Just before half-time, as I was stretching for a ball George Wood, the Everton goalkeeper, collided with me. Thinking back, I think I went into a state of shock. I remember the awful pain, and dragging myself off, and the next thing I remember is someone saying the game had been abandoned. Outside there was chaos with people trying to get away, the ambulance couldn't get through to pick me up, and Jimmy Hedridge put me in his car and drove me to the hospital. It was New Year's Day, so nobody was around, but luckily the specialist Mr Winston came out to see me and put me in plaster, I was sent home and booked back into the hospital the next day.

I remember getting home, and the next thing I remember is waking up after an operation. I didn't know what had happened, or how serious the injury was until later. I'd snapped my medial ligaments and torn all the fibres around my knee, so it had been a big operation. I was in immense pain, and the injury subsequently kept me out for a year, which was the darkest period of my career, because obviously there was a lot of speculation about whether I would ever play again. And obviously I wondered about that myself. That was where Jimmy Hedridge came in, because his personality and his ability as a physio helped me through.

That was the worst time and it started a bad run. First I had a dispute with Bolton which kept me out for a couple of months, when I wanted to join Wolves and they wanted me to go to Everton. I got a lot of criticism over that. Then, with a cartilage injury and a broken leg, I only played something like 50 games in five years. Obviously that really set my career back. It was one nightmare after another. But it doesn't do to dwell on the might-have-beens too much or you would drive yourself mad. And I could at least take some consolation from the fact that they were all different injuries – if it had been one thing which kept recurring, I think it would have been much harder to cope with because you would always fear it was going to keep on happening. As it was I just felt a wee bit unfortunate getting four serious injuries. But it makes you appreciate the good things all the more, and it taught me that you can keep on going and keep your head up no matter how low you get.

England 1 Romania 1   **Wednesday 11 September**
I'm not sure that we've got the balance right with Bryan Robson, Glenn Hoddle and me in midfield. It worked well in Mexico against West Germany, but that was a different type of game. There isn't any such thing as a friendly in international football, certainly not against Germany, and they have a defence who don't concede much, but it wasn't a tight world cup qualifier. They were out there to experiment a bit, and they were looking to play. I don't think they'll be so naive when it comes to the World Cup, and Romania weren't. It wouldn't do to underestimate them. I think they are a good technical side, they are strong, work hard and have one or two very good players, and they are together regularly. They'd been together for the last ten days. We'd come together on Sunday (or Monday for the lads coming from Italy) after a tough game on the Saturday.

I know that's the old, old story, but it bears repetition, because unfortunately it is still true. They were so organised, when one player made a run, another one filled in, they knew where everyone was going. And as an 11, we hadn't played together before. And that just makes it very, very difficult. I mean I give everything I've got, I'll run my guts out for my country, but when you are not that well organised and the other team are, it is very difficult. There aren't any easy games in international football any more. Our approach might have been all right when we were the kings of football, and used to beat people by seven or eight, but those days have gone. We played Canada in pre-season, and in international football you laugh when someone mentions Canada, but they are going to the World Cup, and they will make it hard for teams to beat them because they are well organised and they get everybody behind the ball; it is hard to break them down. At club level the great example we had of that was against the Dublin University side, UCD, in the European Cup Winners Cup. We were champions of England, and we beat them 1-0 over two legs, an Irish college side! Because they were well organised and they just got men behind the ball and stopped us from playing. And it is the same in international football now.

And against a team like Romania it is even harder, because they have got some good players too. Although we played with a winger, I thought we lacked width because of our system with three in the middle. Because Glenn doesn't want to go wide, going wide isn't really my game, and nor is it Robbo's. And against sides playing with a sweeper you can't get through down the middle. I think you need to stretch them, and I think that was why we didn't win.

In my opinion the pattern, the balance, isn't right as it stands. I think

44

we should play four across the middle with two of them wide players. Then of course the boss has to sort out who he plays as the middle two, when there's some competition. There's Glenn, Bryan, Ray Wilkins, Brace and me to start with. It's a difficult job, because I do agree with people who say that there are a lot of players of about equal ability in England, and if you asked ten people in the street you would be given ten different teams – if you ask the press, you are given ten different teams. It is a hard job, but it is Mr Robson's job to take those decisions, especially as we have so little time together to prepare compared to other teams, I think he needs to do it now. Decide who his best eleven players are, get the pattern sorted out, and play them together as often as possible. He has one advantage. We have basically got a good solid defence, which is a base to build on. If you don't give goals away, you've always got a chance, and we aren't giving many goals away.

We were a little unfortunate, perhaps, because we had two goals disallowed and I thought the fellow handled before their goal. I think of our two disallowed, Mark Hateley probably did run off side at the free-kick, which we'd practised in training. But I thought Barnesy's goal was a good one, and watching the high-lights on TV confirmed that. I thought Barnesy timed it well and the flick through for him was great. But it was tight, and the referee gave the decision against us, which is something we'll have to contend with in Mexico if the summer trip was anything to go by.

My achilles – my other achilles – went in the second half. I've been struggling with my left leg. This time I got a ball on the right hand side, and I just checked back to cut inside and I felt it go. I was in a wee bit of pain, but it was a World Cup match, so it was a case of grit your teeth and get on with it, which you've got to do. But it is stiff now, and I'll be struggling.

Thursday 12 September
I was very sore. I went into Bellefield for treatment. I've obviously no chance of playing on Saturday. It is just so frustrating, I can't seem to get a run of games going at all, and it is these silly niggling little injuries the whole time, which drive me mad. What makes it worse is that when I'm playing I feel strong, but it seems I've been with the physio all season.

There was a lot of criticism in the papers this morning, and Robbo came in for some stick for his performance. Well it wasn't one of his best, perhaps, but you have to see it in the context of the game. His great strength, I think, is the runs he makes into the box, and the goals he gets from them. But the ball wasn't coming in for him. We had a chat before the game and he said to me 'I know you'll go out wide sometimes and hit the ball in, watch for me making my run' and we did work it once or twice, but unfortunately he got caught off side on one of them. But overall the quality of ball he needs was not being played in, which is where our lack of width showed up.

The other thing of course is his strength rattling into people and shaking them up. But we just didn't get too many opportunities to catch people in possession. If you went in on somebody they had always got an outlet, which meant that someone, somewhere wasn't doing their bit. Of course Wembley is a big pitch, but I've played at Wembley with Everton and if you are all doing it together you can close teams down. But that again comes down to organisation and knowing what everyone is doing. You don't all have to be tacklers to do it. Kevin Sheedy isn't the best tackler in the world, but you can ask him to make things difficult for his man when they've got the ball, and then you use his abilities when you've got it. You can't have a team of ball winners, or a team of ball players, you've got to have complementary abilities, but then organise things so that you use players' strengths and cover for their weaknesses. But with England it is very difficult to get that sort of organisation because we aren't together enough, which is why we must have a settled side and a settled pattern when we are. And perhaps it is just me, and I'm completely off target, but at the moment I don't think the balance is right.

Friday 13 September

Friday the thirteenth is not a good day to visit a specialist. I ended up on crutches. I've got every confidence in Mr Campbell, who is very good. He has treated me once or twice before. He gave me a jab in my right achilles, and he made it very plain that he did not want me to do anything while the painkilling jab was taking effect. He said that the achilles tendon is not something to mess around with, so I've got to use crutches for a week. Great news! But I do know the importance of the injury, and he was so specific that it is just a matter of getting on with it and hoping that the week flies by. So, probably, does everybody else, because I know I shall be difficult to live with at the training ground and at home. I'm not a good patient.

Sharpy is down to sub again, with Inchy playing at the front, and Alan Harper coming into midfield for me. So we've changed again; Sharpy obviously is not happy, and I don't think the lads are either, because the changes are unsettling.

We've had some interesting games with Luton over the years. Two years ago we beat them 5-0, a game which will be remembered for a John Bailey goal. He'd got the ball in our half, and he pumped this massive ball forward, Findlay came out for it and it bounced over his head and into the net. Bails doesn't score many goals, so he was jumping up and down with delight and of course all the lads ran over to him and he shouted 'Even Pele couldn't score from his own half. Even Pele couldn't do that'. People watching must have wondered what we were all laughing at.

Last year's semi-final wasn't a laughing matter until the end. We had played in the European Cup Winners Cup semi-final in Munich on the Wednesday. It was a difficult game. We drew 0-0 over there, which was a great result because Bayern were a good side, and then we came back for the semi-final, and we got battered for about three-quarters of the game. They worked hard and, all credit to them, they were the better side, but we hauled ourselves back into it through sheer determination more than anything. And we had just started getting on top and right at the death, when they must have thought they had won it, we got this free-kick. And Kevin Sheedy's trusty left foot tucked it in. It just bobbled over the line, and we had got out of jail.

We were lucky to get extra time, but in extra time there was only one team going to win and that was us. It was amazing, because I thought we'd maybe struggle because the hard game in midweek might take its effect, but we just seemed to get stronger and stronger. Which just goes to show how much your mental state affects your tiredness, because we were lifted by our escape, while for them to see that ball bobbling over the line must have been heart-breaking after they had played so well and deserved to win.

We had a couple of chances in extra time. I had one when I went right through and dummied the keeper, but he made a good save, and then we had another free-kick. Which again Kevin took and Derek Mountfield put in.

It was incredible really. Kevin had been troubled by an ankle injury, he wasn't 100 per cent fit, and he hadn't had a kick for most of the game. Brace and I were getting a bit niggled with him, and then he pops up with a major part in the two goals which get us to Wembley again. It's swings and roundabouts with players like him. A brilliant player when he's on song.

It must have been a sickener for Luton, although you don't think about that at the time, because they had played well and we hadn't. But semi-finals are about winning, and at the end of the day that is what you've got to do. Wembley is no place to lose, but losing a semi-final is even worse. We were just elated with our victory.

Everton 2 Luton 0   **Saturday 14 September**
John Clinkard had said that I should spend Saturday at home watching TV, so that was what I did – the Ryder Cup and the St Leger – and listening for news of the game. Apparently we didn't play well, but we

won, which was what we needed. Sheeds got one, then Sharpy came on as sub and got the second.

Lay around the house.

The lads said it was a scrappy game against Luton. They're looking forward to the Super Cup game with United on Wednesday. Personally it's not something I can get wound up about – I probably would be if I were going to play – but as a detached observer for once, it seems meaningless. I know the clubs need the revenue, but in World Cup year I think they missed a great chance to give the F.A. some help, by keeping the weeks free. And the competition is meaningless really – it's a cup, and if you win it you win it, but I can't see any point in winning it.

I'm not totally out of sympathy with the clubs' position. It was a tremendous tragedy in Brussels, we all feel that, but whatever happens you can't bring those people back, and I just think that the ban and a lot of the measures which are being taken at the moment are half cock and punishing the wrong people. The clubs got a lot of flak for trying to get the ban overturned in court, but I thought they had every right to do that, and the critics were just jumping on the band wagon. Last year I earned my right to play in the European Cup, and it is being denied to me because some thugs, who are nothing to do with me or Everton, went wild in Brussels. They aren't football supporters, they are hooligans, who ought to be sorted out by the proper authorities. As Brian Clough said, football hooligans aren't just hooligans between 2.45 and 4.45 on a Saturday afternoon.

It needs the government and the police and courts to get their act together and do something about it, instead of half-baked ideas like identity cards. And I fail to see how the police can stop Kentish miners going through the Dartford tunnel because they might cause trouble in Nottingham, yet are apparently unable to stop football hooligans from going abroad to cause trouble.

Derek Mountfield has gone in for a cartilage operation, so that will keep him out for a few weeks, which is a bit of a blow.

The Gaffer has made his decision at last. He told Sharpy that he is going to have a run in the side, which means Inchy presumably has been told he is permanent substitute for a time. The main thing is that he has taken a decision. The lads weren't happy with the chopping and changing, and the situation was reaching breaking point. Obviously it was a hard decision to make, and I wouldn't have wanted to have had to make it. It isn't like him to be indecisive, but I think Inchy recovered much more quickly than he expected, and it left him with a real problem.

48

Manchester United won again on Saturday, and the press are giving them the full treatment. I read one piece which talked about them being the new Real Madrid, and going to take over Liverpool's European Crown, which is ridiculous after eight games. So I think that has made the lads a bit gee'd up for the game. Because we do fancy playing them. The Cup Final was a serious exception, but we do think we can beat them when we play them. They seem to have a strangle-hold on Liverpool at the moment, and we seem to have one on them. I always feel we can score against them, I always fancy us to get a goal from a dead-ball kick, while I never think they'll get goals against us. Kevin Ratcliffe always plays Mark Hughes very well, so he never looks as dangerous against us as he seems to against other teams.

Tuesday 17 September

I was just doing bodywork. In the evening I went to watch Bolton against Lincoln, who drew 1-1, and had a drink afterwards with Ian Greaves and Sam Allardyce. I still have a lot of affection for Bolton, and I still think that if they could get some sort of success they would get a good crowd. Blackburn, who are top of the second division at the moment, are getting about 10,000, and I'm sure Bolton would do better than that. It's a real football town.

I'm still very close to Ian Greaves. He is a great man. He was very shabbily treated by the Bolton board I thought, and that played a part in my walk out the following summer. I'd been at the club since I was 15, and I thought it was probably time for a change, but I think it would have worked out very differently if Ian had still been there. I was just very disillusioned by the way he had been treated. He'd taken us up as champions ahead of Tottenham and Southampton, but while they were able to spend millions establishing themselves, he had to try and run a first division club with very little money. He spent about £500,000 on Len Cantello and Dave Clements – which didn't really work out – and that was it.

So the summer after he'd been sacked, my contract came to an end and I refused to sign a new one. It was the time when freedom of contract had just begun, so it was still in its infancy, and I was one of the first cases. I saw John Barnwell and agreed personal terms with Wolves. Bolton agreed terms with Everton, but when I told Everton the terms I had been offered by Wolves, they couldn't match them, while Bolton and Wolves just weren't getting together about the fee.

I got a lot of criticism for being greedy, because it was said I was demanding £1,000 a week. The whole package might have been something near that, but I certainly was not asking for that as my weekly wage. Football contracts are quite complex with pension funds and bonuses and loyalty payments to be included, but no one wanted to know about that. It was much easier to grab the figure of £1,000 a week, which some players were on anyway, and use that as a stick to beat me with.

The criticism got worse when Arsenal came in. They'd just got back from a poor pre-season tour, so Terry Neill obviously felt pressured to do something. I went down to see him with my accountant and my agent on the Wednesday before the season started. We sorted something out, but it was very quick, and there were still a few loose ends to be tied, so I asked for some time to think about it. Terry Neill said, 'Ring me at nine tomorrow.' So I did, but I hadn't really had long enough to get everything sorted out, so I asked for a little more time and he said 'No. The deal's off.'

I was a bit taken aback, and the next thing I knew was reading on teletext that I'd failed to agree terms with Arsenal, so I got slaughtered in the papers.

It seems ridiculous now, but at the time I really wanted to go to Wolves. They seemed at the time to be a club going places. They'd bought Andy Gray, won the League Cup, qualified for Europe, were building a new stand, so they seemed to be going places. I wasn't to know that they hadn't got the money to back it up, although perhaps their failure to agree terms with Bolton could have given me a hint.

Looking back, the only thing I did wrong was that I didn't play football. I should have signed a weekly contract with Bolton and played for them even though I was in dispute, rather than staying away. Obviously if I'd known that Wolves hadn't got any money I'd have gone to Everton then, but as it was I fell between three stools, and ended up going back to Bolton. That was a funny experience, because there was a bit of hostility towards me there, which I could understand because I had had some bad press. But once you are out there playing and giving 100 per cent, people see you are trying to do your best, and they come across to support you again, which is what happened. And, as I say, I still have a great affection for the club.

Manchester United 2 Everton 4   **Wednesday 18 September**
I met the lads for lunch at the Four Seasons in Hale. Afterwards the boss called me in and bought me a glass of champagne. He said 'All last season the vice-chairman made me have a glass of champagne in the afternoon, and the results went so well, I think we should continue it. It's a lucky omen.'

It certainly was. The Super Cup may not be a very exciting competition, but it was a great game. There was no doubt both sides wanted to win it, but it wasn't as cautious as a league match might have been, and the result was some really fast, open football. But the fact that we got two goals quickly, after they might easily have had one or two, also helped that, because I think they thought then, 'to hell with it, let's have a go' and it was real cut and thrust stuff.

Kevin Sheedy was absolutely brilliant – his first touch, his passing, everything. It was one of the best games I've ever seen from him. A measure of how good he was was that you didn't see Gordon Strachan. He was just trying to chase Sheeds, and Sheeds was so hot on the night he was just a joy to watch.

John Bailey was delighted. He always has a bet with Jimmy McGregor, their physio, every time we play United, and he is well ahead at the moment.

Thursday 19 September

I went to a promotion for NEC, the club sponsors. Then judged a 'Miss Lovelylegs' competition at Benny's disco, which was fun. I'm looking forward to seeing the photos!

Tomorrow I hope I get rid of the crutches.

Friday 20 September

Yes I'm off the crutches. Pleasure at that however was restricted because everyone was buzzing about the game tomorrow – the Merseyside Derby. I'm absolutely gutted at missing it. Perhaps because I come from Merseyside I feel it more than most, but when you talk about big games, the Derby game is unique.

After treatment I dropped the tickets off at my Dad's, and went to the pub, 'The Quiet Man', which was full of Reds and Blues. The banter going on was unbelievable. Two of my uncles, Uncle Arthur and Uncle Michael, were in there. Typically on Merseyside, one is an Evertonian and the other a Liverpudlian. I think that is the unique thing about Merseyside, it runs right through families. In Manchester you get areas like Stretford which are all United, and others which are all City, but in Liverpool it is all intermingled, and that's probably why the rivalry is passionate but friendly, which is what I find nice about it. It is great to go to games which have this unbelievable atmosphere with the reds and blues standing together. One of the most enjoyable afternoons of my life was the Milk Cup Final at Wembley in 1984, even though we didn't win the game. It was just brilliant to see Wembley with Red and Blue all over the ground, a great atmosphere but no trouble. But saying that just goes to show what is wrong with the game generally, because it shouldn't be remarkable.

Everton 2 Liverpool 3   **Saturday 21 September**

An unbelievable game. Wednesday's game with Manchester United was a great game, but this one had everything, it was something else. Kenny Dalglish got one even before you were sitting down in your seat, and from then on it was just unbelievable, an amazing game. Great skills, great passes, shots, saves, misses, goals, an electric atmosphere. It was a disappointment to lose, but even so I loved every minute of it, it must have been the greatest game I've seen for ages, and I think every one of the 50,000 there would say the same.

After Kenny's goal we might have equalised within two minutes, but Gary Lineker just couldn't catch it right. If the ball had gone in it might have calmed things down a bit, but it didn't. And of course with the crowd willing us forward because we had gone down so quickly, we got caught up in the atmosphere. With 90 minutes left, what we needed to do was calm down, get our foot on the ball and have a bit of patience and try and get people in behind them, but in that atmosphere we couldn't, the adrenalin was going and we just pounded at them. I could understand that, because I got a sweat on just watching.

So we had a lot of the ball, but it played into their hands. They were playing with a sweeper – Molby and Hansen marking, with Lawrenson sweeping – which you have to give Kenny full marks for – and as we were attacking incessantly, they broke on us again. Rushy got one and then Steve McMahon, who had just joined them, got another and we were 3-0 down. All our pressure meant Liverpool got men behind the ball and sucked us in and then broke, which is what they love doing and do so well – they've done this for 20 odd years in Europe.

So we had to do something, and the boss, all credit to him, pulled Ian Marshall off and put on Inchy, and we got one back fairly quickly through Sharpy. And then it was a great game. Gary Lineker got one with about eight minutes to go, so it was a crescendo of a finish. We were trying desperately for the equaliser and twice Liverpool broke, and Kenny was free in front of goal. And Nev was on the floor, because he'd gone for the dummy, and Kenny put it over the bar. And a minute later he did the same thing again. I couldn't believe it, because you would back him of all people to score from those, 98 times out of a 100.

When you got your breath back, you had to say that we had given away some bad goals defensively. For the first one the full-back knocked it long from outside their 18 yard box and Rush picked it up on our 18 yard line, which is not like us at all. I wondered if Ratters was fit, because Ian Rush outpaced him three or four times, and I've never seen him outpaced in four years, and there is no way Rushy can outpace him. Ratters had had a toe injury, so I wondered if that was still affecting him. He hadn't said anything, and when I asked him, he said he was OK, so there you go.

But it is definitely worrying, because we're giving goals away all over the place. I hate to think how many we are giving away. Manchester United won again, 5-1 at West Brom, and they aren't giving goals away. That goal was only the third they've conceded in the league all season, and that's how you win titles.

Sunday 22 September

I've just signed a three year boot contract with Hi-Tec, so I flew down to London today for the exhibition. Steve McMahon is also with them, so we flew down with Paul Bracewell and Gary Stevens, who are with Adidas.

Monday 23 September

Flew back up from London and went in and worked with John Clinkard. Just doing body work and a bit of walking to stretch the achilles. Boredom time. The lads meanwhile were preparing for Wednesday's game against Bournemouth.

Tuesday 24 September

Sheeds is struggling with a knee injury. The boss was quoted in the papers today saying we had got to be mean and not give goals away. Obviously he'll let us know what he feels about it, and that's right. So hopefully we will get tight, and keep a clean sheet tomorrow.

Everton 3 Bournemouth 2　　　　　　　　　**Wednesday 25 September**

If you don't get to your seat before kick-off at Goodison these days you're likely to miss something. It took Liverpool 45 seconds to score on Saturday. Yesterday we were 1 down after 11. It's unbelievable. So we got the ball and started hammering at them, and we got caught again. Two down after 14 minutes, and the last thing the boss said before we went out, 'Whatever we do, we don't concede' and we've given two away in 14 minutes.

Understandably he was not very happy at half-time. Gave the lads a right rollocking. He said 'Get out there and do the job properly', which is right. It is scandalous the way we are giving goals away. Anyone who attacks us looks like scoring, which is very very worrying, and I don't know how we put it right.

We got them back by half-time. Trevor Steven has had a quiet start to the season, but Gary Stevens is in great nick, his attacking play has been just as impressive as his defensive work, and he looked like a Brazilian full-back tonight going forward. Gary Lineker got his head to one cross – another header! – and Ian Marshall got to another, and then in the second half Heffernan headed into his own net, so we won. But it wasn't very satisfactory. We wanted a couple of goals lead to take down there, but that won't be easy. One or two teams have been turned over down there – Manchester United were two years ago.

It is so different to last year. I've a feeling we might be trying to look good, to go out and play like champions and that's no good. Sometimes you've got to scrap. We know there is an onus on us to entertain, it's something everyone is conscious of with the current problems, but I think we are taking unnecessary chances. And sometimes we are almost attacking too much. Against Leicester we had so much of the ball, yet we ended up getting beaten 3-1, which was ridiculous. We've got to get back to the basics, which mean you start by not conceding goals, you defend solidly, and then develop from there. And that is what we have not been doing. Some of the goals we've conceded this year have come from us having the ball, giving it and letting people come at us.

I still have the feeling that Ratters is injured, and that is important because his pace is essential to us. He's been struggling since Tottenham, and we've been struggling at the back since then.

It's not the only problem though. I think it's a general lack of professionalism throughout. We've been trying to play in certain areas where we shouldn't, instead of going for safety first and not conceding goals. When we were winning we were solid, and got the ball into the last third of the field and played there rather than trying to play our way out of trouble, and that's what we've got to get back to.

I had a word with Brace afterwards, because I thought he was going forward too soon. He said that he was getting missed out by the ball over the top for Gary, but I said 'Well, you've just got to stay, because you are getting caught in there, and if it breaks down you're nowhere and people can pick it up if you're forward too early'. And there are just these little things wrong which are costing us.

Andy had said in the *News of the World* last Sunday that part of our problem was that Sharpy and Inchy should be our front pair. They were brilliant together at the start of last season, and maybe they are the best partnership, but Gary has got nine goals already, which is what he is paid for, and how can you argue with that? Nine goals answers any criticisms on that score, because if we hadn't been giving goals away we'd be flying. I know you defend as a team, but we've been very slack, and a lot of the goals have been down to stupid errors.

I hope to be back a week on Saturday. I'm keeping my fingers crossed. It feels quite good at the moment, we'll just have to see how it goes when I start running.

I don't know whether my return will make any difference. That's not really for me to say. Alan Harper does a great job, but I tend to 'hold' in front of the back-four, and perhaps they are missing my talking on the pitch, because I like to get involved and do a lot of talking.

And, to be fair, we haven't had a settled team yet, which makes things difficult. I know Manchester United have had a few injuries, but I think ours have been in the more important positions with Derek Mountfield missing from the back and me from midfield.

Thursday 26 September

Nev injured his ribs against Bournemouth, so he might be struggling for Saturday at Villa. He was in having treatment.

Friday 27 September

Ian Atkins has gone on a month's loan to Ipswich. That should give him the chance of first team football, which he wants. I think he'll do a good job for them.

The lads were getting ready for Villa. I think we'll be a lot tighter down there. Obviously the boss and Colin Harvey are very concerned about giving goals away.

I'm going down too. The boss always involves players when they are out of the team through injury. Inchy was out for eight months, but he was always kept involved in every aspect of things. I think that is a very good policy. Possibly because he was a player himself quite recently, he knows how players feel, although Ian Greaves used to have the same policy at Bolton, so I've been quite lucky. I do think it is important to keep injured players with the party, take them to hotels, keep them involved in the dressing-room, so that you still feel part of things. When you are injured it is such a low time for you, you need to feel wanted and have something to be part of.

The players also play their part in that. With a good set of lads like we have at Everton they'll keep you involved, say 'Come along with us' and that is important.

Aston Villa 0 Everton 0   **Saturday 28 September**

It wasn't a good game. We battled, and we got a result, was about all you could say about it really. And we kept a clean sheet, which I was happy about. Thanks to Nev, who had a jab before he went out, and had a terrific game.

Sunday 29 September

A quiet day. Went to Leeds to do a Charity thing with Bryan Robson and Gary Lineker, but otherwise I've had a rest.

Monday 30 September

I'm driving everyone mad at the moment I think. Just having treatment all the time is so frustrating, and it really makes me pretty difficult to live with.

The lads are preparing for our next match in my favourite competition, the Super Cup.

55

I'm just having massages, heat treatment and a bit of friction on my achilles to try and get things moving.

Everton 1 Norwich 0   **Wednesday 2 October**
The reserves were beaten 2-0 at Liverpool last night; to make matters worse Inchy got injured.

The Super Cup match was just awful. There were only 10,000 in the ground, there was no atmosphere, and neither side looked as if they wanted to play. I was glad Gary Stevens was on the park because he was attacking and defending more than anyone. Gary Lineker got the goal from a deflection, it was going to take something like that to produce a goal, because the game was awful. Awful!

Thursday 3 October
The same thing for me. More treatment. But at least I know I can start running on Saturday, which gives me something to look forward to.

Andy King came training with us today. He's with Wolves at the moment, but not very happy. He's a player of tremendous ability – if he could repeat his training ground performances in matches he would be a world beater, but the tackling isn't as sharp in training matches. He is still a very talented player, a tremendous one touch player, and a good finisher, but you suspect that he can sometimes go missing in the heat of the battle.

My other brother broke his ankle playing football for the university team. My mother is going mad with all the injuries. It's a nightmare for her.

Friday 4 October
We've got Oxford tomorrow. John Clinkard's room was overflowing today. Alan Harper, Trevor Steven and Ian Marshall will all have to have fitness tests tomorrow, so I shall have some company when I start to run.

Bobby Robson phoned to ask about the injury, which I thought was a nice gesture. The game against Turkey is coming up, and obviously I had to tell him I was struggling, but it was a nice boost to know he is keeping me in mind.

Everton 2 Oxford United 0   **Saturday 5 October**
The lads all passed their fitness tests. I didn't. I started to run and it just wasn't right – I felt pain again. I've just been told to rest again, but I am sick with disappointment, and worried. It started on September 9, it's now October 5, and I'm still struggling.

The game was not a classic. We deserved to win, but only a really controversial ending lifted it out of the ordinary. In the 89th minute, they were having a little flurry in search of an equaliser and the ball was played into our box, and Ian Marshall handled it. The ref waved play-on, and we got the ball and Brace went straight down the other end and scored our second. They went mad. There was only just time for the re-start, the goalkeeper went and kicked a bucket of water over and all hell was let loose.

From my position, you could understand it. I thought it was a penalty. But when I went into the dressing-room, Marshy said he had been pushed, and a couple of the lads said he had as well. And because we'd got possession, the referee had played the advantage rule. He was in an unenviable position; but if he had ignored the advantage rule and given us a free-kick it would have saved everyone blowing their tops.

Oxford had clearly come for a point. They worked hard, but they obviously weren't interested in coming at us and making a game of it. If there was going to be a match, we had to make it, and we weren't playing well. We just had to scrap for it really, but at least we kept another clean sheet, which I was pleased to see.

Sunday 6 October

I went in for treatment. Inchy has asked for a transfer. He just wants first team football, and the manager has decided to give Sharpy a run, so there's no place for him. Obviously the boss wants to keep him, but Inchy is adamant he wants to play so it is an impasse really. Something has got to happen.

Inchy is quite a single-minded lad. He has got a very good, positive attitude. He's a player I fancy a lot, I'd always want players like him in my team. He's a little terrier, he doesn't like getting beaten, and he'll always have a go when the chips are down, which is the attitude you need in a team to be successful. So there's a bit of a problem.

The lads are going down to Bournemouth tomorrow for the second leg on Tuesday. It should be a bit of a game. Alan Harper's not fit, but Richo is now, so he'll play.

Monday 7 October

The lads travelled down to Bournemouth. I'm not going to this one, I'm staying behind for treatment. There is no progress though, it just seems to be standing still, and I'm going spare with boredom and frustration. But there's nothing I can do except grit my teeth and wait, because I've just been told to rest.

Tuesday 8 October

I went to watch Bolton play Forest, who won 4-0. It was a bit of a tanking really. Forest looked solid. Bolton had one chance in the first half, but after that Forest just won quite comfortably. Bolton have got a few problems. David Cross isn't playing – he's discovered he's played for the last three matches with a fractured skull, which is typical of his attitude, and which is the sort of attitude they need. But they've got a few experienced players there, so they should really be doing better.

We won 2-0. A good result for us down there.

Wednesday 9 October

It turned out that we had had to weather the storm early on, but we got control in the second half, so we were quite pleased with the way it went. Richo marked his reappearance with a goal.

I'm just doing body work trying to keep myself in some sort of condition. I'm not doing anything on my ankles though.

Thursday 10 October

I saw the specialist again today. He said try and give it another two weeks rest, which seems like back to square one to me. But he got my left one sorted out, so I have to accept what he says.

Friday 11 October

The lads went down to London to play Chelsea. I didn't go with them. I didn't feel like it. I think that when you go on away trips when you aren't training you tend to eat and drink too much. And at the end of the day when you are fit again you've got to get back match fitness, and it's a hard enough game to play when you are fit, so you've got to be in some kind of condition. So I prefer to stay at Bellefield and have a good hour on the weights and bicycle which at least keeps you in some sort of nick.

Saturday 12 October

We lost 2-1 at Chelsea, which is very disappointing. When they said on TV that Nev had been sent off I couldn't believe it, because he's not one to go shouting at referees. But it turned out he'd committed two bookable offences, so according to the rules he had to go.

Monday 14 October

Bellefield was like a morgue. Everyone is away on international duty – there's only a few of us in. Sharpy was there because he had burst a blood vessel in his ankle, which has blown up massively. John Clinkard however said it was one of those injuries which look a lot worse than they are, which reassured Graeme considerably.

Talking to the lads about the game, it sounded as if we were a bit unlucky, although they were quite impressed with Chelsea. They thought everyone worked hard for one another and they all had a go, which confirmed my feelings about them.

We evidently did quite well after the sending off, and might even have got a point. But we didn't. We could have done with a point. We aren't playing well at the moment, and we are losing too many games.

The sending off of course didn't help. It sounded like two peculiar incidents. His first booking was for bringing down Speedie, which cost us a penalty as well. He was not very happy, because he said afterwards that he hadn't made contact. The second one he came running out for a through ball, misjudged it and handled to save the situation, which you can't argue about. I suppose, given that he had already been booked, he had to go, but the lads weren't very happy about it, and as he didn't like the first booking, neither was he.

I can imagine he'll be more upset than anyone. He is a perfectionist, which is why he is such a great keeper, and he will be reproaching himself for letting the lads down. He won't show that outwardly, but you know that's what he will be feeling. He has a tremendous attitude. He is always in at 9.15, an hour before everyone else, and I'm sure he'll have gone out for a run and worked it all out of his system.

Tuesday 15 October

The rest seems to be doing my ankle some good. It seems a wee bit better.

Wednesday 16 October

We're going to Mexico. England beat Turkey 5-0, with Gary Lineker getting a hat-trick, but we were already on our way thanks to a great performance by Northern Ireland, who won 1-0 in Romania.

That was a tremendous result. I must admit I didn't fancy them at all out there. I was very impressed with Romania when we played them at Wembley, and I thought they'd batter the Irish. I'd have backed them to win by a couple of goals, which just goes to show what a good judge I am!

Our game was satisfactory as well. We'd won out there 8-0, so obviously they are not first class opposition, but that just means you are a hiding to nothing. But Chris Waddle got an early goal, which the goalkeeper threw in really, and that settled us down. The Gary Stevens–Gary Lineker partnership worked well again, with Gary Stevens' crosses setting up a couple of Lineker's goals. Gary Stevens in fact had a tremendous attacking game down the right hand side from what I saw on TV. He is a superb athlete, and I think he is going to be a good player. It's said that wingers can get at him a bit, but I don't think there's a full-back born who hasn't been done by a winger once or twice. I remember Tony Dunne, who was an outstanding player, getting hammered by Terry Curran when he was at Forest. Gary has had trouble with Fereday at QPR on their pitch, and with Peter Barnes, but on the other hand he's played against John Barnes and Jesper Olsen, who are good players, and not given them a kick. I think he has got a great future ahead of him, because he is the type of lad who will always learn and he looks after himself. He gets a lot of recognition for his attacking work, but I think he is a good defender, and I think Mr Robson fancies him, which is great for him.

The other Evertonians were less successful. Russia beat Eire, which puts them out of the World Cup, and Wales lost a friendly at home to Hungary 3-0, so Sheeds, Nev, Pat van den Hauwe and Ratters didn't have such good days.

Thursday 17 October

Kevin Ratcliffe, who is Sheed's great mate, went into a travel agents and got a stack of holiday brochures, wrote a card saying 'Kevin Sheedy – book early. Not Mexico This year' and left them for Sheeds.

Friday 18 October

Watford tomorrow. I'm sure there will be goals. Over the years when we've played them we've had 5-4, 4-4 results, always entertaining games.

Inchy is back in – in midfield. Richo has been left out. So Inchy is getting his wish to play, although he said that he's not a midfield player and would prefer to play up front. As long as he is getting a game he'll settle for that.

Everton 4 Watford 1   **Saturday 19 October**

True to form in the end although it was tight for the first half. Inchy and Brace played well together in the middle of the park and both scored. Sharpy, who had a good game, got the other two.

I've always rated Keith Hackett very highly as a referee, but he had one of those days – he certainly made one important mistake and possibly another, although in a way they cancelled one another out. He disallowed a goal for them in the first half, which most people thought was all right. And then, just after half-time, when we were winning 1-0, he gave them a penalty for hand-ball which brought them back into it, and could have made it a bit dodgy, because we'd been a bit rocky at that stage. In fact we bounced back and played so well that we steam-rollered them in the end. But the video showed afterwards that it was Lee Sinnott who handled Terry's header, not one of our defenders.

I couldn't really judge about the disallowed goal, because I was watching from the bench. And down there you aren't a neutral observer. You get so caught up in the battle down there, willing your team on, that you see everything in just as biased a way as anyone on the pitch. So if there's a debatable decision, you can't give an objective verdict – if a goal for the other team is ruled out you don't think, 'That was a good goal', you agree with the decision. And if a penalty is given against you, you're as outraged as the defender even if the decision was right. Besides which, it isn't the best view in the world. But I still prefer it. You do get a much better view from the stand, but it is impossible to concentrate on the game because you are having to sign an autograph every two minutes. Even if you go in the directors' box, you tend to have people asking for your autograph and wanting to chat to you, so you can't attend to the game properly. Of course being asked for your autograph is part and parcel of football, and I accept that, but I prefer to avoid it while a match is on. And sitting on the bench also means that I'm not being asked when I'm going to be fit every two minutes, which happens on a match day. When you are injured you must get asked 'When are you playing again?' hundreds of times, which just rubs in how frustrated you feel. Match days are the hardest time when you are injured, your frustration just builds up, because the lads are getting worked up in preparation for the game, and you know you want to be out there with them.

Monday 21 October
I started running. The lads were getting ready for the Super Cup game at Norwich on Wednesday. The name 'Super Cup' makes me laugh. I mean, all respect to Norwich, who are a good little club, but the idea of Everton going to play Norwich in the Super Cup seems funny.

Tuesday 22 October
No humour today, just sheer despair, frustration, you name it. I worked a bit harder today, and immediately felt a reaction in my achilles, which is not a good sign to say the least. I shall see the doctor.

Wednesday 23 October
I saw the doctor and after an examination he said I might have to have a stripping operation – the sheath on the achilles being stripped off, because it's full of adhesions. To say I was angry is putting it mildly – I was blazing mad at the time, because we have been messing around for six weeks. When I had calmed down a bit, I had to admit that resting it had worked with the other one, but it is still frustrating to think that I've wasted six weeks, so I am not in the best of moods.

I shall see the specialist on Friday to confirm it, but it is likely that I shall have an operation. So I'm putting as much pressure as I can on the doctor to get me in straight away. I just want it done quickly.

I went in to do some body work. The lads lost 1-0 at Norwich last night. They evidently didn't play well – I don't think they put much thought into the game, because I don't really think they were in the mood for it. Getting excited about playing Manchester United in a meaningless competition is one thing; being motivated to play at Norwich is another matter.

I saw the specialist Mr Campbell, and I'm having the operation on Monday at 4.30. I tried to persuade him to take me in there and then. If he could just have knocked me out and done it straightaway I would have been delighted, because I just want to get it over with. It won't be a very nice weekend, with that to look forward to.

It has been a day of upheavals. Bails has signed for Newcastle, and Ian Atkins for Ipswich, where he's been playing on loan for the past month. We shall miss them both, both great characters in their different ways. But that is football, and you get used to good lads coming in and going out. It is part of the game. But Bails really made his presence felt. A tremendous joker, a really lively character, the type you want around at a football club, and it's a shame when these people go. There have been a few great lads who have gone – Terry Curran, Andy, now Bails. But then you get new ones coming in, like Gary Lineker, who is a bit quieter than them, but brings other good points, and it all goes to make up the club.

Manchester City 1 Everton 1   **Saturday 26 October**
                                             Sunday 27 October

I expected us to beat City. I think the lads will be a bit disappointed at not getting three points there, particularly as we went 1-0 up quite early. Bobby Mimms, who played because Nev was on a one match suspension for being sent off at Chelsea, played ever so well, from what the lads told me on the phone. I'm delighted for him, because when he came he just didn't look confident. I wasn't that impressed with him but the gaffer got Alan Kelly, the old Preston goalkeeper, onto the staff to work with our goalkeepers, and there was a marked improvement. Since Alan's been with us, Mimmsy has looked sharper, looked to have an appetite which he didn't have before. Whether it was lack of confidence coming to a big club or what I don't know, but he has trimmed down a bit, and it seems he has turned the corner.

Apart from the phone calls it has been a lost weekend for me. I just want to get tomorrow over with.

Shrewsbury 1 Everton 4   **Tuesday 29 October**

I woke up to a pain in my leg, which I expected. I've had a cartilage and
a ligament operation on other occasions, so it was not a new experience.
It doesn't get any better though – I still don't like hospitals. I'm in
Lourdes, which is a private nursing home in Liverpool. It is first class,
I've got no complaints about the hospital, and I've every confidence in
Mr Campbell, who did a terrific job on Adrian Heath. But it just drives
me mad being here.

I listened through a haze of drugs to our game on the radio. It was a
great result to get down there. Shrewsbury have turned over a few big
clubs in their time, and going to grounds like that is always difficult. The
way we've been playing it wouldn't have surprised me if we'd gone out.

Wednesday 30 October

Still lying here feeling drugged.

Thursday 31 October

They let me out – I think they'd had enough of me and just wanted to get
rid of me. I was delighted to be going home.

We found out that we've got to go to Fulham or Chelsea in the next
round of the Milk Cup. Not easy, but if you want to win things you have
to overcome games like that. Liverpool are playing United, which will
be a tester. It is amazing how many times Liverpool, Everton and
United seem to get drawn against one another.

West Ham 2 Everton 1   **Saturday 2 November**
                                                Sunday 3 November

We were one up again, then McAvennie got two goals. The difference to
last year! Last year if we went one up, that was the end of the story. The
referee could have blown his whistle there and then. I know it would be
a boring game if whenever you went one up you were going to win, but
that is the way it is with successful sides. Last year I always had the
feeling that if we got in front we'd stay there. We did at West Ham last
year. We went there in November when they were doing well, really
buzzing, and Inchy scored and that was that. We won 1-0.

   This year Trevor scored, and then we let them get back in the last 25
minutes. It's a nightmare when that keeps happening. I spoke to Ratters
about McAvennie, asked him if he'd had a chance to catch him with any
tackles, and he said he hadn't; that he was the elusive type of player who
gets it and gives it and then gets on his way, and does his stuff in the box.
It sounds as if West Ham have a good player there, because all the lads
were impressed with him. They said he looks the part.

Tuesday 5 November

The most exciting thing that's happened was lighting the fireworks for Louise this evening, which shows how I'm enjoying myself at the moment. The other high-lights are talking to the lads on the phone. I'm just sitting at home with a big crêpe bandage on, not knowing what's happening.

Thursday 7 November

I went down to have my stitches out. Looking at my ankle was frightening. I had this sudden wave of fear that I would never be right again. I think you always get that fear after an operation, because if your leg has been immobilised you always seem to lose a bit off your calf anyway, and your leg always looks wasted and weak. But the surgeon was quite happy with it, and I was pleased to have the stitches out. Now I just want to get back to work as quickly as possible.

We've signed a new player – Neil Pointon from Scunthorpe.

Friday 8 November

I went in today for a bit of therapy and watched the lads training for half an hour. It was the usual gentle Friday with head-tennis, but they then had a practice match to fit Neil Pointon into our way of doing things. He is playing tomorrow because Pat van den Hauwe has gone down with measles. You can't get a lot out of practice games against the kids, and we never have tackling in them, it is all very low key, but he obviously was given a lot of the ball, and he did look very confident on it. He is a chirpy, confident sort of lad, quite quick, and he looked quite impressive.

Everton 6 Arsenal 1   **Saturday 9 November**

As I'm on crutches I didn't go to the game, I just listened to it on the radio. Astonishing result really. They are up there – they were fifth until today – and they hadn't been giving many goals away. They hadn't been scoring many, but they had been winning games 1-0, not conceding many, so to get six against them was outstanding. By the sound of it, it was a bit tight at 2-1, but then we got on top and paralysed them.

Manchester United got beaten at last, 1-0 by Sheffield Wednesday, Lee Chapman, who is Inchy's pal from his Stoke days, got the goal, so we'll buy him a drink for that one. At least it means we've pulled a little bit back.

Manchester United were the subject of an altercation I had with Tony Dunne. Alf Davies, the commercial manager at Bolton, had a celebration of his 25 years at the club in the evening, and even though I had to be a bit careful on my crutches, I really enjoyed the night, seeing Ian Greaves, Frank Worthington, George Mulhall and people like that again.

Tony said that United should have won the League for the last two seasons, because they have so many world class players. I had had a couple of glasses of wine, and I got a bit heated. I said, 'Well I don't agree with that. We were the best side last year. You only win the title when you deserve it.' I do believe that. I'm absolutely adamant about it. I went through the United team with him and said, 'Yes, they're all good players, but you win things with team football, not good individuals.' It's always hard to define world class. My answer was that if you want to win titles you should get good club players, it is alright being world class, but you've got to do it week in, week out for 42 games. I always think the best team comes out of the 42 games as the champions and that's all there is to it. You don't get anything for 'We should have won this and we should have won that.' I think we should have won the F.A. Cup last year; but we didn't. Their name is on it.

Last season I don't think there was any argument that we were the best team. The year before United pushed Liverpool quite close, but I remember them coming to Everton at the beginning of May, when we were already in the Cup Final, and we had about four players missing. Ratters was injured, we had Gary Stevens at centre-half, we had a kid Rob Wakenshaw playing at the front, yet we controlled the game. Some games stick in your mind and I remember that game vividly. I came off the pitch at the end and said Liverpool were going to win the title, because United didn't want it enough. I remember thinking during the game, 'These don't want it'. They didn't show any real desire for it, they didn't do anywhere near enough for a team chasing the championship.

People explain that failure away by saying that United were in a state of disarray at that time. They'd been thinking of selling Bryan Robson to Italy, then they were selling Wilkins to Italy and Ron Atkinson was being linked with Barcelona. There was a lot of disruption. But that's no excuse. I haven't signed a new contract, nor have Graeme Sharp, Adrian Heath or a few of the lads. Obviously the boss is concerned about it – well, I should imagine he is – but there is no way it will get in the way of what I'll do for Everton, and I wouldn't want to pick up any wages if it did. I don't know whether I'll be at Everton next year, although I hope we can sort something out, but if I'm not going to be there I want to leave with a trophy, and if that means me going into a 50-50 tackle and risking getting injured again, I wouldn't even think twice about it. That's the way I've always played the game and the way I always will. And if any of the lads in our side aren't doing it, I'll tell them, or someone else will, and they won't get away with not doing it. And that's why Everton and Liverpool have been successful. After all, that year Graeme Souness knew he was going to Italy at the end of the season just like Ray Wilkins, but it didn't stop him or Liverpool. And I just couldn't believe Tony saying that, because last year we were the best side.

Sunday 10 November
Talking to a few of the lads on the phone, it sounds as if Neil had a tremendous debut. Coming from Scunthorpe to make your debut at Goodison against Arsenal must be quite nerve racking. I'm not sure how I'd have coped with it at 20, but he's obviously come through with flying colours. I wonder what the boss will do when Pat is fit?

Monday 11 November
International week again, so half the lads are away. I went in. I'm still on crutches, but I'm off the drugs now, which is good news, and I'm trying to get the ankle going after the operation. The main thing is being able to go in and see the lads and getting involved again.

Neil was absolutely delighted with things, playing at Goodison and being part of a win like that on his debut. It was quite a week for him.

Steve Williams of Arsenal had got a few of the lads wound up. Inchy said that Williams had tried to be niggly at times, but it just hadn't been productive. On one occasion it had been counter-productive. He'd tangled with Inchy, who'd caught him in a tackle and brushed him aside, and one of our goals came from that. Inchy said, 'Well, I'm not a big lad!' There was also one other thing which made me laugh. Someone had shouted at Charlie Nicholas to shut the goalkeeper off, and evidently Charlie shouted back 'I've done that twice already' or words to that effect. I felt sorry for him. Of course I wasn't there, so I can't really comment, but saying that doesn't sound as if he'd be my cup of tea. Of course I want my strikers to play with the ball, but sometimes you've got to do a little work off the ball too.

Tuesday 12 November
There was no one in today. The boss doesn't believe in killing you on the training ground, so he's given the lads today and tomorrow off. We heard that Brace is playing for England in place of Bryan Robson, who did his hamstring in the Turkey match. I'm really pleased for Brace, because I think he is a very good player, and a winner.

Wednesday 13 November
I watched the England–Northern Ireland game on TV. Not a good game, but a great result for Northern Ireland, which takes them to Mexico. The Romanians won't be very pleased, but Northern Ireland deserve it for the results they got against Romania, and objectively I don't think anyone can argue with that.

Also if Scotland beat Australia, which they should, it means that three home countries are going to Mexico, which is a tonic for the game after an awful time. If we can go there and do well it will give the game the boost it needs. But, to be fair, I don't think it is as bad as it is painted anyway. I have seen some very good games this season, they have been entertaining, with some good attacking football in them.

The international wasn't one of them really. Obviously I'm a little biased, because I hope to get my place back, but I didn't think the midfield looked right. I would play 4-4-2 rather than 4-3-3 anyway, because I think it is a better balance. I think you need the pattern which playing four across the middle gives you, especially in Mexico where the build-up is slow, and where you are playing against top class opposition. If there are holes to penetrate, world class opposition will penetrate them. And when we played Romania at Wembley they got at us a wee bit because there were holes for them to exploit.

Friday 15 November

Neil has been left out – a nice reward for a great debut. But I think the boss has made the right decision. Pat has done well this season, and I'm a great believer in playing what you think is your best team. There's plenty of time for Neil to come again, this is just part of his education.

I got off my crutches yesterday. I'm delighted – I'm just down to a walking stick now.

Ipswich 3 Everton 4   **Saturday 16 November**

I went to Old Trafford to watch United play Spurs. They kept giving the scores over the tannoy. We were two down; Liverpool were one down against West Brom, and Old Trafford was buzzing. At half-time we'd pulled one back, and Liverpool had equalised. So I felt a bit better, and after having the better of the first half, United were held to 0-0. At the end I went down to the players' lounge, and the scores were coming up on the TV. And it came up Ipswich 3, and I thought 'OH NO' and then it came up Everton 4, so they were at it again giving us heart attacks. A great result, and an old fashioned scoreline which must have given the fans a really entertaining game.

United started very well. In the first 20 minutes they could possibly have had one or two. Barnes was getting down the left flank against Gary Stevens and knocking in some good crosses. Gordon Strachan was playing in the middle and looking very busy. But slowly Spurs started to get a grip, and at the end of the day they had the better chances. Steve Perryman tightened things up in midfield, Glenn came into things and started opening United up with little balls through between the right back and the centre-half, and if Galvin's crosses had been better United would have been in trouble a few times. As it was Chris Waddle missed a couple of fair chances, heading straight into Bailey's hands and not even hitting the target, which is a bit disappointing for a striker, when he'd got through for a shot. United looked as if they were missing Robbo a bit. I think he is a tremendous influence on them, and they are missing his fire and his influence as much as his ability. He has a terrific attitude, cajoling people and getting them going, and I think they are missing that.

It was a great result for all the teams chasing them.

I saw Glenn Hoddle in the players' lounge afterwards, and discovered he had had the some operation as me, which I hadn't realised. I asked him how long he'd been out with his and he said, 'five months'. I nearly died. But then he said he'd tried to rush it to play in the UEFA Cup Final, which he didn't advise. He said, 'Take your time and you'll be spot on, you'll have no problem with it.'

That was reassuring. I've had a few injuries, but every one you get you have this doubt in the back of your mind that you won't recover: so it was nice to hear. Because, from the way he was knocking his passes around, he has certainly got over his.

Thursday 21 November

When I arrived without my crutches for the first time I got some terrible stick. 'Who said they don't believe in Miracles?' Ratters demanded, and comments were flying around. I got my own back. It was really wet, and the lads came in after training soaking and muddy and I said, 'I've grafted like anything in that gym'. The language was choice.

Friday 22 November

I'm quite pleased with the way things are going. I've spent the week doing body work and trying to get movement in my ankle, and it has seemed to improve steadily every day. I've actually been working harder than the lads. They've had a couple of days off again this week – more of Everton's hard training. But it seems to be working. I'm looking forward to the game against Forest tomorrow – I haven't seen us for a few weeks now, so I'm looking forward to watching. And a win will be handy because it will put pressure on the others, especially with United beginning to drop points. I fancy us to win, we've beaten Forest three years on the trot at Goodison, and we always seem to do quite well against them.

Everton 1 Nottingham Forest 1   **Saturday 23 November**

Sitting on the bench when Brian Clough is around adds to the fun of the afternoon. To be fair I was wearing a rather loud suit, a black suit with blue checks, so he said he'd have that when I'd finished with it. I said, 'Well, I think you'd suit it.'

Later on he said to their Gary Mills, 'Mills, you're a winger. Get that ball and go past the full-back. That is what I pay your wages for. Do it please.' His presence certainly keeps things lively. Personally I enjoy his

68

style. And he does well with his teams. He has a good side, and he uses them very well, he knows how to play the game. They keep it tight, make it very difficult for people to play against them, but when they do break out they get people forward very quickly. I've been very impressed by Peter Davenport, and although he is only just getting back after injury, so it wasn't one of the best games I've seen him play, he and Nigel Clough are a good combination.

We saw their strengths today. We had a lot of the ball, but Steve Sutton made a few good saves and they looked quite strong. And I was sitting there thinking 'It stinks a bit, does this', because it was so reminiscent of the Forest of the old days when they just soaked everything up and then suddenly broke out and 'Bob's your uncle', you're one down.

And that was exactly what happened. I'd heard the half-time scores, and United were three down at Leicester, and I went in and told the lads, because obviously that was great news for us, but when we went out again it was Forest who got the goal, not us. A quick break down the left, a cross was whipped in and Nigel Clough stuck it away.

So then we were struggling a wee bit. And it was looking a bit grim, until we knocked a corner to the edge of the box and Brace came on to it on his left peg and it flew in. After that we had a couple of chances, but we couldn't really say we should have won it.

Of course the lads were very disappointed afterwards, because United had been beaten. But we are closing the gap gradually. It's 12 points now, which doesn't seem nearly as big a gap as even 14, let alone the 17 which they had over us at one stage. Liverpool are sneaking up too, and there's a pack of clubs chasing now. It's not all over yet by a long way.

I never thought it was all over anyway. I was never convinced even when they had that tremendous start and were playing such tremendous football. Of course injuries have let them down, but that is part of football. I still think we and Liverpool are the sides to watch.

Monday 25 November
I'm made up, delighted, relieved etc. I went to see the specialist today and been given the go-ahead to start jogging. He says it will break up the adhesions, so I was able to start.

The pleasure I got from doing some jogging was indescribable after all those weeks of inaction and frustration. I only did some light work because John Clinkard has gone with the lads to London for the Milk Cup tie with Chelsea.

Tuesday 26 November
I went to Anfield to watch Liverpool play United. At half-time it came over the tannoy that we were drawing 2-2 at Chelsea and Kevin Sheedy

had been sent off. I couldn't believe it, Kevin is the last person to get sent off in our team, and the comments from all around me suggested the fans couldn't believe it either. 'He must have hit somebody with his handbag' was a frequent comment. To be honest I didn't fancy our chances when I heard that, because getting a result down there was always going to be hard even with 11 men, but the lads obviously battled it out because that was the way it ended.

That kept me happy while I waited for half an hour to get out of the ground. Mr(!) Robson had got me tickets, the worst tickets I've ever had in my life, so of course they were in the United end, and I was locked in with the United fans at the close. I was well pleased about that. I spent half an hour trying to get out, but rules are rules, and if I was in with the United fans I had to wait until the police were ready to escort them to their coaches. Eventually I did get out and went into the lounge for a drink, and saw Dennis Tueart, who had had an achilles operation. He was also reassuring. I think he had done a physiotherapy course because he seemed very clued up on the subject and gave me some helpful hints. In fact I have been using the wobble board – a board with a ball underneath it which you use the ankle a lot to balance on – but he gave me further reassurance, particularly as he now runs marathons and has no trouble at all.

So in the end I quite enjoyed the night out, especially with the news of the Chelsea result. The game itself was a good one. A bit unfortunate for United, who had had the better of the first half, deserving to lead 1-0, and then lost to a debatable penalty: at least I couldn't tell from the view I had, but the general feeling afterwards was that it was outside the box. But that's Liverpool. They ride their luck when they have it, and the signs are that the old red 'Mean Machine' is rolling again. They are making progress in the League too – they are only a couple of points behind United, and have now knocked them out of the Milk Cup.

And to be fair, the Liverpool equaliser asked a few questions about United's defence. Molby, who hadn't had the best of first halves, as sweeper, was pushed back into midfield after United scored, and he went on this run after McMahon broke off Whiteside. And United just backed off him and backed off him, and he hammered this ball in. It was a terrific shot, but United had let him run a long way without a challenge.

The penalty came a minute or so later, and at the end Liverpool were the stronger side. They do just grind people down if you give them a break. And United had further injury problems. Barnesy had done his hamstring after Saturday, so they had pushed McGrath into midfield with Strachan moving out wide again. McGrath had a tremendous game. I'm very impressed with him. If he had been less honest he might have got a penalty in the first half when he got a yard on Lawrenson and showed his pace by keeping it on a run. He got into the penalty area and

Lawrenson made a last ditch tackle, and if he had gone down it would have been a penalty, but he tried to stay on his feet and the chance was lost. Olsen had quite a good game until he tired, but Strachan had a quiet game. Johnston over ran Blackmore in the second half, so even though Rushy still couldn't get a goal against United, Liverpool finished in front.

Wednesday 27 November

It turned out that Sheeds was sent off for swearing. Rules are rules, but . . . personally I think there are worse offences like going over the top, which are more deserving of sending off than swearing.

I'm running half pace now.

Thursday 28 November

Running again, and feeling no reaction, so I'm delighted. Obviously I'm a bit stiff after the operation, but that's only to be expected.

Our reward for the draw at Chelsea is a visit to QPR if we win the replay. Another game on the silly pitch. Really entertaining that will be. We are all looking forward to that one.

Friday 29 November

The lads went off to Southampton. I stayed behind to do some more work. In the evening I went to see Tranmere Rovers play Stockport County, managed respectively by my old colleague Mr Frank Worthington and an old opponent from our Bolton and Oldham days, Mr Les Chapman. Stockport won 3-2. It wasn't the best of games, although there were some quality goals, but I love watching football. I don't really enjoy watching us play, because I get too tense, but I like going to games and getting involved. And it is always nice to come across players who you have lost track of. Barry Siddall, who I used to play with at Bolton, is on loan to Tranmere, and other players I knew were Andy Hodkinson, who also comes from Bolton, and two lads from Everton, Johnny Morrisey and Mark Leonard, who got two of Stockport's goals, were all playing. When you look through the teams it is surprising how many people you know.

And it was funny to see Frank in a typical loud suit going off into the directors' room.

The only trouble was that it was a bitterly cold night and it took me about an hour to get warm afterwards. My arthritic knees were playing up.

Southampton 2 Everton 3   **Saturday 30 November**

I went in in the morning and did a bit of training, then dodging the

Anfield traffic – they'd played in the morning, and were evidently a bit lucky to get a draw against Chelsea – went home and tried to keep track of our game. I had the radio, the TV and Ceefax on.

It was all exciting listening too. We were without Graeme Sharp, who has gone to Australia with Scotland, so Paul Wilkinson was playing. It is a difficult place to go and win. It's a small ground, and the crowd are right on top of you and get at you a bit. We won there 2-1 last season when we were going for the title. It was another of those games which showed what a good squad we had, because Kevin Richardson came in and got both goals in our 2-1 win. What a good player he is coming in as a cover player, because he would certainly get into most teams. The lads who came into our team did a great job for us last year.

Today we were one down after 60 seconds. It's getting to be too much of a habit – Chelsea, Liverpool, Bournemouth and now Southampton. I'd say the moral of that one was that you've certainly got to get there on time if you want to see us, but the Southampton game started late – they've got an old players' reunion or something, and there was a veterans match to celebrate their centenary first.

We were level at half-time, then we went 2-1 down. Manchester United were having a tight game with Watford, but then Alan Brazil scored. Obviously that was disappointing with us losing, but I was pleased for him because he is a very good player. He has been having a bad time, and he needs a run of games, so I was pleased he had scored.

Then as it got near twenty to five all hell broke loose. We'd equalised. Watford equalised and then, because our game was running late, the news came through after the others had finished that we had gone on and won.

This is just great, because with Manchester United and Liverpool drawing, things are getting closer. United are still two points ahead of Liverpool, but we're now only nine points behind United, which is only three results now. It is very, very pleasing. I think people will be looking at us now. They said we'd had a shaky start, but going down there and winning is a great result, and with that and the win at Ipswich I think we are on our way.

The only thing which worries me a bit is that we are still conceding too many goals. It is our achilles heel – if I can use that word – at the moment. 3-2 wins and 4-3 wins are great for the spectators, but I don't think the gaffer will be too pleased with the number of goals we are conceding, and it is too many for my liking.

Monday 2 December
Further progress I'm pleased to say. My running is getting stronger – I'm just over half pace, and I started kicking the ball today, so I'm building up towards full training and feeling quite pleased with it.

The lads were talking about Trevor Steven's goal for the winner at Southampton. It was supposed to be an incredible goal – he'd got the ball out wide, cut in and slammed it in from 30 yards out. It must have been a hell of a shot to beat The Shilts from that distance.

Everton 1 Manchester United 0   **Wednesday 4 December**
I've been stepping up my running the last two days. I've started doing doggies and a lot with the ball. I'm training really hard now – I'm having to have a sleep in the afternoons. I don't know whether that's my age or because I'm working harder than usual, but I need a new pair of legs. I'm really enjoying it though. We're having a lot of rain, but it's lovely and mild, and I'm loving it. There is nothing to equal the feeling of getting out in the mud with a ball.

That's three times we've played them so far, and we've won all three. Frank Stapleton put the ball into the net for our goal. I thought he was a bit unlucky. He was trying to bring it down, and it was an awkward height and it spun off his foot – but I suppose that's what happens to a forward in a defensive position. But I think we deserved to win anyway.

People will say that our beating them doesn't mean very much, but I think when Everton play United there is always a bit at stake and a bit of interest involved. And I'm sure that when we play them in the League on Boxing Day we'll win that too. I'm sure all my team mates would say the same thing. We expect to beat them. I don't know what the United players would say, but I would think that they don't fancy playing us.

Thursday 5 December
I had my first game today – just a practice match with the kids. I played for half an hour. I felt absolutely tremendous. My right achilles, the one I had had the operation on, was great. I felt no reaction at all.

But I came off after half an hour because I felt a slight strain in my left one. I could probably have run it off if it had been a serious match, it was nothing drastic, but I thought I wouldn't take any chances, so I came off. I mean, I've been out so long, there was no point in keeping on playing with the risk that it could get worse. I'm so experienced with injuries these days!

So I came off after half an hour, but I got on the ball, played a few one-twos and really enjoyed it. I'm really feeling I'm on the way back. I know now that the achilles has healed after the operation, and that is the crucial thing. If I'd felt this strain in the right achilles I'd have been a bit worried wondering what was going on, but as it is in the other one there's no problem. I shall just have a couple of light days and then after the weekend I shall be bombing again. I can't wait. I can see myself playing again within a couple of weeks.

If it hadn't been for the strain I might have been ready to play this

73

weekend. I had thought of playing in an 'A' team game on Saturday, but we'd already decided against that because it is against South Liverpool, and some Scousers are really tough lads! There would be a few young lads in there trying to make a reputation, which is great, but you don't want to be on the receiving end of it. So it hasn't really set me back.

We had a PFA meeting. Inchy, who is our PFA rep, called us together. There has been a lot of talk about a Super League, with the big clubs pushing for it. In fact they have already backed off a bit from the original idea, which was a totally separate league with no promotion or relegation. But there has been talk about the top two divisions separating, with the third and fourth divisions not having automatic promotion and relegation. The PFA had a meeting on Monday in which they said they would go on strike if the big clubs tried to force things through without everybody agreeing. Inchy got us together to tell us about it. Mr Adrian Heath, our shop steward and voter for the strike! I said I'd be a scab. Seriously I support the PFA, although I don't think there's any question of us going on strike. It won't come to that. But we had a discussion about it, and Adrian put the union's position.

I think you have to keep promotion and relegation. Perhaps the League should be streamlined, and if it is, I think it might be an idea for the lower divisions to be regionalised as they used to be. But there has to be a place for the Boltons and Blackpools and Bristols and Southends down south. We have a very difficult, demanding league, but one of the great glories of our game is its competitiveness, on the field and for clubs, lower clubs, striving to reach the top. On the field I think our competitiveness, strength and will to win have been at the heart of our club successes in Europe over the years, and I think you need that. And I think the lower divisions contribute to that as well. It is the bread and butter teams who keep the game going. Players like Kevin Keegan and Ray Clemence came from those clubs, and they might never have come through if there hadn't been lower division clubs for them to start at. I sometimes think it is better for a youngster to go to a small club than go to a club like Everton or Manchester United, where it is very difficult to come up through the youth sides, because if they've got a problem they can afford to go out and buy a player, rather than take a chance on a youngster.

I do think that cutting down the number of games we play would be a good move. The England players in the Everton team played 70 odd games last season. That is an awful lot of games when you are going to have to play against the Italians or Brazilians in the World Cup at the end of the season. But they are saying that if they cut down the first division they will bring in a British Cup, so from the players' point of view you are back to square one.

Some people are surprised that Inchy is our representative – his baby face again. In fact he's been around for a bit longer than you would think to look at him. He is a good rep – he is very interested in that side of things, so we are kept better informed than we would be if we had someone who wasn't too bothered. He was quite funny at the meeting. I took the chance to bring up my big moan at the moment, which is the number of complimentaries you get when you are injured. Players get three tickets, all the staff get three tickets, the physio, everybody. But when you are injured you only get two. Discourages you from swinging the lead I suppose. So I said, 'I'm not happy with this'. Inchy said, 'Rules are Rules, Peter'. And that was it – a democratic decision that I get two tickets until I'm fit.

I was thinking again about the way things change at football clubs. Alan Kelly is looking after the reserves now. Terry Darracott, a tremendous Evertonian, one of those characters who are the life and soul of a football club, has gone to work with Mike Lyons at Grimsby, and Alan, who came in to work with the goalkeepers, has taken over. He's got that dry Irish wit about him, which is different to Terry's. One of the fascinations of football for me is seeing team photos from year to year and the changing faces. But the clubs just roll on, and you meet an awful lot of good lads in the game. And everyone brings something to the group. I was saying a month ago about Bails leaving, but now young Neil Pointon has come in and he's another lively confident character, a great personality. He is a good player too. As a defender he is very quick to people, he shuts them down very well, and he uses the ball well too. Obviously we knew what we were doing when we got him, yet he'd been there for a lot of people to see, because he'd played nearly 200 games for Scunthorpe.

Yesterday he did one of the best warm-ups I have ever seen. We were on the bench and the gaffer told him to warm-up, and he ran up and down the pitch six times without stopping, full pelt – tremendous action. It made me shattered just watching him. So he went on. Then a bit later on Gary Lineker went down and the boss told Sheeds to get warmed up. And he stood up and did a couple of groin stretches. It was hard to imagine two more contrasting warm-ups; we were killing ourselves laughing about it on the bench.

Paul Wilkinson, Lord Lucan, is another player who is coming into things more now. I've had a high regard for him from the time Grimsby knocked us out of the Milk Cup last season. We'd battered them, had them on the rack all through the game, and he was grafting and grafting. Then in the 89th minute they got a free kick and he put a header away. It's devastating when you lose a game you've dominated in a situation like that, and you can imagine what I thought at the time.

Obviously coming to Everton from Grimsby is a big change, and he is a quiet sort of lad, but he is beginning to get into things now. And you know he is going to improve. He wants to learn. He is an awkward customer, one of those players who are all hard, bony angles, and a strong runner. Last night he had a yard on McGrath, who is quick, in the first half, and McGrath got back and got there. But in the second there was a ball played into the channel, and Wilky did him for pace, which I thought was great, because he had been beaten for pace earlier, but he had come back and kept going and going, and been rewarded.

And he is one of those players who look like natural finishers, a real goalscorer. When we have finishing exercises, he'll bend a few great goals in, but then he'll miss hit one, but it'll just bobble into the back of the net anyway. I always think, 'That's the sign of a striker'. Real strikers get goals with ones that just bobble in, not just with ones that are perfectly struck.

Gary Lineker's got that too. Although he strikes them beautifully as well. He hit one waist-high volley last night, rather similar to a goal he got for England, and it flew out off the cross bar. He has got tremendous strength in his legs.

And of course he also gives us that extra bit of pace over the top. I was sick when Andy left, because he had done tremendously well for us, he was a close friend and his attitude was great. But as I said before in the Cup Final, with Sheeds and Trevor Steven not at their best, when United pushed us up onto the half way line we couldn't get anything over the top because we didn't have any pace, and Gary gives us an outlet. Obviously he is not as rough and tumble in the penalty area as Andy, so it is pros and cons, but put the ball over the top and he's away, because he plays on defenders' shoulders so well, and once he's gone they never catch him. And you cannot argue with his scoring record. Even at Leicester, where they weren't a very successful team, he did it for them consistently. His record is second to none, and that's with Leicester.

One thing defenders hate is getting turned, and he gives us the option to get it over the top and get them turning. We did that a few times last night.

I'm really bubbling at the moment. I was absolutely delighted with that little game today. No reaction at all. The only thing is I have to have a good warm-up beforehand to get it really loosened up – a bath, then 20 minutes in the gym doing exercises, but I'll settle for that. I certainly reckon to be playing by Boxing Day. But the whole place is beginning to buzz again. You can feel it. We've had a few wins and that little bit of extra confidence is flooding back in.

Friday 6 December
I had a bit of ice treatment on my left achilles, then travelled down to

West Brom with the lads. The good news is that the right one feels fine. Sharpy was back from the Scotland trip to Australia, but Wilky is playing.

West Brom 0 Everton 3   **Saturday 7 December**

We were always in control. From the kick off there was never any doubt really, it was a bit of a battering for them. I felt a bit sorry for West Brom, because they looked like a team playing with no confidence at all. Just like at Goodison they played tippy-tappy football, which looks nice in certain areas, but just puts you in trouble. Kevin Sheedy, Pat and Gary Lineker (again!) got the goals. It was George Reilly's first game for West Brom, so he played up front with Varadi and Crooks. Three men up front is a system I've never really liked. I always feel that teams who play that way are just trying to accommodate people. I know we have done it a few times with Adrian, but it isn't a formation I like. I prefer two front men with four in the middle. Front men are always at their best hunting in pairs. They play with their backs to the game a lot, making cross-over runs, and I think three front players just get in each other's way and end up making runs which are alien to them. They just look lopsided.

Some people believe that is true even if one of the three is a winger. I'm less dogmatic about that, because we played that way at Bolton with Peter Thompson and then Willie Morgan, and it worked for us. If you've got a wide man who knows his job, you've got an outlet, and you can give it to him. It works for Chelsea at the moment with Pat Nevin, who does play it well. If you've got a good player there, you can give him the ball in tight situations and he can hold it or do things with it. Deep down though I prefer four in midfield. It works for Liverpool, it has really been successful for us because it means we are solid, but we still get a lot of goals. Obviously if you have got four in the middle, it means they have to get in the box, and it means you have to have quality players to play, but given that I'm a great believer in that way of playing.

Sunday 8 December

Went on 'A Question of Sport' with Allan Lamb in Bill Beaumont's team. A really enjoyable day, but we lost on the last question. Down to me, as usual. If you can believe it I got Garth Crooks and Ossie Ardiles mixed up! It was one of those picture questions with a flash from a Forest–Tottenham game with a white shirt going into the box with three Forest players behind him. The Tottenham player was brought down, and I was concentrating so hard on who the Forest player was, because they had both Paul Hart and David Needham there at that time, that I saw a dark skin and just assumed it was Crooksie. I got Needham right, and messed up the easy bit!

We've got the replay with Chelsea tomorrow. Sharpy will be back, but Sheeds is suspended after being sent off down there, so Richo will play. It should be a good game, I've always fancied Chelsea a bit – I said at the start of the season I thought they'd be possible outsiders for the championship, and they are in the frame. I expect us to beat them even so.

Everton 1 Chelsea 2   **Tuesday 10 December**

Yesterday's entry offers some famous last words. In fact Chelsea looked a very good side. We were at it again, one down after less than two minutes. We don't seem to be learning our lesson, and it was a simple goal too. Full-back played it up to Speedie in the centre circle, he turned and knocked it through to give Dixon a clear run and he chipped it over Neville. We've got about the fourth worst goals against record in the division. It's just as well we are the top scorers. I suppose you have to say it makes us an entertaining side to watch, but it is not like us.

Gary Lineker got a great equaliser, just getting away from McLaughlin for a header and putting it away brilliantly. Then their full-back Wood got sent off, which should have opened it up for us, but we never got on top of them, they really battled and worked for one another, and they got a great winner. McLaughlin stabbed it in after Nev had done well to block Nevin's first effort.

The thing which made it such a good goal though was the quality of the first ball in. When I was watching it I thought we looked very static. I thought 'No one's moving' and I wondered if Nev should have come. But watching it again on the club video it was just such a good ball. Rougvie came off the near post and got the flick-on, and from that moment we were struggling. Perhaps we didn't attack the second ball quickly enough, but it was very hard to counter. Chelsea scored against Liverpool that way. Manchester United used to do it with little Lou Macari, just putting it onto his head in front of the near post, and then Stoke used it for a time with Maguire hitting O'Callaghan. And if the quality of the ball in is good enough, it is almost impossible to stop. You just have to attack the second ball quickly, and we didn't attack the second ball. Which is a bit disappointing, because we rarely concede goals from dead-ball kicks.

Wood had to go off. It was a diabolical tackle and Pat had a really bad injury – he's spending the night in hospital – but apart from that I had nothing but admiration for Chelsea. They fought and they battled and they played with great spirit and a lot of ability. Speedie was brilliant, he and Dixon looked tremendous. Of course I always watch people in my position carefully, and I thought Spackman looked a very good player. He is underestimated. But Jones and Bumstead did a good job for them. Possibly they've got little weaknesses at the back, although

Pates does very well for them, but they work so hard for one another they cover it up. You can see they are getting a belief in themselves, and there seems to be something really good developing there.

I never thought I would say this about an Everton side, but I thought on the night that Chelsea wanted it more than we did. That was one of our great strengths last season. I always think that a lot of games come down to the amount of winners you've got on your side. The will to win is paramount. And this game provided a great example of that, because they wanted it more and it just shows what you can do even with ten men.

Obviously that raises the question, 'Have we lost it because we won last year?' I don't think so. I think we have still got that tremendous will to win generally, but every so often you need a kick up the backside to keep you on your toes. Last season Chelsea beat us 4-3 up here at Christmas and that provided it, and set us off on our terrific run. Hopefully this will have the same effect. And I think the lads recognise it. I was in the dressing-room afterwards, and I got the vibes coming back, and everyone was sick and I think realised we had been out battled on the day, which I don't like and we don't like. It just reminds you that you can't go out and take things for granted, you've got to go out and battle in every game, as well as being skilful and playing good stuff.

Wednesday 11 December
The lads had the day off. I was in doing body work. I'm still feeling my left achilles, so I was whisked off to see Mr Campbell, and I'm having a jab tomorrow.

Ratters got a booking against Chelsea which takes him over the limit. The boss moved quickly and has taken Kevin Steggles from Ipswich on loan, obviously to play the couple of games Ratters will miss. We've also signed a young lad, Coyle, from Ireland.

Thursday 12 December
I had the jab, which means I can't do anything for a few days. Mr Campbell doesn't believe in letting you do anything for anything from four days to a week to let the painkiller take effect.

The lads had a practice game, which is a bit unusual for us. We've got a few injuries though, so it was to sort the team out. Sheeds is out, so Richo will play. Pat's out, so Ian Marshall comes back in with Gary Stevens going back to right-back and Neil Pointon coming in. Alan Harper will be sub.

It turns out though that Ratters' booking was only a two pointer, not a four point offence, so he is available. Which leaves Steggles a bit redundant, because I'm sure we got him to cover for Ratters' absence.

79

We play Leicester tomorrow. I know we lost there earlier this season, but it was a funny sort of game because we seemed to have all the ball. I'm not denying they deserved to win, but I expect us to win tomorrow.

Everton 1 Leicester City 2   **Saturday 14 December**
That's twice in a week I've put down that I expect us to win tomorrow, and twice that we've lost. I'm not putting it down again. Today I couldn't understand it. We just didn't seem alive. It was similar to Chelsea only more so, because this time we had a goal start. Their big centre-forward Alan Smith proved a handful, and he got the winner, but it was a strange sort of game. We just looked lethargic all through, as though we thought we only had to go out there to win. I couldn't understand it because we had this great start and we needed the points to get back into the championship race. That's two home defeats on the trot, which is unusual, so we need something to get us going a wee bit.

I'm not in the best of moods either, because my left achilles doesn't seem to be getting any better. We've decided I should work it on Monday and see where we stand. At least that means I'll know where I stand. I shall be sick if it means another operation, but I've got to do something, I don't want to waste six weeks as I did with the right one messing about, and it seems the same old routine to me as before. But that is perhaps because I'm so fed up. If it meant another six weeks waiting to see if it would settle you're talking about the end of the season, and I'd sooner have the operation now and get it over with.

Monday 16 December
I had a run out. It's not an agonising pain, but it is there, and it is just getting worse and worse. So I saw Mr Campbell and he decided to operate again. I'm in on Wednesday.

Friday 20 December
I went AWOL for 2 days before going in – at least as far as this diary was concerned. Couldn't bring myself to write anything. The final straw was being told that he'd wondered whether to do the left achilles while he was doing the right one because he knew I'd had trouble with it earlier in the season.

I spent Thursday recovering from the effects of the anaesthetic. I've been allowed out today on crutches. I can't put any weight on my feet for two weeks.

Coventry 1 Everton 3   **Saturday 21 December**
The lads showed we've got a bit of mettle after all. Coventry's not the easiest place to go and win at – it hasn't been one of our most successful

grounds, so it was terrific to hear we'd bounced back and won. And United were beaten at home by Arsenal, which means we've pulled back a bit on them. We're playing them on Boxing Day, so that is an extra incentive.

Tuesday 24 December

I'm not going in. I've been told to stay at home and rest, so I'm just lounging about the house feeling sorry for myself.

Wednesday 25 December

My first normal Christmas at home for a few years. It was the first Christmas Louise has really been old enough to get involved in, so that made it even nicer. So if there is a silver lining to the whole thing it was being able to enjoy Louise's Christmas. Having Christmas Day and Boxing Day at home is a change from training Christmas Day and playing Boxing Day. But if I'm honest, I'd happily settle for training on Christmas Day.

Everton 3 Manchester United 1   **Thursday 26 December**

I listened on the radio. We might have had a penalty early on; we went one down even though we were playing well, but then we came back and got a tremendous result. We needed it desperately. It means we are only six points behind them now – if we'd lost it would have been twelve, which might have been just too much to drag back. They know now we are breathing down their necks and it is not all over. Mind, they must be sick of the sight of us. That was the fourth time we've beaten them this season. I didn't dare write it after what happened against Chelsea and Leicester, but I did expect us to beat them. I think we would beat them nine times out of ten. I always fancy us against them, and even though I didn't see the game I have been proved right. We play Sheffield Wednesday on Saturday, and in spite of our result at Hillsborough early in the season, that will be harder because their style tends to make you rush your game and knock it longer than you normally do. So if we can get another result against them it will be terrific.

Friday 27 December

Spoke to Adrian on the phone. He was bubbling, said all the lads were looking forward to tomorrow. Obviously the game last year was the one he had his ligament injury in, and now he is back, playing in my position and getting a few goals. It is always good to see a player coming back from a serious injury and doing well. Tottenham's Gary Stevens had a similar injury and when I spoke to him after their game at Old Trafford he wasn't altogether happy with it, but Adrian has recovered from his quite well.

Everton 3 Sheffield Wednesday 1 **Saturday 28 December**

Obviously I didn't go again, but by all accounts it was a tougher game for us than the score suggests. Gary Lineker and Sharpy are really bustling now as a partnership. Sharpy got two and Gary one against United today Gary got two and Graeme one. There's been a lot said about Gary and fitting him into our team, but he just keeps scoring goals and goals and goals.

We apparently had to scrap for it, but it's another win for us. It is nice to get three wins after two defeats. I think we will keep on winning now. And United's game at Newcastle was snowed off, so the gap is only three points now.

Monday 30 December

I had my stitches out today, which is always a relief. Looking at my leg it hadn't got as much wastage as the right one had, so that was cheering. I needing cheering up a bit last week, because *Match Weekly* did my stars for 1986, and it sounded as if I might as well stay in bed for the year. I don't usually look at the stars, but then I bought the *Daily Star* for some reason – I'm a *Mirror* reader usually – and the ones in there said 'an exciting time in the middle of 1986', which ties in with the World Cup so I'll settle for that. I'm feeling more positive now. I was very disappointed about having to have another operation, but I've got over that now. It's just a question of going in and getting on with it and getting fit It's happened and it's no use moaning about it. I'm pleased with the way it looks, and I'm looking forward to going in tomorrow and doing some body work.

Tuesday 31 December

John Clinkard came and collected me because I can't drive at the moment, and I went in and started getting my left ankle moving again. It immediately seemed easier than the right one was after the first operation.

The lads came in later to travel up to Newcastle for tomorrow's game Newcastle are always difficult on their own patch, and anything we get there will be a bonus, but the lads seem confident. They've had a great Christmas and are buzzing and looking to go up there and win.

Newcastle United 2 Everton 2 **Wednesday 1 January, 1986**

I went in to do more movement exercises for my ankle. Pretty boring stuff, but it has to be done.

The game sounded a real ding-dong affair. We were 1-0 up, then 2-1 down with ten men, and got back to a point from a penalty. So getting a point there with ten men is quite good really.

It turned out the lads were disappointed rather than pleased with the point. Quite a few of them thought that for half an hour in the first half it was the best we'd played all season, so we must have been in good nick. We were 1-0 up when the referee gave them a free kick which we weren't at all happy with and they equalised from it. Then it all went a bit haywire. Brace was still upset about the free kick, so he launched himself into a reckless tackle and injured himself, and came off with an ankle injury. Trevor Steven had to have stiches on the top of his foot so he was just hobbling about, and then Sheeds walked off with a groin strain. So we struggled on with ten men, but really battled and then someone got on Sharpy's back and we got a penalty, so we got a point.

The injuries we've got though, are amazing. Other clubs go on about their injury problems, but the whole midfield from last year, Paul Bracewell, Kevin Sheedy, Trevor Steven and me, are all injured. All the other three are struggling to be fit for the weekend.

Friday 3 January

I've just been working on my own with John Clinkard doing these ankle exercises. It is soul destroying being by yourself and doing it without all the lads and the fun of ordinary training. But it is a necessary part of your rehabilitation, and I'm lucky to have such a good physio, who appreciates what I'm going through and keeps me gee'd up.

Liverpool and Everton have both been drawn at home, so we are playing Exeter on Sunday in the third round of the F.A. Cup. Obviously we should beat them, but with our injury list you can't take anything for granted.

Everton 1 Exeter City 0   **Sunday 5 January**

The midfield was Heath, Harper, Richardson and Wilkinson, which is amazing. They are all good players, but you've got a full-back and two strikers playing with Kevin Richardson, who is a genuine midfield player, which just show how depleted you can get. But you have to adapt and, as I've said before, it is people who have come in as replacements and done terrific jobs for us, like Richo and Bertie Harper, who played a big part in our success last year. They did so well that you would have thought they were regular starters, not replacements, but now with two strikers playing out of position, you just have to hope they will get their heads down and do the job for you.

Which they did, although we were grateful when Gary Stevens hit in a beauty from the edge of the box. Really the game was always under control, but in the F.A. Cup it is always tense. It gives you grey hairs and you get a sweat on just watching, if it goes on a long time without your getting in front. I kept thinking, 'I hope these don't nick one', because the longer it goes on the more nervous you get. Even crosses into your box, which you deal with easily enough get you panicking. Ratters slipped and Nev had to come out and charge a lad over, which had us on the edge of our seats. We were getting increasingly impatient when Gary got one, because we didn't want to go down there for a replay. I think we would have beaten them if we had had to go down there, but obviously we didn't want to.

Against teams like Exeter you need to get a goal early on to settle yourselves down. If you don't, you feel the crowd getting restless, always more so in F.A. Cup matches, which is part of the magic of the competition, and that affects the players. It all then becomes a vicious circle, and that I think is why you get so many upsets in Cup competitions. We had to wait until 10 or 15 minutes from the end for Gary to get the goal, and by then, although it was freezing cold, I had a sweat on watching.

Exeter did well really. They weren't an attacking force, but they were organised and worked very hard and made it very difficult for us. Obviously coming to Goodison for a club like Exeter is like a visit to Wembley for us, and they didn't want to let themselves down. And they didn't. They had terrific support – they must have had 8–9000 with them in full voice, and they took a lot of credit. They put their two wide midfield players in the holes making it very difficult for us to get balls wide, and it was tough.

I'm going to see Mr Campbell tomorrow, a week ahead of schedule. Derek Mountfield, who is still having problems with his cartilage and Paul Bracewell are coming down to Lourdes with me.

Monday 6 January

Good news. Mr Campbell gave me the go ahead to start running. It means I've pinched a week. I'm delighted, it's great news. And the achilles does feel fine.

I listened to the Cup draw at the hospital on a clapped out old radio I borrowed from one of the nurses. We were about the fifth team out. A home tie with Blackburn or Nottingham Forest, who drew 1-1 at Forest on Saturday. A good result for Blackburn, obviously, but I still have the feeling we will play Forest because they always do well away from home. They looked a good side at our place, they break so well. But you can't ask for more than another home tie.

I like Lourdes – the nurses are a wonderful friendly bunch. There is one old dear who is a Liverpool fanatic, and she always bends our ears whenever we go. She loves Kenny Dalglish, and I always have a joke with her. I told her they were a good side, the fourth best team on Merseyside, next to Tranmere and our reserves, who are bottom of their league.

It was starting to snow when we left the hospital, and really cold. I thought, 'That's typical of my luck, because I don't think I shall be doing much running if this keeps up.' And it has, so it might set me back a couple of days.

Tuesday 7 January

I couldn't train outside today because of the snow, which was a bit disappointing. I went into the gym instead. It's astroturf, so I just did walking exercises and some very very light jogging, because its obviously not the best area to train in. The lads have got two days off, so I'm just jogging with Brace.

Mark Higgins popped in to Bellefield to say hello. He was meant to be making his debut for Manchester United against Rochdale, but their game has been postponed again – their undersoil heating obviously isn't working as well as ours.

He looked tremendously fit and I was delighted for him. I'm sure he will do well if he does play when the game takes place, because he was always a good player, a solid, quick defender, who never gave anything away and did very well for Everton, playing through a lot of pain.

With Derek likely to be out for the season, you wonder if the boss was right to let Higgy go when Derek came back and started training again at the start of the season; but when I look at Higgy now he looks a new man, and maybe he needed a change of scene after the horrific time he'd had. Sometimes you can stay at a club too long, but it must have been very difficult for him having played through all the club's bad years, to be out injured watching us win all those trophies and not be part of it. So although perhaps we could have done with him now, in the long run it might have been better for him to go to a new club and a new challenge.

Friday 10 January

The last three days I've just been in the gym with Brace following the same routine. Nothing strenuous, just getting the ankle ticking over. It is still bone hard and icy outside.

Mark Higgins played last night for United – and tweaked his ligaments. I complain about my luck, but when you look at the time he has had, being out for two years, being told he is finished and fighting his way back, it make you realise how lucky you are. At least I'm starting to get going again and, thank God, I've got no more sheaths to be taken out, so I know I won't have any more trouble there.

Really the game swung on a penalty. For once I sat in the stand along with Brace rather than on the bench. We were 2-0 down, Brace and Trevor Steven had both failed fitness tests, and it looked as if we had a real struggle on our hands, because QPR looked quite solid. Sharpy had a good chance. All he had to do was head it straight but he headed wide, and I thought at the time, 'It's going to be one of those days'.

Then, just before half-time, the referee gave us a penalty. He was in a great position to see to be fair, and it probably was a foul, but it was the type where the defender is climbing on the striker, which referees give free-kicks for outside the box, but nine times out of ten don't give them for inside the box. So from QPR's point of view it was a sickening decision. So that put us back in the game and in the second half we got three goals in 12 or 15 minutes and were never in any danger. Even when Sheeds' groin went again and he had to come off, Wilky came on and got the fourth, to add to the inevitable two from Sharpy and one from Gary Lineker. The penalty was the turning point, but even so QPR went in 2-1 up, and I wasn't too impressed with their response really. They didn't seem to come out again with any conviction. They are going to Carlisle for a Cup match on Monday, and they'll have to show a bit more resolution up there, because that will be a hard game. They need a few more with Terry Fenwick's attitude.

So it was three more points even with our depleted forces. Trevor and Brace may be fit for the next game. Brace's ankle is getting a wee bit better, although it is a slow job. Trevor has just got a big hole in the top of his foot. He can run and turn on it without any problem, but he can't kick with it. It is in a really sore position, and you can't get away with it however much padding you put over it.

We are still conceding goals though. Certainly the fans are getting their money's worth watching us, and I suppose in the state football is in, we have to think about entertaining them. And probably they would sooner watch us win 4-3 than 1-0, so I suppose my views aren't important. But I don't like to see us conceding goals, and I don't think the boss is over happy with the amount we're letting in at the moment.

I trained really well today, not a twinge, so I'm hoping I shall play in the 'A' team on Saturday. But I'm just delighted to be joining in with the lads again.

Blackburn beat Forest 3-2, so that's another of my tips gone down the drain. I really thought Forest would do them. We'll be quite happy with that result though, because we will fancy ourselves against Blackburn at Goodison.

Tuesday 14 January

The lads have got a couple of days off again. The gaffer really believes in working us hard. I did a few sets of doggies. We've got a bank at the back of the gym which you run up and down. I started off doing eight, then seven and so on down to one. Then I did a one to six, which is hard work. You run one up to the top of the pitch, then jog one, then run two and jog two, and so on. I felt quite good again, so I was pleased.

Wednesday 15 January

I did a 12 minute run, then a set of doggies. I'm just looking forward to Saturday. No, I'm looking forward to joining in with the lads again tomorrow.

Thursday 16 January

Joined in with the lads in a game of possession followed by a five-a-side. The boss was watching and he pulled me aside at the end and said he didn't want me to play in the 'A' team. I was not too pleased with that, and said so. But he was winding me up, because he then said he wanted me to play in the reserves, providing I don't feel any reaction tomorrow. He only wants me to play half a game, but I'm delighted.

Friday 17 January

I woke up feeling a bit stiff, so I went in early and had a warm bath and did my stretching exercises. Then I joined the lads in our usual Friday head-tennis. A triumphant and profitable return – my team, Sharpy, Richo and me, won and scooped the pot. We all put £1 in.

Nev had got a bang in training on Thursday and it turns out he has broken a rib. I think he will play though. Last year I cracked three ribs at one stage, and had a jab to freeze the nerves on the bones, and it looks as if Nev will have the same thing. I think he will play with a jab.

Brace is still struggling, Sheeds is as well, but Trevor might be fit. We're away to Birmingham, and I'm sure we'll be going there for three points. We've got designs on the title again, and the way things are going it's all quite pleasing. I'm sure the boss is pleased as well, because in spite of the injuries we keep ticking over and picking up results.

I'm going to play for the reserves, which is sooner than I had expected, so I'm delighted with the way it's gone. The boss has said he's quite happy for me just to play a half, but he has left it up to me, so I shall just see how it goes tomorrow.

Birmingham City 0 Everton 2   Saturday 18 January
Everton Reserves 2 West Brom 1

I didn't break any pots, but I got through the game without any problems. I wasn't really extended, I played well within myself, and I felt fine at half-time so I played the full 90 minutes. They had Tony Grealish playing, along with Gary Robson, Bryan's brother, and Gerry Armstrong. I've had a few battles with Tony in the past, so I had a little word with him. I said 'First day back after four months, so take take it easy' and we had a laugh.

One of the good things about it, was that I was able to ease my way in without any publicity, because the boss had kept it quiet, which I appreciated. It is very different to Bryan's situation at Manchester United – he's gone to some physio in Amsterdam for a different opinion on his injury, and every step he takes he's followed by the press. I prefer our way, because I think it takes the pressure off you. You can go out and enjoy the 90 minutes without feeling you've got to prove yourself and show you haven't lost anything during your lay-off.

Our game had kicked off at 2 p.m., so we were changed in time to watch the results on TV in the players' lounge. We'd won 2-0 at Birmingham. Gary Lineker scored both goals. What a surprise! United were 2-1 up and then it flashed across to Old Trafford and there was a picture of Nigel Clough walking off, and Forest had done us another favour – they'd won 3-2, so the gap is down to two points now.

Funny incident in our game. There seemed something strange about the pitch, and after about two minutes I noticed there weren't any corner flags up. So I pointed it out to the referee, who said he had already noticed and asked for them. We played for about ten minutes without any, which is a bit unusual. It was odd that no one noticed at the start.

Sunday 19 January

A bit stiff, but no reaction in the tendon itself, which is encouraging.

Monday 20 January

Went in and did a bit of training with the lads. Again it went well. There's a reserve team game with Derby on Tuesday. The boss has left it up to me to decide whether I play or not. I hope I shall, because I feel good. He said again that he'll be happy if I just play one half.

I hooked Ratters today beautifully. I was having a cup of tea after training sitting with Kevin, Kevin Sheedy, Colin Harvey and a couple of the groundsmen. We were slaughtering Dougie Rose, who is the Bellefield groundsman, for not having the corner flags out at Goodison. Of course he said that it's not his job, Bellefield is his responsibility, not Goodison. Then we started talking about the different types of corner flags – if you win the League Championship, you get special ones. And I said, 'Yes, and they're having special sombrero-shaped ones at the World Cup'. And Mr Kevin Ratcliffe, Captain of Wales, dived in, 'You must be joking', which had all the lads laughing. A typical defender Ratters – he's quite a mickey-taker himself, but he's always likely to dive in. You

88

can always get him. A pity Wales haven't qualified so he won't be there to see the sombrero-shaped corner flags for himself.

Everton Reserves 0 Derby 1   **Tuesday 21 January**
The lads have got a couple of days off again. I played. It was a very competitive game. Arthur Cox, the Derby manager, is one of those people who always gets his players wound up, and they were a good side – they're top of the League – and it was a very hard game. I enjoyed it. I got one or two late tackles – I mean tackles of course – in, but I didn't get too involved. I just had a good run out, and lasted the 90 minutes without any discomfort, so it was quite pleasing again. It's just a question of getting my sharpness back and building up my strength, and having had two games in four days I'm delighted with the way it is going.

Wednesday 22 January
Basically I had the day off – I just went in for a hot bath and a few loosening exercises.

Thursday 23 January
The lads were back in after a couple of days off. I really enjoyed joining in with them and the training; it is one of the joys of being a footballer.

A rare sight at Bellefield – the old enemy coming through the gates. The Prudential Insurance Co. are sponsoring a Merseyside Unites campaign – an attempt to get together after the Brussels tragedy, and photographs and posters will be given to schools and community centres free of charge. So the Liverpool first team squad came over for the joint photo. It must have been nice for them to see a proper training ground for once, which I told them. Kenny had a dig back about the streaks I've had put in my hair. He looks in really good nick – he still looks 21.

A nice bit of news as well which shows the fans haven't forgotten me. I've won the *Liverpool Echo* Sports Personality of the Year Award. I just pipped Jan Molby, who has really settled in well in English football. I think when he came it was all a bit quick for him, but he has slimmed down a bit and he looks a very good player. He's got a thicker Scouse accent than I have, so he must really be settling down here.

I must thank all the readers who voted for me – perhaps it was just a result of having a large family to vote in a small poll!

Friday 24 January
There is no reserve team match tomorrow, so I shall just go in and do a little training in the morning. The boss obviously wants me to wind down after two games in four days, and he told me to take it easy over the weekend. There was some speculation in the press that I might play

tomorrow against Blackburn, but there is no way that that is on. I trained OK again, but I don't think I'm ready.

Inchy is struggling with a groin strain, but the good news is that Brace and Sheeds are fit. We can't take Blackburn for granted. They've asked for another 2000 tickets evidently, so they'll have around 12,000 with them. They are a good solid side, a team who have been knocking on the door of the first division for a few years now, without quite making it. They've got some good old pros like Fazackerly, a good solid back four with Branagan, Keely, Fazackerly and Rathbone, who have been there for a time and know each other's game inside out, and they've got Garner, who has always got goals in the second division, so it won't be easy.

Everton 3 Blackburn 1   **Saturday 25 January**
Gary Lineker got another two. His finishing was world class. For his first goal he sold a dummy and three of their defenders went for it. So did Inchy and I, sitting on the bench! Then he just chipped it over the keeper. The second one was a similar effort. I've said it before, but he and Sharpy are looking an incredible handful up there. I know I wouldn't want to have to play in the back four against them.

Pat van den Hauwe got the other goal. He's playing centre-half and is taking over Derek's mantle in that respect too – it's his second this year. He's not a great goalscorer, but he put it away well. Chris Thompson, who I played with at Bolton, got Blackburn's goal. He has been in and out this season, but he got two goals against Forest and now this one, so it is nice to see him doing well.

I felt sorry for Sheeds, who had to come off again. This time he felt a tweak in his knee. He must have had about 12 fitness tests this season. He's never really been able to get into his stride. I know I've had four months out, but he has had these continual niggling injuries, which are equally frustrating. He has had groin strains and hamstrings and knocks on the ankles, and he hasn't really been able to train all through the season; he's been getting off the treatment table to play all the time, and considering everything he has done a terrific job playing when he isn't 100 per cent fit.

Sunday 26 January
Watched Liverpool win at Chelsea in the live match on TV. They have a poor record at Stamford Bridge, but I just had a sneaking feeling they would do it somehow, and had a £25 bet with a friend on it last night. And I was right, although it wasn't very convincing. Chelsea had a few injury problems – they lost Dixon, who is one of their great assets, and then Lee and ended up with 10 men, but Liverpool still had to struggle to hold on.

Liverpool were playing their sweeper system again, which I'm no great lover of. I don't think it really suits them. I've seen them use it twice now, and it doesn't seem their game really. But they've got results both times, and Kenny obviously thinks it's right, so who am I to say?

Last night I was presented with a Manchester Students' Trophy as Sportsman of the Year, which was very nice. I seem to get more awards when I'm not playing than I do when I'm playing.

Monday 27 January

Had a session in the gym with John Clinkard. I missed the Cup draw, but we're away to Tottenham or Notts County – with the replay at White Hart Lane. I expect it will be Spurs, which means we'll be playing them about four times in a couple of weeks – we're playing them in the Super Cup semi-final.

Apart from our game, there were one or two other mouth-watering games. Manchester United and West Ham, if they both win their replays – West Ham's is at Ipswich, which will be tough – Arsenal and Luton. Liverpool are at York, which isn't a bad draw for them.

Playing a team four times quickly is always a daunting prospect. It gets very frustrating because you get to know how each other play. It tends to become very sterile and niggles can carry over. I don't like it. As I've said before I'm not really in favour of the Super League, and if it meant playing each team four times, like they do in the Scottish Premier division, I wouldn't fancy it at all.

Tuesday 28 January

Did a really stiff running session up and down the hill at the back of the gym. It's only a little hill, but when it is heavy, it is really hard and gets you blowing a bit. It feels like that hill of sand which Sean Connery runs up in one film – I can't remember the title.

My achilles feels fine though, so I expect to play in the reserves against Hull tomorrow.

Our treatment room is like Emergency Ward 10 at the moment. I think John Clinkard is getting suicidal he is so overworked these days. Brace started training in the gym and felt his groin. Ratters, who got a thigh injury in a tackle with Branagan on Saturday, felt his back. Then there's Sheeds, Adrian Heath, the list just goes on.

We've bought a lad from Wigan, Warren Aspinall, which was a bit of a surprise – to me anyway. He's going to stay with Wigan for the rest of the season. Bryan Hamilton, whose opinion I respect, came up to Bellefield today and he was saying he thinks Aspinall will make a first class player.

I met the lads at Birch Service Station on the M62 for the trip over to Hull. The snow was coming down relentlessly, so we stopped again at the next services, Hartshead Moor, to phone up to see if our journey was really necessary.

Alan Kelly got off the coach to phone and came back saying it sounded as if their secretary thought he was talking to an idiot, because he said they hadn't had any snow at all in Hull. I couldn't believe it, but when we got there, there wasn't any snow. The pitch was muddy on top, and then hard a couple of inches down. We lost 2-0, but from a personal point of view it went superbly. I got a few good tackles in, which always helps. I hadn't thought there would be any problem with tackles, but it was nice to have it confirmed by getting a few good ones in and not even thinking about it. In fact everything went well, there was virtually no stiffness at all, which reassures me that I am going to have no problems with my achilles tendons from now on, so I was delighted. The only thing wrong was losing.

On the coach home we had the radio on listening to the Cup news. We're playing Tottenham, who thrashed Notts County. United got through against Sunderland. I got off again at Birch, and went into Manchester to meet a friend, Paul Ingham, who has a nightclub, and Bryan Robson for a drink. Then we went on for a Chinese meal, and talked about Bryan's visit to Amsterdam, which was interesting, hearing about the different views on injuries of the man over there. Bryan had come back very convinced, said he had worked wonders with friction, using his fingers, and ice and stretching exercises. I'm a great believer in body exercises, perhaps doing 200 a day, but Bryan was saying this man believes that you should do them as slowly as possible, rather than with quick jerking movements.

Of course I had to wind him up about getting sent off and missing the Liverpool match as a result. He obviously wasn't very happy about it, but I think he's resigned to it now. I can't repeat what he said about the linesman, although he didn't really blame the referee.

I think you can become a victim of your own publicity though in certain ways. I know I was very glad that no one knew I was having my first game in the reserves. When Bryan played his first reserve team game at Barnsley a week or so later, the TV cameras were there, all the newspapers were there, so everything he did was under the microscope. And I know that in one or two of the reserve team games I've played in the last ten days, because I'm an international, I've found it difficult to find a yard of space playing against these young lads who want to test themselves and you. But that is a responsibility you just have to live with.

Just went in and had a bath, and did a few stretching exercises. Everything feels great. I might even play on Saturday, because Sheeds is struggling, Adrian Heath is struggling and Gary Lineker is struggling. I'm not 100 per cent yet, but I don't think I'll let anyone down. It is a funny thing about match-fitness. You can play 100 reserve games and you won't get match-fit. They'll get your mind right and get you to a certain level, but the only way you get fit for playing in the first team, is by playing in the first team. And I'm sure if I'm picked for Saturday, once the adrenalin gets going, I could last the game.

But if I don't play against Tottenham in the League on Saturday, I'm sure I'll play against them in the Super Cup in midweek. It's really up to the boss now – I've had a chat with him about it, and I'll leave it to him. He's not a bad manager after all.

It's not a bad time to be coming back either. There's definitely a buzz about the place now. You can almost smell it. In fact I think you can smell it. When you go to a club with relegation in the air, I think you can smell that. And vice versa, when you go to a club where things are about to start happening, it is a different buzz, a different smell, but it is there. There is something in the atmosphere, something about the place.

People walk with a spring in their step if you like, there is a lot more laughing and joking; there's just a general buzz that makes you feel that you could be on the brink of something good. Things are more or less in our own hands now. We're two points behind United, and I think it is a question of one of the top four – United, us, Liverpool and Chelsea – winning it. Chelsea have had a couple of knock-backs in the Cup competitions, so it remains to be seen whether they can bounce back. I think they will. But if we win our games we'll win it.

Bryan's return is obviously an important boost for United, because he makes the others play. I think Whiteside has been missing him, although Bryan was saying last night that Norman's been suffering with a knee injury and he played all the second half last night with a groin strain, because Strachan went off with a hamstring. That must be about six they've had, which is extraordinary. It does make you wonder a bit, because you never hear of us or Liverpool having hamstring injuries. I don't know what United do in their training, although Bryan says they sometimes have a hard running day, which we never do during the season. The boss leaves it up to us if we feel we need a set of doggies, or an extra blow, but he's basically a great believer in letting the games keep you ticking over. I took a friend down to watch training one day and his actual quote was, 'You flick the ball up in the air twice and then you're having a shower and you get paid a fortune for that?' Well, we do a bit more than that, but our training is so simple, it does border on the ridiculous. But if you get fit in pre-season, and the lads who went on the

England tour only had about three weeks' break anyway, so they hadn't had time to lose their fitness, you don't need much during the season, you are playing so many games. That's always been Liverpool's philosophy too, and no one ever queries their fitness.

England won 4-0 in Egypt on Wednesday. Obviously with all the Cup replays it wasn't the full squad. There's another game against Israel in a month's time, and I hope I shall get a call-up for that. I shall be disappointed if I don't, but I'm determined to get to Mexico, so I shall battle on. Mr Robson must have the nucleus of the squad in his mind now, but I think there are still a few places up for grabs, and I am confident of my ability to get one.

And if there is a silver lining to my injury and Bryan's, it means we'll have relatively fresh legs. I haven't done anything yet this season – I've only played half a dozen games, and I wasn't fully fit in any of them, so I can come in now and be really buzzing. While some of the other lads will have played 60 games by the time we go to Mexico. Gary Lineker for example has played 40 already. It's a crazy way to prepare for the biggest tournament in the world, and other countries will be a lot better equipped than us, but that's the way our game is run, so we just have to make the best of it.

I'd been a bit disappointed with the attitude of some of our reserves in the games I've played. I had a word with the boss about it today, but he just said, 'You keep on with your own game and it won't be long before you are in'.

Friday 31 January
I got a shock when I picked up the paper this morning. 'Reid to the Rescue', saying that I was playing on Saturday. The boss hadn't given me any indication he was thinking of playing me when I saw him yesterday. In fact I took Barbara and Louise out for dinner last night and had a few bottles of wine, because there's no reserve game on Saturday. If there's a game we never go out on Thursday.

Anyway I got to Bellefield and the boss called me in and said, 'Do you feel all right?'

So I said 'Yes' and he told me I was playing tomorrow, which is typical of his style. He doesn't mess about. I think he hadn't said anything to me yesterday, because he didn't want to give me too long to think about it, as it is my first game for five months. He is very good like that. He protects you very well. When I had to have my second operation he kept that out of the press, and he let me start my come-back quietly.

Obviously I'm delighted. It was a surprise. We've had a few injuries,

TOP *Champions 1985: tired but happy. I'm not sure if the linked arms are because we couldn't stand up, but they show our togetherness.*

BOTTOM *Keeping tight and hustling together: Ratters, me and Brace are too much for Holverda in our European Cup Winners' Cup quarter-final v Fortuna Sittard.*

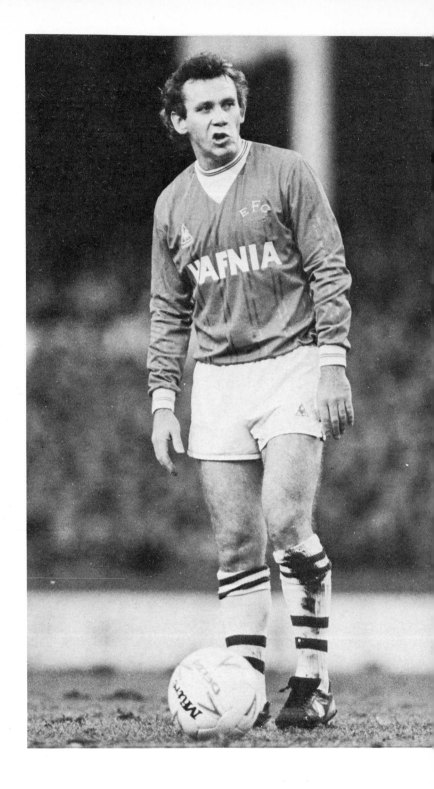

FAR LEFT *I'm Sheeds' dummy at free kicks, and it looks as if I know it.*

LEFT *A picture that sums up our 5th round Cup match in the mud at Tottenham.*

BELOW *Fortunately we had some composed moments too.*

TOP LEFT *The reason for playing football: to play in the big games and win them.*
TOP RIGHT *As our faces suggest, in spite of the sending off, the 1985 Cup Final didn't work out as we hoped it would.*
BOTTOM *Andy Gray's reaction to the controversial tackle in the 1985 Final was voluble.*

LEFT *One of the reasons Alan Robinson is not Everton's favourite referee . . . Sharpy goes for the ball, Steve Nicol goes for Sharpy. I thought it was a blatant penalty, but like Alan Hansen's handball in the 1984 Milk Cup Final, Mr Robinson decided otherwise.*
Sporting Pictures (UK) Ltd

BELOW *When you've got 4 in midfield you can keep together: Brace and I side by side in the 1985 Charity Shield – the game that ended any inferiority complex about Liverpool. Keith Hackett, one of my favourite referees, looks on approvingly.*

The game that started my run of injuries but took us to Mexico: England v Romania in September, with Rednic and I finding that you win some and you lose some . . .

TOP *Giving Billy Hamilton a free header cost us the match at Oxford.* P. Floyd
BOTTOM *Gary Lineker's fortieth goal of the season should have been the most important, putting us in the Cup Final. But then we blew it . . .* All-Sport/Dave Cannon

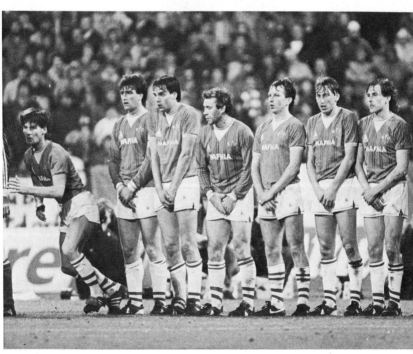

Sheeds and Adrian Heath are missing, but it is nice to know that he is quite happy to stick me in. He probably had good reports back from the game at Hull. Anyway I just went and had a game of head-tennis and came home.

Everton 1 Tottenham Hotspur 0   **Saturday 1 February**
It was quite an eventful come-back, because I got the goal about seven minutes from time, and we went to the top of the League – at least until tomorrow when United play West Ham in the TV match.

It began quietly enough. I was up early, as usual, had scrambled eggs for breakfast, but then I got a phone call saying Radio 2 wanted me to go on to open the programme with Alan Green, so I went in to the ground early to have a little chat with him.

The fans were tremendous – I had a terrific ovation from them, which was very moving. It's always nice to know that you haven't been forgotten.

The game itself was not a classic. There was a swirling, cold wind, which didn't help us, and it was very tight. I think with the Cup games coming up, Tottenham's main concern was not to get beaten, and they made it very difficult for us. They never really threatened us, but they got men behind the ball and made life extremely difficult, because although they were having a bad time, they have got a lot of good players.

Garry Mabbutt had an outstanding game playing as a central defender I thought, especially when you consider that he was up against the pair I think are the best strike force in the League.

I don't think I played particularly well. I didn't expect to. It will take me four or five games to get anywhere near match-sharpness. As I said earlier in the week you could play 100 reserve matches and you still wouldn't be match-fit for the first division. It's a different ball game, it's so quick. I kept getting caught on little things, and I was shattered when the goal came. Gary twisted and got a cross over, Sharpy and Trevor got headers to it and it came to me on the edge of the box. I chested it down and just got my shot in, as Steve Perryman and Chris Hughton rushed out to try and block it. I saw it hit the underside of the bar, and I saw Gary Lineker, who was making a run into the box, turn round and I turned away. I didn't see it actually cross the line, but all the lads assured me it had.

Obviously I was delighted, because coming at that stage it meant we had won. All we had to do was keep it tight for the last few minutes.

The boss had just about been going to take me off when the goal went in. I wish he had taken me off straight away after it, because a couple of minutes later I nearly threw the points away. I got the ball somewhere around the half way line. I could have done anything with it, but then I got shut down and I turned towards our goal. I'd got nothing on, so I should really have belted it into the stands. But when you're down physically I think you go mentally as well and I tried to hit this back pass, and put it straight into Chiedozie's path. Luckily for me, Nev made it hard for him, and although he went past Nev, he ran the ball out. Getting caught on a back pass is something I never do, well, almost never, but when you are exhausted you make mistakes. I froze watching it. Time just seemed to stand still for those few seconds. Someone said afterwards I'd picked the right person to pass to. No disrespect to Chiedozie, who is a good winger and pacy, but I don't think he's the best finisher. If it had been Clive Allen I might have paid for it. If it had gone in, I think they'd have found me in the Mersey, but as it was we got away with it.

Obviously it being my first game back for five months and me getting the goal which took us to the top, I got all the attention afterwards, even though I'd had a quiet game. I said I wanted to thank Brace for doing my running for me, because he had had a super game even though he is really struggling with his ankle. He never gets much attention, but he is an outstanding player. He came into the players' room and I asked him how his ankle was and he said, 'killing me', I said, 'Well, I hope it kills you every week, if you're going to play like that'. Because he had nicked the ball off Glenn and started things for us half a dozen times.

He does a hell of a lot of running. I thought he had a great year last year. When we bought him some people said that he and I were very similar in style and might not work together too well, but I think we complement each other. We work together really well on certain things. I can hold people up and then he can come in and tackle them, and vice versa. I can remember countless occasions when one of us has someone tight, so that the other can come in and nick the ball off them. We have a combination which works really well. You find out how good a player is when you play with him, and Paul may not be spectacular but he is a very, very good player. There's certainly one thing we've got in common – our finishing ability is a standing joke among the lads. Barbara said today that that was the first goal she'd seen me score, because the few I have got have come in away matches. I think Paul's done quite well this season – he has got three so far. Funnily enough I had four shots against Tottenham, more than I usually do in games. Perhaps I was trying to impress! Usually I get a nose bleed or come out in a rash if I get into the opposition penalty area. In our promotion year at Bolton I got about ten goals from midfield, which is not bad. I should improve on my current rate.

I had a laugh with Steve Perryman during the game. We're neither of us the quickest players in the world. He caught me once and I said, 'I was trying to get out of the way there, but I was a bit too slow'. He said, 'Yes, if we had a race it'd be a selling-plate'.

He's given them a bit of steel since he moved back into midfield. I think at the moment they could do with one or two more players like him and Mabbutt, who are steady. If you've got players like that running through your side you've always got a chance.

After last year, they've really fallen away. At the moment they show all the signs of a side lacking confidence. I don't think their crowd is helping them. They are a terrific crowd and White Hart Lane is one of my favourite grounds, but I think their situation at the moment is similar to Everton's two and a half years ago. The crowd want success so much you can feel their impatience, and it becomes intimidating. There is such a thin line between success and failure at football, and confidence is a deciding factor. If you like, a bad back pass at Oxford changed Everton's history. From a side which was going out of the Milk Cup to a third division team, we went on to reach the Milk Cup Final, win the F.A. Cup, lose only two or three games in the remainder of the season and win the Championship and the European Cup Winners Cup.

But you have got to make it happen as well, and I think some of the Tottenham team aren't doing that at the moment. I hate picking people out because it always seems like tempting fate, when you've got to play a side again quickly, so saying Chiedozie isn't the best finisher in the world, probably means he will go and score against us. But I was a bit disappointed with Chris Waddle. He proved at Newcastle that he can win you a game with his ability, but I think it is fair to say that he hasn't set the Thames alight, since he's been at Tottenham. If I were him, as it is not going for him on the ball at the moment, in that situation, I would definitely try working a bit harder. I think that is something he needs to get into his game.

So much in English football depends on the character of your players. We play sides who can match us for skill and ability, because in England players are much of a muchness, and it comes down to how much you want to win. I was critical of us against Chelsea and Leicester on those grounds, but since then we've responded tremendously. And we now have the confidence to go on winning. It won't matter if it is a very tight game, we'll hustle and battle and force people into errors. And everyone can be pressured into errors. In the Charity Shield we scored because we forced McGrath into an error, and he is a tremendous player – I've voted for him as my Player of the Year, because I think he kept United going while Robbo was out. Against Bayern Munich, people like Augenthaler and Matthaus have tremendous skill, but we hustled them into errors. It is the basis of Liverpool's success over the years. Of course they are a great passing team, but they have tremendous strength when they haven't got the ball.

And when you look at our side we've got great tenacity. Take Gary Stevens. You can go past Gary with the ball, but he'll get up and catch you. So will Kevin Ratcliffe. In midfield Paul will hunt and nick things and you need people like that.

Of course we've got some class as well. No one's asking Gary Lineker to knock people in the face or be an Andy Gray, but he gives us his pace and his finishing. Graeme Sharp has been outstanding over the last couple of months. He is a real quality centre-forward and he looks as if he is improving all the time.

So at the moment there is a similar feeling to last year. It is different, because Andy's charismatic personality is not there now, but there is a belief that we are going to win something. And we are very close as a group. I think if you got into our players' lounge you could feel the warmth. I know Brace had a grump on when I was chatting to him, because of his ankle, but it is a happy place where we all take the mickey out of one another. I've been in one or two where I've had a nice drink after a game, but they haven't got the same homely feeling. That is nothing against the players, but I think you feel a nicer atmosphere in our lounge. Everyone mixes. A lot of it comes down to the boss having got a good set of lads together, which I think he must get a lot of credit for. You get someone like Pat van den Hauwe, who has come from a club like Birmingham, where they have a few lively lads to say the least, and he has come in and fitted in perfectly. But we aren't a glamour side like United, which puts a lot of pressure on them. We prefer a low profile, and that is something Liverpool have managed to have, in spite of all their years of success.

Sunday 2 February
I was meant to go down to London today to do the England World Cup record, but I was so stiff when I woke up I decided to give it a miss. Going down to London and back wouldn't have done me any good at all, with another trip down there for the Super Cup match on Wednesday coming up. So I spent a couple of hours in the bath and took Louise for a walk.

Then I watched the West Ham–Manchester United game on the box. West Ham won 2-1, which kept us top. The perfect advertisement for English football. It was a terrific game, everything about it was absolutely fabulous. United were coasting it I thought, until the keeper let two in. That's a damning statement, and I'm not much of a keeper myself, so possibly I'm talking through my hat, but I put them both down to him. One was from long range at an angle, and with the other I thought he looked at the forward coming at him and took his eye off the ball. I'd be very disappointed if my keeper let two in like that, because I really thought they were coasting it, I couldn't see West Ham scoring.

It was sickening for Bryan Robson going off like that, because I thought he and Colin Gibson were both playing magnificently. But to be fair to West Ham, they were trying to get back at United. And it is incredible what a difference a goal makes. From the moment they got the first goal, things started to tick. I thought McAvennie was left a bit isolated in the first half, because they were trying to get Cottee in between Gidman and McGrath, and I don't think they caused United any problems. But then suddenly Wardy hits one in, and suddenly Cottee is getting in closer with McAvennie, and Devonshire is running down the left and they looked an altogether different proposition. But it was magnificent entertainment.

Monday 3 February

I got to London after all. When I was going out training, John Clinkard said there was a call for me from Andrew Clements at the Terry Wogan office. I just thought it was the lads taking the mickey, so I went out and trained and didn't think any more about it. But when I came back in, they had been on about four times, so it obviously was genuine and I spoke to him. They wanted me to get the train down and go on the show. It was about 1 p.m. then, so I thought it was too late, because I had to go back to Bolton to change. But they booked me on the 5.20 shuttle from Manchester Airport, and the boss said I could go, provided I was booked into the Westmoreland, which is the hotel we stay at. The lads are coming down tomorrow, but he said he'd see me there later, because he was going to watch the Watford–Manchester City Cup replay. We're playing Watford on Saturday, and City the following Tuesday.

So it was a bit hectic, but I caught the shuttle and did the show. I hadn't had time to get nervous, so I quite enjoyed it.

Then I booked in here, had a sleep and phoned Dad. I don't know what sort of team we'll have on Wednesday, because he told me Brace, Sheeds, Gary Lineker, Alan Harper, Sharpy, Kevin Ratcliffe and Inchy aren't coming down tomorrow, so there will be a lot of changes. I don't think that's a bad thing in a way, because if you are playing a team several times, by law of averages you are bound to lose sometime. I'm sure at a pinch – if it were the F.A. Cup tie for instance – some of the lads could play, but I think it's sensible to leave them out of this one.

Tuesday 4 February

The boss took me out to Wheelers fish restaurant for lunch, then we had a walk round Fortnums before coming back to the hotel to meet the lads. Aston Villa were staying there as well, so I spent the afternoon in Andy's hotel room chatting to him.

My appearance on Wogan brought back his embarrassing moment on A Question of Sport. They had to identify a ground from a photograph, and Andy said 'Hillsborough, no QPR, . . .' and mentioned a few. At the end it turned out to be Glasgow Rangers, which for a Scot to get wrong . . . He got some terrible stick from the lads. And about a week later this envelope arrived for him. Inside there was a big photo of Ibrox with a huge arrow pointing at the ground and 'This is Ibrox' written on it. It was from Derek Johnstone. Andy's never lived it down, although I think my getting Ossie and Garth Crooks mixed up is in danger of becoming a legend too.

They were playing in a Milk Cup replay at Highbury tonight. Talking to Andy he wasn't overjoyed with the way things were going. He said they needed a bit more steel, although he was very impressed with Elliott, the centre-half they'd got from Luton. I got the impression Andy thought they might get a tanking at Highbury, but it turned out they won 2-1, so they are in the semi-finals. So Andy is still in line to keep his record – every time he joins a club, they reach a final in his first season.

The lads arrived. A bit of stick flying around about the Wogan show, then we went into Regents Park and had a game of head-tennis. The boss, Colin Harvey and Doc Irvine all joined in, nothing very strenuous.

We are a young group, and it is going to be difficult for us. I know it is a nonsense competition, but with the Cup game coming up, Tottenham will want to show us they mean business. We've got Darren Coyle, who was playing in the Irish League three months ago, and Peter Billinge who was playing for South Liverpool then, in the team along with Ian Marshall. Darren looks as if he can become a good defender, he's quick and good in the tackle, and Peter Billinge is a big, strong tackler, but both lack experience. On the bench there's Derek Walsh, who is a brother of Colin, the lad at Nottingham Forest, and Jason Danskin.

Tottenham Hotspur 0 Everton 0　　　　　　　　　　**Wednesday 5 February**
It started snowing in the late afternoon. By the time we got to White Hart Lane, it was thick on the ground. It was obvious the game was going to be a bit of a farce. You obviously weren't going to be able to play any sort of football on it, and I was just glad that it wasn't in a more important competition. I certainly didn't expect to enjoy it, but it was another 90 minutes to get under my belt, and I was happy to look at it like that.

We had Ian Marshall playing in the back four instead of Ratters; Paul Wilkinson was up front with Trevor Steven; and in the middle I played with Kevin Richardson, with Darren on the right-hand side and Peter Billinge on the left.

For twenty minutes we got battered. Glenn didn't play, they had the young lad Ian Crook playing midfield, and Steve Perryman kept shouting, 'Plant it over the top', which they kept doing, because we do play a bit square at the back, and they had a few really good chances. Nev was brilliant, but Chiedozie got in a couple of times and missed good chances.

So the boss changed the formation, because they were getting down the right-hand side all the time. Richo went out to the left-hand side, where he's played before. Peter Billinge came in the middle with me and Trevor Steven dropped back to play on the right, with Darren moving up as a makeshift front player alongside Paul Wilkinson.

That meant that at least we had a pattern which looked a bit more solid. It didn't get us into the game, but at least it stopped them getting a chance every other minute, because they had had four great chances.

In the second half we looked a lot tighter. They were still in charge, but we had a few attempts – Wilky had a goal disallowed because he was supposed to have leant on Miller – and we did make it more difficult for them, we were competing a wee bit.

It will be interesting coming back here for the Cup tie with our full side. Of course I fancy us, but it is the last trophy they've got to go for, and they have got some good players, even though they aren't getting the results at the moment.

I think we can expect them to try and play the same way, with Glenn Hoddle and Steve Perryman looking to knock the ball in behind our back four, and hitting the corner flags to try and get their wingers beyond our back four. I think they've decided that is the way to play against us, and that is good thinking on their part. When we won 2-1 in that vital League match last season, they had a lot of the ball and played some pretty little patterns in midfield, but they didn't really get at us until they started slinging balls into the box from corners and things like that. They can play their pretty patterns in front of us all day as far as I'm concerned, and I think they've realised that now, and I think they are going to knock it long. But at least we'll be prepared for that, and I'm sure we'll have something up our sleeves. I think it will be a real hell-for-leather game, and there will be a few interesting individual battles.

Thursday 6 February

We had a really long journey back through the snow last night. What made it seem even longer was that we are running a dry coach this year. It's part of our application of the government ban on alcohol at football. Other clubs have a drink for players on the coach, but we don't – perhaps because our chairman is President of the League, I don't know. But we don't, although you can always do with a lager after a game. It helps you relax.

So I just had a quiet day today. I'm not doing very well with my predictions though. Watford won their second replay at Maine Road, which I'd expected City to win with home advantage. But I was right about West Ham finally doing Ipswich.

101

We were due to report in at 3.30 to go down to Watford, but at 10.30 we got a phone call saying the game was off. I don't think they'll be too sorry after two Cup replays in four days, but obviously I was a bit disappointed, because it might have been a good time for us to play them. I don't think they'd have been at their best, particularly if they had had a bad journey back last night.

So we just went in and did a bit. The lads went into the gym, but I found a soft area outside and did a few doggies and shuttles with Kevin Sheedy, who is getting back to fitness. At least the delay gives him an extra couple of days to get right.

I got a sweat on and then arranged with Kevin Sheedy, Kevin Ratcliffe and Adrian Heath to go and watch City play QPR tomorrow.

It wasn't a very good game. City's attitude after their Cup defeat was terrific. They worked hard and got the result. QPR looked as if their minds were on the Milk Cup semi-final with Liverpool. For the second goal Terry Fenwick missed a tackle on Nicky Reid, and if Fens, who is a terrific competitor, was not attuned to the game, you can imagine that QPR weren't right for it. There was one tremendous result for us. Chelsea lost 4-1 to Oxford, which has done us a favour.

I thought watching City, that because they lack pace at the back they play very deep and make the pitch very big for you. I think McCarthy is a good competitor, but he lacks that yard of pace necessary to be top class, and he overcompensates by drifting back too far. I fancy Gary Lineker to get one or two against them.

Caught the shuttle down to London with Brace, Trevor and Gary Stevens to do the England squad record 'Around the World with England'. There are a few classics on there! We also did an anti-smoking campaign aimed at youngsters, which is something I believe in strongly.

We were at the Abbey Road studios. The Tottenham lads were away, and United were playing Liverpool in the live match, so there were a few missing.

I had a word with Fen, told him we'd been at the game yesterday and he mentioned he'd missed the tackle on Nicky Reid, which I'd have expected him to. I used to think he was a dirty player, because I've had a few bust-ups with him, but you don't know a player until you've played and trained with him, and for attitude and will to win he is tremendous. I think he might just lack a yard of pace and that's why his tackles can look bad.

I also had a chat with Alvin Martin. West Ham have done ever so well. I wasn't really convinced that they would go all the way, although obviously beating United last week was a great result for them. Talking to Alvin they clearly fancy their chances, and why not after winning that match. They've got games in hand, but I'm not sure that they have the squad to come through a pile up of fixtures. That might prove Chelsea's downfall as well, going by yesterday's result, because they've suddenly had a burst of injuries, which we've had and Manchester United have had, and it makes you appreciate people like Richo and Alan Harper and Neil Pointon who have come in and kept things going and got results.

We watched the last 25 minutes of the Liverpool–United match at the studio. It was like the Alamo for United. They were really under siege. Turner made a great save from Rushy, McGrath and Moran battled tremendously, and they held out for a draw. Which I think was the result we wanted.

It turned out afterwards that there had been a nasty incident before the start, with United having something squirted at them from an aerosol can when they got off the coach. It makes you despair.

We got the shuttle back. My car wouldn't start at the airport, which is good news at 10 o'clock at night. I had to get a taxi home.

Monday 10 February

Apart from Derek Mountfield, who had to go into hospital with his cartilage, everyone is fit for tomorrow; must be the first time since the win at Hillsborough in September. Fit is perhaps overstating it, because Brace is virtually getting off crutches to play, but everyone is available for selection. With the amount of games in England you never get a side with everyone 100 per cent fit, people just play through niggling injuries.

The papers were full of the incident at Anfield. There does seem to be something between Liverpool and Manchester United fans which transcends the usual rivalry, perhaps because there is a bit of feeling between the clubs. When we play United it is hard and keen and we both want to win, but it doesn't go beyond that. There seems to be more to it with Liverpool and United. When I went to watch their Milk Cup match I was in with the United fans and the feeling was ugly – vindictive and hostile.

I was a bit disappointed, though, with the things Ron Atkinson, and the Manchester United Chairman came out with, about having trouble at Anfield and being spat on, because I think that is just fuelling the problem. I've been spat on at Old Trafford and other grounds a few times, but I haven't made a public issue of it. Trevor Steven had to take a corner through a hail of pennies at Old Trafford last year. It isn't just Anfield's problem. Of course the aerosol attack was terrible, but a

103

young lad suffered as well as Clayton Blackmore, and they are equally bad. It is the sickness in English football at the moment. Most people who go to football are decent ordinary people, whether at Anfield, Old Trafford or Goodison, but there are a minority of idiots, who need catching and putting in jail. The violent people who use Stanley knives and Aerosol cans should be sent down for a long time. But pointing the finger at Liverpool just inflames things.

I watched the tape of the game in the afternoon. It was another great advertisement for English football, which made the malice of the fans seem all the more difficult to understand. Liverpool looked terrific, even though they had to change the team around a bit when Walshy got injured. It was nice to see Sammy Lee coming on and playing as if he had never been away. I thought he and Lawrenson were outstanding down the right-hand side.

I felt sorry for Sivebaek – a two month winter break in Denmark and then flung into that as his introduction to English football. He looked like a fish out of water, and knowing how hard I found it coming back after three reserve games, I sympathised. The pace of English football is something overseas players generally find totally foreign to them. At West Ham last week the game just passed Jesper Olsen by. He evidently had a good game in the replay against Sunderland though, and one or two press reports compared him to George Best, which is ridiculous. Best was the best player I ever saw, and he used to do it week in week out against the likes of Tommy Smith and Emlyn Hughes. When it's fast and furious, our game doesn't suit Olsen.

Everton 4 Manchester City 0   **Tuesday 11 February**
All the other games were off because of the weather. Goodison was in perfect condition, a credit to our undersoil heating system. It was bitterly cold though, and there was a swirling wind, which had its influence on the game.

City hasn't been beaten for 10 games, so they aren't a bad side. Not top class, but workmanlike. They had the wind first half, and they began quite well. We got an early goal – Gary Lineker picked up a Paul Power back pass and stuck it away. People said afterwards it was down to a bad back pass, which it was, but they ignored the finish, which was brilliant. He was at an angle and Nixon had a good position, but Gary somehow scooped it round him into the far corner.

City did quite well for the rest of the half. They had one or two snatched chances, Davies should have scored on one occasion, but Nev made a great save. We were due to see Davies miss one, because he got a hat-trick against us, when Chelsea beat us 4-3 just before our good run started last year, and it was an incredible hat-trick – goals he had no right to score, knee high volleys from the edge of the box, swervers, all that sort of thing. But Pat van den Hauwe had a tremendous game against Lillis, who had looked really sharp against QPR, so they didn't threaten that much. Pat has done so well in Derek's position, he gets up well, and although he is not the strongest, he is an awkward customer. I haven't seen any forwards get the better of him since he started playing there.

They had a lot of the ball in the first half, because we found it difficult to get out against the wind. And they played a strange system with three against Brace and me in the middle, so it was a question of hanging on and keeping it tight until half-time. In the second half, Nicky Reid stood on the ball very early on, Gary was in like a flash and tucked it away, and at 2-0 the game was virtually over. We just kept them penned in their box, which I had a feeling we might do, because of the conditions. And once we get our teeth into something we are very hard to shake off. There was one ten minute spell when we had them so rattled, they didn't know whether they were coming or going. The keeper made three or four great saves, including two from Richo, who had come on for Sheeds, in about five seconds. Then Sharpy, who had another great game, put Gary in for his hat-trick, where I think the keeper made a mistake in deciding to come. And Sharpy got the goal he deserved when Redmond made a mistake. He had had a very good game playing instead of Kenny Clements against QPR, but I think he found playing us a different experience. He tried to have a touch too many, instead of hooking the ball away and Sharpy nipped in and put it away.

You could say all four goals were down to defensive errors, but that overlooks the fact that we put them under so much pressure, they were forced into them. Even the first goal; it was a bad back pass, but Sharpy had put Power under so much pressure, he forced it out of him. And in the second half with Gary Stevens charging forward, Trevor Steven getting around Power and knocking crosses in, there was just no respite for them. We often seem to attack the Gwladys End second half, and have a lot of success there at keeping teams penned in. And we capitalise on errors, whether it is against City, or Manchester United, or Bayern Munich, so we should get some credit for that.

The three points give us a bit of breathing space at the top. It is nice to be up there. Last year people were waiting for us to crack and we didn't, so I just hope we can keep it going again. People talk about pressure, but we don't mind feeling the pressure at the top. There is much more pressure being 17 points behind and trying to get back into the race.

We've now got two days off – we're playing Tottenham on the Sunday in the Cup. The ground is rock hard, so we wouldn't be able to do much, but anyway the boss is a great believer in not overworking us, giving our bodies plenty of rest.

Friday 14 February

We went in for a game of head-tennis and were told Sunday's game is doubtful, which is no surprise, because it is so icy.

Saturday 15 February

Travelled down to South Mimms via Luton to see Arsenal play them in their fifth round tie. We're playing Luton in a couple of weeks. Whatever Mr Pleat and Mr Smith say, I think games on plastic pitches aren't football, it's like playing on ice.

For all that though, I quite enjoyed the game, which ended up 2-2. Luton were slightly the better team, but I thought the draw was about right, because Arsenal had a real go. Viv Anderson played well, and Tony Woodcock looked as lively as I've seen him for some time. But although Arsenal have got them back to Highbury, it won't be easy for them there – they looked like two evenly matched sides.

If every first division club had undersoil heating which worked, like ours does, that would be a better answer than plastic pitches.

Sunday 16 February

The game was off. The boss, Colin Harvey and Mick Heaton went over to the ground and they said it was just too dangerous – flat on the wings but badly rutted through the middle. It's a bad time to start missing games, but you can't play on that sort of surface. It's been provisionally rearranged for Wednesday, but even that must be doubtful – it'll require a hell of a thaw.

So we drove home, this time via Coventry to watch Coventry play Birmingham. The boss loves us watching games. Coventry have got undersoil heating and although the pitch was a bit heavy it was in good nick considering the country is covered in ice. It was quite a ding-dong game too. We left just before the end with Birmingham winning 4-3, but then Kilcline got his second penalty to tie it up.

Monday 17 February

Sheeds has gone in for a cartilage operation with the new 'scope' method. This isn't good news, and he must be totally frustrated, because he hasn't really been fit all season; it's been one fitness test after another. The lads have been taking the mickey wondering when he's going to finish a game, because he keeps on having to come off.

It was too hard for us to train outside, so we just did a bit in the gym.

We want to play. The way we are at the moment we are confident of playing anyone, while Tottenham are a bit down at the moment, so we don't want the game to be put off all the time, but it is obviously already doubtful for Wednesday. At least there's the Derby at the end of the week, we know that will be played, and you can feel the excitement for that one building up already.

106

There was one piece of good news – I'm in the England squad for the game in Israel. Considering I've only had a few games, that is terrific news. Obviously I'm part of Mr Robson's plans, I just hope I can get in the side. I played against Romania, and I thought I did quite well even though I didn't feel the pattern was right, so I just hope I can get a game in Israel.

In the evening I went to the St George's Hotel for the Liverpool Echo Sports Personality of the Year award dinner. A really enjoyable night – Stanley Matthews and Stan Mortensen were there, and so was Tommy Smith, one of my idols as a boy, so it was nice seeing him again.

Tuesday 18 February
Tottenham is off. Fortunately we know the Liverpool game will be played on Saturday – they've got good undersoil heating too – so that gave us something to concentrate on. We had to train in the gym again which is not ideal. It's got a synthetic surface like QPR and Luton, but you can't have a proper game of football, tackling is virtually out and so are quick turns. It's just a case of getting a bit of a sweat on, although we play well among ourselves in there. I don't feel any ill-effects on my knees or ankles from going in there, fortunately, because I know some players do. I just get a general stiffness afterwards and have a long soak, and sometimes a massage from the physio. If we could train outside all the time we would.

Wednesday 19 February
A day off. I went to a testimonial dinner for Des Drummond, the Leigh Rugby League player, who is a good friend. I don't really like going to too many dinners, and that's two in a week. But I'd been careful on Monday, because I thought we might be playing tonight, so I didn't feel too guilty. And rugby players aren't the best paid in the world, so it was in a good cause. I enjoyed it – I like the Rugby League crowd, and Peter Parfitt's speech was good.

Thursday 20 February
Just trained in the gym again. Nothing strenuous.

The atmosphere is really building up for the Derby. The demand for tickets is always hot, but this one has been similar to those I remember as a kid, when you couldn't get a ticket for love or money. We used to bunk off school to get tickets and things like that. I think because we are at the top with Liverpool right behind us, it has made it even more exciting than usual. They are still tremendous occasions anyway. The last one was a good football game, which they usually aren't, you can't find room to breathe in them normally. But with the League title at stake there's even more interest in this one.

107

My Dad is on the phone every two minutes – 'Have you got any more tickets?' I've only got him 45 ground and 20 seats so far, and he still wants more. Half our family are Red and half are Blue. My mother has always been an Evertonian, but my Dad was a Red, until I started playing for Everton. It is one of the unique things about Merseyside, that support tends to be split right through families, which is why the rivalry is friendly as well as intense.

Friday 21 February

I'm really revved up for this game. Usually I tend to be quiet on the Thursday and Friday. I start cutting off and concentrating on Saturday's game, but I'm finding it a bit difficult to get away. The phone is ringing constantly.

Also perhaps having been out for so long, and this game having that extra bit of bite to it, the tension is getting to me. They are buzzing and they want to beat us. We owe them one from Goodison, so it's all quite interesting. You can't predict the result, only that it will probably be the usual Derby – so tight that you won't get time to play football.

Liverpool 0 Everton 2   **Saturday 22 February**

I always wake up early on match days. I had poached eggs on toast, and went in to Bellefield for lunch at 12. The lads have combinations of eggs, beans and toast to taste, but I just had a cup of tea, having had a big breakfast. I had my bags for the England trip with me, because we were driving straight down to Luton after the game.

We had a 15 minute drive to Anfield through streets thronging with red and blue all walking together. It makes you wonder how there can be trouble at any ground when this game probably produces the most intense rivalry of any match in England, but the fans all mix together so happily.

The game itself was as tight as I expected. We were the better side, but there weren't many chances and it didn't look as if we were going to get a breakthrough, until Bruce let Kevin Ratcliffe's shot slip under his body. It was an unfortunate error for him, because he has been getting some criticism recently, and he was playing with an injury, but he should have stopped it. To be fair to Bruce it was the first mistake he has made against us. In Derby games and the Milk Cup final he's played brilliantly coming and claiming crosses which we've put in where we wanted.

That opened the game up a bit and Gary got a second a few minutes later. Liverpool weren't very happy, because they thought it was offside. I couldn't tell from where I was, but with a player like Gary, who is so quick and plays on defenders' shoulders the whole time, you are going to get these narrow decisions. Sometimes he'll beat the off side trap but be given off side because he was so quick it deceived the linesman, so it is swings and roundabouts. And he said afterwards that he was onside.

Gary is so quick you've always got a chance with him, even with a punt forward. And that was what we were looking for, because Liverpool like to squeeze up on you in a similar way to us. And Alan Harper pushed it forward and Gary was away. Gary thrives on things like that. He's not the best touch player in the world, but he's a hell of a reader of a through ball, or even of a hopeful punt. He has that ability to read where it's going and he will do his damnedest to get on the end of it. And when he gets there he finishes brilliantly. Bruce came out and he chipped it over him beautifully.

So we were quite pleased really. There hadn't been many chances, but Bruce had made some good saves, and we were more dangerous than they were throughout the game. Trevor Steven turned and hit one shot, which Bruce did well to get. I set up Richo for a volley, which he made a brilliant save from. And I thought we might have had a penalty, which we didn't get.

That was the good news. The bad news was that I've had to pull out of the trip to Israel. About twenty minutes into the game Steve McMahon caught me from behind and opened my knee up. I had ice treatment at half-time. I was struggling a bit, and I thought that Clinks was going to pull me out. But Brace was also having trouble – he'd only just passed the fitness test with his ankle, and he was struggling too. So while I was lying down having ice, the boss was talking to Brace, and then he came over to me and said, 'Will you carry on?'

So I said I'd have a go. Brace was clearly in real trouble, so I just had to try and get through the game.

It was a bit of a struggle, but I just tried my best to keep it going. I think I did quite well considering, because it was a physical game. I got involved in it and quite enjoyed it. But obviously afterwards I wasn't going to be fit. The boss said we'd say it was a groin strain. That wasn't being deceitful, he was doing it to protect me from pressure, because obviously I've had knee injuries before and if I said I was pulling out with a knee injury, people would think the worst. So that was thoughtful of him. I think he does well on things like that.

Gary Lineker has also pulled out with a back injury, and Pat van den Hauwe is out of the Wales squad with a hamstring. He had another tremendous game. He just seems to be improving all the time ever since we bought him. I think he is a top class defender now, and I don't say that lightly, because it is something I'm concerned about. I'd rate him on a level with the Lawrensons and Hansens now, which is a great compliment as far as I'm concerned.

To carry on the tale of woe, Brace is being put into plaster. He has been struggling with his ankle ever since the Newcastle game. He has played on, done a great job, but it has got steadily worse. So they will give him a jab and put him in plaster for five days and see how it goes.

It was a physical game as you'd expect. I got involved a few times. I caught Jan Molby with a tackle. I think I caught him on the ankle, and he went down and a few words were exchanged. The adrenalin is going and you are excited, and I let him have a mouthful, because in the heat of the moment you say things which you shouldn't really. So I was running back frothing at the mouth and Sammy Lee, with this big smile on his face said in this nice, calm, posh voice, 'Oh Peter, since I met you, your language hasn't half deteriorated'.

I just burst out laughing. There were 50 000 baying at us, and he just took the heat out of the moment. It was typical of him. He gives everything he has got in a game, but still has time for a joke.

I got booked later on for a tackle on Alan Hansen. I might have just caught him, but in Derby games no quarter is asked. It wasn't malicious, I'd gone for the ball, so I thought I was a bit unlucky. But I was probably booked for a tackle a few seconds earlier on Craig Johnston, which was a bad foul. It was probably the two incidents coming on top of one another.

Having said that, and that I thought we should have had a penalty, Joe Worrall had an excellent game. Derbies aren't easy to referee, and I thought he did very well. I might be biased, because whenever we have him we seem to win, but I would certainly place him as one of the top three referees in the country, along with Keith Hackett and Neil Midgley. There's always a lot of chat in games, and the three of them will let you have your say – they give as good as they get, and let you get on with the game.

Ratters was a bit excited about his goal, and allowed himself to be a bit critical of Liverpool to the press after the game. I always think that is a mistake, because things like that can rebound on you. It's tempting fate.

But with Paul Walsh and Kenny out, Rushy was a bit isolated. They had Craig Johnston playing wide on the right and I suppose linking with Rush, and then they had Jan Molby just behind them. We'd expected them to play Molby as sweeper, but they played this funny system and it didn't really work. Molby went off at half-time, whether because of my tackle or to change the system I don't know, although they said he had a shin injury.

I don't think it had worked for them really. They had a lot of the ball, but they didn't look very fluent, and they only really threatened us when they pushed forward after we'd scored and Rushy started getting through. But we always thought we had the upper hand.

I don't think they're hitting it off at the moment, but for a team which isn't quite on song they aren't doing too badly. Semi-finals of the Milk Cup, still in the F.A. Cup, and up there in the League. All in Kenny's first season when he is obviously learning the job. But I'm sure they will get it right in the end, because he has got a good football brain.

Sorry to go on about plastic pitches, but on the TV at lunchtime, they had David Pleat and Jim Smith trying to defend them. They were attacking the Leicester chairman, who wants them outlawed in the first division. David Pleat had a go at Highbury being icy, but as far as I'm concerned there is no difference between an icy pitch and a plastic one. If all first division clubs were made to have good undersoil heating like that at Goodison and Anfield, there wouldn't be any need for plastic pitches. They were trying to defend the indefensible. The next thing they'll be wanting is 11 robots to go out and play on their plastic pitches. I know some Luton and QPR players who don't like playing on their own pitches. It makes a false game. Tackling is an art in football and that goes out of the window on a plastic surface. So does taking men on, unless you are George Best, because the ball just runs away from you. You can't knock a through ball because it runs too fast. All you can do is knock it up to the front men and support, and that's all you can do on ice too. I've got a great regard for Jim Smith, I think he is a great fellow. I don't know David Pleat, so I can't say. But I think they are both quite mistaken when they talk about these plastic pitches. And I won't say any more about it – at least until we have to play on them again.

Sunday 23 February

I stayed over in Liverpool at my Mum and Dad's last night, because I had to go in for treatment early this morning. I must admit I had a few drinks last night – half celebration at winning the Derby, half to drown my disappointment at having to drop out of the England squad. I need games at the moment, and going to Israel would have been an ideal opportunity to get another one in, as well as obviously wanting to get back into the England set up.

I had all morning having treatment – ice and ultra-sound, just trying to get the swelling down.

Monday 24 February

Ice and ultra-sound all day again. It was still icy outside, so the lads were in the gym. My knee is sore and swollen, so it looks as if I might be struggling to play against Villa at the weekend. I'm really depressed. You get a lot of time to think just sitting on the treatment bench. You aren't allowed to have cups of tea or read papers in the treatment room, which is a rule I agree with, because it shouldn't be like a holiday camp when you are injured, it should be boring, so you don't want to be injured. But it left me just getting more and more depressed, thinking about missing out on the England trip and thinking, 'Here we go again'.

Tuesday 25 February

More of the same – ice and ultra-sound. I'm feeling a bit more philosophical today – it is a ligament injury, but they don't think it is a serious one. I can bend the knee. It's just a niggling injury, which at the moment I will settle for, because when Steve caught me it opened my joint up.

Wales won 2-1 in Saudi Arabia. That was a bit of a shock, because I didn't think Nev would concede, but then I heard it was a penalty, so that explains it.

Liverpool was our fifth consecutive clean sheet, which is a terrific advert for the keeper and the back four. I don't want to be a kill-joy, but it is a lot more reassuring than it was earlier in the season, when we were winning games 4-3. It is nice to know that if you get a goal or two you are in with a great chance of winning, and we are on that sort of run at the moment. We've got that sort of feeling in the dressing-room at the moment. We all want to keep it tight.

It is a great compliment to the defence, especially as we've had Pat at centre-half and Neil Pointon coming in and doing well at left-back. Pat I've mentioned, but Neil must take a lot of credit as well, considering he came straight in from playing at Scunthorpe, which, with respect, is a big jump. He's had his off days, but overall he has done exceptionally well. He is the type of defender the boss likes: quick to the ball, stops people playing. He can use the ball and he has got a good football brain, but first and foremost he defends. When it needs booting out of the danger area, he makes sure it goes.

Wednesday 26 February
More ice and ultra-sound. It is a bit sore and swollen still, so I'm carrying an ice bucket around with me. It's a wee bit tight, but I can walk without pain. I'm just hoping it will be alright for the weekend, although it will be touch and go. The weather doesn't help because I can't even go for a jog outside. If I want to test it, it might have to be in the gym, and with the synthetic surface, I'm a bit worried that it might flare up again.

I got away quickly to watch the England match, which was live on TV. We went one down quickly – I thought the lads were having a kip at the corner, in any standard of football it was a diabolical goal to give away.

That made it difficult, because a few teams have gone there and got bad results. But we didn't look as though we had got a pattern, at times it just didn't look as if we knew what we were doing out there. And we got terribly stretched out as a result.

And it wasn't just in midfield, which obviously is the area I look at first, but from back to front. Barry Davies was commenting that Gary Stevens was not getting forward. Well, I didn't think Gary had one of his better games, as I'm sure he'll say when he gets back, and he did have acres of space to go into, but he is a right-back not a right midfield player or a right winger. His first job was to get his defending right. As there was no midfield man in front of him, which he is used to with Trevor Steven, it meant there was all this space, but if he went into it, as opposed to going on an overlap he left this great hole behind him. And defensively he was getting exposed because of the gap too. I don't care who the full-back is, if there's a winger running at you from 20 yards away and he has got a bit of pace, it's very difficult for the defender. I'm sure that Gary would be the first to say that he gets a lot of help from Trevor down that side, they have a good understanding, and you need the extra man in modern football. But I thought we had those problems all over the pitch. They had a lot of time and space in midfield, which is worrying, because you think a better quality side would really exploit that, because we couldn't get to them to close them down, because we were so stretched out. I don't think it works with three men in midfield, particularly with Ray going so deep to take the ball off the back four. If they pushed up more and gave him the ball 20 yards further up, it would be better, because Ray could start doing things that much nearer the opposing goal.

I know I keep harping on 4-4-2, and having a pattern, but it does matter. I think that unless Chris Waddle or John Barnes really stamp their authority on things fairly soon Mr Robson is going to have to decide to do without a winger.

We have only got three months to go to the World Cup, and we must have a pattern. This was the first time that that group had played together, so that obviously doesn't help, but if you have an established pattern it makes it easier for people to fit in. Against Romania if you got the ball in midfield and played it square, you never knew whether Chris Waddle was going to be on the left, or the right. You didn't know if you played a through ball, if someone was going to be running into the box, or if the forward had come short. When I play for Everton I know I've got Trevor outside me and I can knock it to him; if I want to play it up to Sharpy, I can hit him; if I can knock it over the top, Gary Lineker is going to be there; or I can give it to Brace, to switch it to the other side. In the England side you have 11 quality players, but you have got to have an established pattern as well before you can do anything. It is no good having 11 quality players with some of them getting in one another's way, which was what it looked like.

In the end it was thank heavens for Bryan Robson. He was the only one making inroads in the box, getting on the end of things and really making things happen. He got a couple of goals, so at the end of the day it was another victory. It has got the lads together again, so although Mr Robson can't be over happy with the performance, it is still positive. I know I wish I'd been playing rather than watching it at home. Someone said it might not have been a bad one to miss, but you always think, 'Perhaps I could have helped organise things, got us to push up more and not be so strung out, got a few tackles in and tightened things up.'

But even if I'd had a nightmare I'd sooner have played; I always want to play for England.

In the evening they showed the high-lights of the Derby County–Sheffield Wednesday Cup tie. The ground was rock hard, and I thought Martin Hodge had really injured himself badly when he went over a defender's back and landed on his head. It looked awful, but being the lad he is, a tremendous character and brave as a lion, he played on and really he got Wednesday out of jail, because he made some terrific saves.

I love the Baseball Ground. The atmosphere is fantastic. I remember playing there for Bolton, against the likes of Archie Gemmill and Charlie George in a League Cup tie, the year we reached the semi-finals and it was really electric.

Thursday 27 February

My leg is improving slowly. I did some straight running in the gym and I didn't feel it, or at least only a little, so I've asked the boss if I can have a fitness test at Goodison, where the heating will ensure that the ground will be soft. So it looks as if Gary Lineker and I will be having fitness tests.

Those scope operations are amazing. Sheeds is back running and looks really good. Ten days after the operation! Derek Mountfield has been off for six months. But his shattered, so he had to have the knife to get it all out.

Brace had his plaster off. He has got no chance for Saturday though, which is a bit disappointing. And if I'm honest, I think I'm struggling. The running went quite well, but I still feel twinges when I'm walking around.

Friday 28 February

The treatment room is getting like Emergency Ward 10. John Clinkard is going up the wall. Today Gary Lineker pulled up with a hamstring injury, and was packed in ice.

I had a similar day to yesterday. Ice and ultra-sound and a bit of straight running. I'm having a fitness test tomorrow, so I'm just keeping my fingers crossed. Brace said his leg felt a bit better today, but he obviously is not a starter for tomorrow.

Everton 2 Aston Villa 0   **Saturday 1 March**

We reported at Bellefield, then Gary and I whipped down to Goodison in the car for our fitness tests. We both passed. If Gary has got a hamstring injury, you wouldn't notice it in his running. And I twisted and turned and had a few block tackles with the physio, and came through all right.

My knee was a wee bit sore, but I felt it was an injury I could get away with, it wasn't going to get any worse, so I played.

They watered the pitch while we were having our tests, but there was a swirling wind and by the time of the game it had dried out. It was like an end of season pitch, but still in good nick considering. It wasn't a good game. We didn't play well. Andy was suspended so he had to watch, but I could imagine he had wound them up beforehand, because they really had a go, and although they only had one really threatening moment, they stopped us playing quite well.

But we stuck at it. It was one of those games where you get your result through character, because we weren't playing well at all, and those are the times when you just have to battle and pick up your wins, if you are going to do anything. And in the end two opportunist goals in the last 15 minutes won it for us. The scorers, surprise, surprise, were Lineker and Sharpy. It was announced before the start that Sharpy has signed a new four year contract which is terrific news, because he and Links must be the best pair around at the moment.

And we didn't concede again, which is terrific.

My knee survived quite well. It was still sore, and I didn't break my neck in any tackles, but I got through the game just trying to keep the ball moving.

Had fun with Andy afterwards. Inchy, Sharpy and I were giving him a hard time about the big Birmingham Derbies – the relegation specials Villa v Birmingham, and the Baggies (West Brom) v Villa, another game that rolls off the tongue. He took it in good part, and we had a good night out with him. I just hope that Villa get out of trouble, and make it to Wembley, although Oxford will be a tough game for them.

United lost, which means the Championship is now in our hands. If we win all our games no one can catch us, and you can't ask for more than that. We've got West Ham and Chelsea to come to us and United away, so it's up to us now. And we've certainly got the hunger for it. We're not giving goals away. And even when we are not on song, we battle and still get a couple of goals. I get the impression we'll always score a goal in a game. It is very rare that I get the feeling, 'Oh, we're not going to get one here'. We always look like scoring, so it is nice when you've got a tight back door. And as I said, there's that scent of success, that confidence in the air. Kevin Sheedy's on the way back, Derek Mountfield is on the way back, so there's going to be some healthy competition for places, because the lads who have come in have done well. United and Chelsea have had a lot of injuries, but we've had our fair share too – we just haven't splashed it all over the papers, we've just got on with it, because injuries are part and parcel of the game, and it's no good moaning about them. The team that goes out on Saturday is the

Everton team that you succeed or fail with, it's no good complaining that X, Y, and Z are missing.

Sunday 2 March

My knee is still sore, so I had ice treatment before watching Tottenham get beaten 2-1 by Liverpool. The Cup Tie has been rearranged for Tuesday, when there's a thaw forecast, because although they played today, it is still cold and icy. I don't know if we can learn much from today's game. Tottenham were 1-0 up at half-time, but I thought that was because Liverpool were awful rather than Tottenham playing well. In fact they should have been two up, because Chris Waddle had this close range header, all he had to do was hit the target and it was in, but it hit his head rather than him heading it.

I thought at the interval, Kenny will have a few words to say, and Liverpool had a bit more urgency about them during the second half. And Spurs looked as if they had just crumbled, they were in total disarray. There were people just running around, and I didn't know where they were going, and I'm not sure that they did. At one stage Chris Waddle and John Chiedozie were out on the left wing about two yards apart. I can't imagine that they will be as bad as Tuesday. But it still needed a great finish from Rushy to win the game for Liverpool in the last minute, which puts them seven points behind us, which is nothing really.

Monday 3 March

Trained in the morning – a bit of head-tennis in the gym – then travelled down to South Mimms.

Gary Stevens didn't come with us, which is a bit of a blow – his knee had swollen up on Sunday, so he stayed behind to see the specialist. We just hope he is fit. Probably Alan Harper will come in. He doesn't look like a footballer, but what a great player he is to have in your squad.

Brace however is fit – he says he feels fine, which is great news.

Tuesday 4 March, Teatime

We had the usual pre-match routine. Woke about 11 a.m., had a walk at 12, followed by lunch and bed for the afternoon. Gary Stevens travelled down this morning, but won't play, so Inchy was pulled out of the reserve match against Liverpool and came down with him to be sub. Kevin Sheedy is playing in the reserve match, which is quite incredible, two weeks after having his cartilage out.

Inchy's arrival though meant I didn't get much sleep. There wasn't a room for him, so they put a camp bed in the room I share with Brace; there wasn't room to swing a cat. We chatted all afternoon, but at least we had our feet up.

And the thaw has come. I phoned home and it is raining up north. It hasn't arrived here yet, but you can feel it is a lot warmer, and you can feel the ground is softer, so the pitch might be in good nick.

Tottenham 1 Everton 2   **Tuesday 4 March**

The pitch was in brilliant condition, a good stud hold, everything was fine. I love White Hart Lane, the atmosphere is terrific – and I can't believe our record here because we did it again.

Tottenham had a real go. It was a bruising first half, and some of the tackling was a bit dodgy, but it is the last trophy they have any interest in, and in their position I could imagine myself responding in the same way. It was a good, hard Cup Tie, and I think it must have been an entertaining one to watch as well. There were a few controversial incidents.

I thought we should have had a penalty early on. Brace got through, and although there wasn't much danger because he was only going to get a cross in, Ray Clemence took his feet, but the referee John Martin wasn't interested. I appealed loudly, but he wasn't having any of it.

Then Ratters got injured – Falco caught him so late that I think the ball was out of play before he made contact. Ratters hobbled on for five minutes, then he went off and we played with 10 men for the next 10 minutes, just trying to keep it tight and get the ball over the top for Gary and Sharpy. They strapped Ratters up and gave him a jab and he came back to play on the left side of midfield, which I don't think is his position! So he hobbled around there for another five minutes, but it was obvious that the ankle was not going to get going again, so he went off and it was time for a big reorganisation.

Richo went from left side of midfield to right-back. Alan Harper moved into the middle alongside Pat. And Inchy came on to play on the left side of midfield.

And for the rest of the first half it was just a battle with chances few and far between. They had one with the ball knocked across the face of the goal which we just scrambled away; and we had one which Gary Lineker just got a flick to, which knocked it away from Adrian Heath, who was coming in at the far post.

And that was about that in a bruising, really tough first half. The second half was similar but we got a break five or six minutes into it. We'd got the ball in their box and Gary Lineker pushed it out to the right, where I was coming up on the overlap. I could see what was on and hit a hard cross in on the six yard line, going away from Clem and towards Sharpy, who was coming in for it. I thought Clem did well just to get a hand to it, because Sharpy was steaming in, but it spun off to Adrian. From where I was it looked a difficult angle for him, but he got a good strike on it and it was in the net. I thought it was a great finish, and a goal which was typical of us, because we do hit quality crosses into the box, and if your strikers get on the end of them, it gives you a chance.

117

They came back at us really strongly, but then we caught them on another break. Sharpy got away to start with, turned back and knocked it out to Trevor Steven, who went outside his man and hit in a tremendous cross to the far post. They were all over the place, we had dragged them so far over that Gary Lineker was by himself, and Adrian Heath was free on the edge of the box too. And Gary put it away beautifully, so we were two up.

They were still coming at us really strongly. Between our two goals they had brought John Chiedozie on. I was surprised they hadn't done that as soon as we lost Ratters, because even if he isn't the world's best finisher, he has got pace, and after the Super Cup match, I thought they'd have decided that playing the ball over the top for him, worried us a lot more than all their clever play in front of us. Because he stretches you and makes you turn, and when you are doing that to a defence you get chances.

And we were a bit anxious, because it was dodgy for a time with them knocking balls over the top for him, and that was how their goal came. Alan Harper was close to him and Neil Pointon was in support, and I was shouting to Harpo to shut down the cross.

Chiedozie knocked in a great cross however and Falco got it above Richo and struck it in beautifully. It was a good goal for them, because Falco had been trying to get one-on-one against Kevin at the far post, obviously knowing that Richo is not our best header of the ball at the back. In fact Graeme Sharp had spotted that that was what Falco was doing earlier, and I'd had a word with Pat van den Hauwe about it, as Falco had done it a few times before, and it worked for him this time. I like Falco. He might not be top class, but he has a real go. On the occasions I've seen Tottenham he has been a lone battler up front, and on the night he was absolutely terrific. He'd had another header blocked on the line in the corner, and had bustled about all night.

After the goal they threw everything at us, but we stood firm and defended well. And when Chiedozie got through, and I thought he was off side anyway, Nev made a brilliant save. Chiedozie lobbed him, and it looked a good finish, but Nev twisted round somehow in mid air and palmed it away. I think we're getting a bit spoilt by him, because we almost accept that as par for the course. Peter Shilton is a great goalkeeper, but there is no doubt in my mind that Everton have got the best goalkeeper in the world.

Then in the last minute or so it seemed as if they had scored, and it was down to me. For the first goal I'd had a go at Harpo, because I thought he should have been tighter on Chiedozie and stopped the cross, because we were two against one. This time they had a throw-in on the other side up by our corner flag. It was thrown to Chris Waddle. I went with him, and Richo said, 'Stop the cross', and having had a go at someone else, I committed the cardinal sin. Chris checked to come back on himself and I bought the dummy. He turned to the by-line, where I should have been, forcing him to turn back, and he whipped a great ball in.

Nev got a hand to it, it hit Gary Mabbutt on the shoulder, and although it was difficult to see from where I was standing, it looked as if the ball had crossed the line, when Pat's leg came from nowhere and knocked it out. Then there was this almighty scramble on the line, and the referee gave us a free-kick. We assumed he had disallowed it for hand-ball, and I think at the end of the day the referee's decision was a bit lucky for us. So we got through. Now we have to wait and see who wins tomorrow between Luton and Arsenal, to see where we go on Saturday. I think it will be my favourite type of pitch again, now that they are replaying back at Luton.

Wednesday 5 March

A day off. Slept in late, went out to cash a cheque, stopping off for a couple of bottles of Guinness, and watched our high-lights and the Liverpool–QPR Milk Cup Semi-final.

Our high-lights didn't shed any more light on that disallowed goal. I think we were a little fortunate to get the decision. The thing that stood out for me in that incident, was that there were about five Everton bodies in there, all trying hell for leather to keep it out. I was trying to get there but obviously couldn't, but there were all these bodies diving in with a 'they shall not pass' attitude which is great to see. I remember during the game we had an attack which broke down and I was sprinting back. The ball went up to Chris Waddle, and I looked up to see what was happening, and I could see Brace, Neil Pointon and Adrian Heath all haring back, and I thought at the time, 'Well, we've got a chance', because it was typical of our attitude. We have got 11 lads with a great attitude, all wanting to do everything they can, and I'm just happy to be involved in a team which does that, because it doesn't happen at every club. I can't imagine there are any dressing-rooms which are closer than ours. We ruck one another on the park, but the lads are all fighting for one another and they'll do anything for one another, and it shows on the pitch and off it.

Liverpool went out to QPR, so that's another of my predictions gone wrong. They played some lovely controlled football, but they just weren't threatening enough, and even when they got a rather fortunate penalty, the keeper made a good save. It confirmed my feeling that they need a striking partner for Rush, because although Craig Johnston was lively, he should play wide on the right. So QPR rode their luck, got two own goals, and they are at Wembley. And you have to hold your hands up to them, because going to Anfield with only a one goal advantage isn't easy, so I was delighted for Jim Smith.

I got one prediction right – Luton trounced Arsenal 3-0, which I'd expected once Arsenal failed to finish them off in the first replay at Highbury. So it is back to plastic for the quarter-finals. But once you are in the quarter-finals you've just got to go out and do the job, there's no excuse. It won't be easy though, because they aren't a bad side. They were a bit unlucky in last season's semi-final, so they'll certainly be fired up for this one. And they've made some good signings. I like Preece, and I think Peter Nicholas does a good job for them. They've got a solid back four, they don't give many goals away at home, so it should be interesting.

Thursday 6 March

As I said, Sharpy signed a new four-year contract last week. At South Mimms Inchy got on the coach carrying this large brown paper bag and shouted to Graeme, 'Here you are Sharpy, Mr Chairman's told me to give you this bag full of money, but you've got to keep it quiet.'

It's come out in the papers that if Inchy doesn't re-sign, Liverpool are interested. So we've been winding him up in training too.

We told him today, 'Kenny's watching from behind the fence', and he blushed. He'd love to stay at the club, but it is difficult for him because he wants first-team football, and at the moment there just isn't a place for him, which is a shame.

We've got a few injury problems at the moment though. Ratters is definitely out. We're still waiting to see about Gary Stevens. Gary Lineker's back is still sore, and he had a jab for his rib injury to play on Tuesday.

Friday 7 March

We didn't train this morning. We had a sandwich at Bellefield around 1 p.m., then travelled down so we could have a run on Luton's pitch. It was an eventful journey, because the coach broke down when we arrived in Luton, and they had to send for a replacement – Jim the coach driver got slaughtered. Funnily enough I'd seen some smoke on the way down and I thought it was John Clinkard having a quick fag at the back. Of course you aren't supposed to smoke on the coach, so Clinks nips up the back when he's desperate.

The pitch is supposed to be better than QPR's, and it is, but I'm still not happy about that type of surface. I tried out flats and rubbers, and decided to play in rubbers, which weren't bad at all.

Luton 2 Everton 2 **Saturday 8 March**

We were delighted, really bubbling on the way home, because we came back from two down. We really showed our character and determination to keep the run going.

I thought we'd played quite well even when we went two down though, so I never felt we were out of it. They had a good 20 minutes leading up to the first goal, which was disappointing for us, because it came from a dead-ball and we knew what they were going to do. It was from a throw-in, and everything was aimed for Foster. It's sometimes difficult to stop him getting a touch-on, but we always like to make sure we're first to the second ball. This time they were quicker than we were. I was in the area and I thought I could have been on my toes a bit more, but Hill got in there first.

But then we came into it and I thought we were doing quite well on the pitch, when they got their second. We tried to squeeze them but Stein beat the off side trap. But we'd had one flowing move which ended with Gary Lineker heading just past the post, and Sharpy had one kicked off the line, so even at 2-0 down it wasn't the end of the story.

I'd felt a twinge in my ankle, but I was OK, and at half-time the boss took off Neil Pointon and put Inchy on. Gary Stevens had passed his fitness test and Alan Harper and Pat were playing at the back, so we just played the three at the back for the second half, with Richo working up and down the line on the left and Inchy having a go at trying to attack them.

It went right for us. We got one goal back immediately. Gary Stevens hit in a good free-kick which Sharpy got on the end of, and from then on I felt quite confident. Inchy got the equaliser, and we could even have won it in the end. It was a good 'character' performance on a pitch we don't like.

They must be gutted though. One up and in control in the semi-final last year, and now they've seen a two goal lead taken away from them. That sort of thing starts to have a psychological effect, and I thought they went a bit when we started putting pressure on. But to be fair to them, they have had a lot of games on top of one another, and you have to take that into consideration. But physically we were stronger.

When we came off though the boss said, 'It's not over yet' which is right, because they went to Highbury and got a draw in the last round. They are a well-balanced side, and you've got to admire what David Pleat has done there. Harford does a great job for them at the front. There's a lot of talk about him coming into the England reckoning, but I'm not sure about that. I don't think he is international class, his touch isn't good enough, but he is very effective for them. Peter Nicholas is an underrated player too, he has got a good brain and he is a better user of the ball than he is sometimes given credit for. He uses it simply, doesn't try to be too ambitious, but he keeps things ticking over. And Hill is a good player. I read somewhere that David Pleat said Hill just lacked a little bit of devil, and I think that is right, but he has good skill, and he is very effective on that surface.

I was incredibly stiff and a bit sore in my achilles – a result of playing on that pitch – so I went in and had a bath and some ice.

Then I came home and watched the United–West Ham match on TV. It was an entertaining game, but a strange one – I felt we would have done well against both sides. People got a lot of room. There wasn't much shutting down in midfield, and both teams played on a big pitch – both sides were strung out, and there was a lot of room for players to turn and run at people. West Ham did well, John Lyall has obviously got them going, they went up there with a very positive attitude.

United had a lot of the ball, but I didn't think they put enough pressure on West Ham at the back. They play a lot of good football, but they play it in front of the defence, they don't really get in behind defences. And they don't sling enough into the box, and when they do get into good positions there's no real quality on the balls going in.

Possibly that's because Hughes and Stapleton don't get in there at them. They do well in holding the ball up and in joining in moves, but you want strikers to get in there and get on the end of things sometimes, and they don't really do that. Yet in the end it was decided by two penalty decisions, and Frank was unlucky in both of them, because I thought the one given against him was doubtful, and he should have had one when he was brought down a couple of minutes later. So it just goes to show how thin the dividing line between success and failure is, because in the end those decisions mean that United are out of the Cup.

I felt a bit stiff, so I spent 20 minutes in the gym doing stretches on the achilles and the legs generally before going out. We had our usual big game with everyone involved. It's always fun, you have a laugh, we play with no off sides, you do a lot of running and get a good sweat on.

The boss had a quiet word with us today, telling us not to expect an easy game tomorrow. I think we know that. Quite rightly he has refused to have a toss of the coin to decide the venue if it goes to a third game, because that pitch is too much of a disadvantage. Arsenal did that in the last round, lost the toss and went out. We will be playing at Birmingham if a third game is necessary. Sheeds is back in for Richo. He has had a remarkable season. All those niggling injuries, and now he is back playing three weeks after a major operation.

Richo must be shattered, because he played very well at Luton. He put quality crosses into the box and worked up and down the line, so it is very tough on him. But I'm a great believer in playing what you think your best team is.

122

Manchester United bought Peter Davenport today. He is a very, very good player, very good with his back to goal, and quite sharp, but I can't help feeling the strikers they are getting are all too similar. I don't think Davenport is a player you can knock the ball over the top for like Gary, or someone to battle for high balls. I think they could do with someone like Harford, who would give them another outlet. You've got to get balls and strikers into the penalty area, and you've got to mix your game up. Sometimes you can thread the ball in for someone to turn and strike, but you've also got to have crosses whipped in and someone getting on the end of them; and sometimes you've got to play big ugly balls for people to battle for, or play them over the top for people to get on to. And I can't help thinking that Ron has gone in there and bought someone for the sake of doing it.

Everton 1 Luton 0   **Wednesday 12 March**

Nightmare time. I'm back in Lourdes. I'm gutted, because I felt so good in the morning. I'd got a few games under my belt, I was feeling so pleased about the way I had got through the game at Luton, when I was really apprehensive about playing on that pitch, and I thought I'd got away with it and was really feeling life was all hunky dory.

We had lunch at Goodison at midday. I had my usual halibut. We had our afternoon sleep at the Atlantic Tower, because St George's, our normal hotel, was fully booked.

We got a great start because Gary Lineker got a great goal. It was one which proved what I said about sometimes just playing big ugly balls, because it is remarkable how many goals you get from them. Trevor Steven didn't even look – he just punted this ball upfield. Gary got a couple of yards on Donaghy and Foster and got on to it. From then on it was a great goal, because he got a couple of superb touches on it and finished brilliantly. A perfect example of why he's the leading scorer and why he cost £800,000.

But 15 or 20 minutes into the game I just turned on a ball and felt this stabbing pain in the muscle in front of my calf. It was an unusual pain because I'd never had a muscle injury before, and I just didn't know what it was. I thought at first a muscle had gone into spasm.

I went off for treatment and said to Clinks, 'It's my muscle. I think I've torn it'.

He said, 'No. You're not quick enough to do one of them'.

I didn't know whether to laugh or cry, because it was so sore, and there was the game going on behind me in full fury, and he had time to make a crack. Anyway he sprayed it and said, 'See if you can work it off' and I went back out. I just wasn't comfortable with it, though.

At half-time the boss asked how it was, and I said, 'Well, I'm feeling it, I'm struggling a wee bit' but he decided to keep me going. Trevor had missed a penalty just before half-time, which was a bit unfortunate, because if we had scored that, I think I could have come off then, I could have pushed to come off if we had been two up.

Instead Clinks put a stirrup on me under some strapping. A few of the lads wear them regularly in games – Alan Harper and Pat both do – to support ligaments or weak areas.

So I went back out. I was in pain and I wasn't doing the side or myself justice. But we had problems with Sheeds, who had nothing left in the tank as it was his first game back, so he went off and I had to try and struggle through it. I was no use out there, I was just trying to sit in front of the back four and make it difficult for Luton, but at the end they pushed Foster up with Harford and were just knocking in high balls for headers, and they had us under a lot of pressure.

And in the last minutes they hit the post. They should have scored because it was a great chance, and if they had gone and taken it into extra time we would have been really struggling, because we were virtually playing with ten men.

At the end of course we got away with it, and we were just delighted to go through. I was in a fair amount of pain and I went into the dressing-room, and the doctor wanted me to go to hospital. We had a bit of an argument about it – I was so sick that I told him where to go, and he stormed out saying, 'If you're not going to listen to my advice there's not much point my coming here'.

He was right, and I was out of order, but it was just disappointment, a reaction to being injured again. I was so frustrated and angry. But I calmed down and had a word with Clinks, and when the Doc came back in I said, 'You're right. I'll go'.

But then he wanted me in for two nights, and I only wanted to come in for one, so we started arguing again. Then he phoned Lourdes, and they said they only had the bed for tonight anyway, so the argument was for nothing. But I'm still frustrated, I just can't believe it has happened. And the way it feels I shall probably be out for a month.

Thursday 13 March

I didn't get any sleep last night. I was in a lot of pain, and they couldn't give me any pain-killers because I'd had about 10 cans of lager to dull the pain and my disappointment before going in. I just had ice treatment right through the night, 15 minutes on, 15 minutes off.

Then at about 6.30 a.m., when I had just started dozing, a Mass came over the tannoy. And that was that.

The Doc let me out in the morning, and I went to Bellefield and had ice treatment all day. At least John gave me some pain-killers, because it was really sore.

There were a few people in. Alan Harper has got a sore achilles tendon. Neil Pointon has tweaked a ligament. Ratters is still out, so if Neil and Harpo can't play on Sunday, we are down to the bare bones.

The only good news is that Derek Mountfield is playing in a Lancashire Senior Cup tie at South Liverpool, so he might come into the reckoning if Harpo is out.

This couldn't have come at a worse time, it's really depressing. We've got a few games coming up. There's Chelsea on Sunday, which I was desperate to play in, then there's the Super Cup match with Tottenham, which doesn't matter so much, but then there's Luton again. Then over Easter there's Newcastle and Manchester United, which are really important, and then there's the semi-final with Sheffield Wednesday. And the way I feel I'm going to miss them all. If someone told me I'd be fit for the semi-final, I'd settle for that right now. But having said that, it's always hard going into a semi-final, when you haven't played games or trained, so I don't know.

I had a chat with Brace and one or two of the others who were in, and I'm convinced it is a hangover from the Luton pitch. I know I keep going on about it, but I just can't believe I've got a muscle injury. I've never had a muscle injury before.

Brace said that some of the Liverpool players said the same, that it is at the game after you've played at Luton or QPR that things go wrong. I think those pitches are just too physically punishing on your joints to play football on. And no one can convince me they are good for skilful football. I think teams who want plastic pitches should go' off and form their own league, so that all games home and away are played on plastic, and that will end all the arguments.

Needless to say I'm on crutches again. I'm getting so used to them, I can do anything on crutches, even rock and roll. Anything except what I want to do, which is play football.

Friday 14 March

I had another restless night. I brought some ice home with me, and iced it through the night.

Now that the first 24 hours are over, it is just a matter of seeing how it goes. Our medical team are great believers in the theory that the first 24 hours after an injury are very important in treating it.

It was a bit easier this morning. There was still a wee bit of pain, but a lot less than there was originally. I couldn't believe how much it hurt, I really thought I'd done something serious. I didn't think a muscle tear could give you so much pain.

I went in and had ice and ultra-sound treatment. The Doc is speaking to me now. When he came in I told him he was right.

I can't drive, so I've organised a couple of friends to act as chauffeurs. John Ritson, who was right-back in the Bolton team and looked after me as a young lad when I first played there, got the job today, because I'd promised him I'd go to the opening of his new café today. I went and quite enjoyed it – I sank a few white wines, which took my mind off my leg for a bit.

I cannot believe it. My leg feels absolutely brilliant. The improvement in a day is enormous, there's just a bit of stiffness. When the Doc came in I told him and he said to get off the crutches – he's read a new book which apparently says that if you can get the muscles working as quickly as possible, it improves your healing time, so I'm walking and I can't believe how good it feels.

I'm sure it is down to ice. When I was talking to Bryan Robson a couple of weeks ago about his trip to Amsterdam, he said it wasn't any miracle cure, it was simply ice and friction.

I think I shall be getting friction on Monday or Tuesday – it is a bit painful, but it's worth it.

Alan Harper and Neil Pointon have both improved, and they've got a chance of playing tomorrow. Clinks is a miracle worker.

United lost 1-0 at QPR, but Liverpool beat Southampton after being one down, so we need a result. It will be hard, because Chelsea always seem to play well against us, and they are still in contention.

Everton 1 Chelsea 1   **Sunday 16 March**
In the first half they looked half a yard quicker than us, a bit sharper. It was more like a semi-final than a league match, there was so much tension there was no room, no space to play, nothing flowed and we desperately needed someone to put their foot on it for a moment. It is difficult in games like that but it can be done, even if it means you have to go square rather than forward, just to put one or two passes together and get a bit of composure into your game and build from there.

They got an early goal which didn't help. Speedie had already had a run in with Pat, collided with an elbow, and this time he went up arms flailing and Pat headed it across goal. Then Derek Mountfield and Gary Stevens got mixed up with one another and we didn't react quickly enough.

In the second half Inchy came on for Richo, and we got at them a little bit. He got a few balls played to his feet and he went at defenders, and got into the box and put some crosses in and the crowd got roused and we began to create a few chances. Eddie Niedzwiecki made two incredible saves, one from Brace in the first half, and then another from Gary in the second, and he looked unbeatable. Wales are lucky to have him, because with Nev as well it means they've got two very good goalkeepers.

In the end we got the equaliser with about seven minutes left. Inchy wriggled round Spackman and crossed, Gary's header was blocked, but Sheeds put it in. It was tough, and at one stage I thought we weren't going to do it, but it was a tribute to the way we kept going and forced a result even though we didn't play well.

Alan Harper passed his fitness test before the game, and then the gaffer left him out anyway to play Derek. Harpo said, 'That's a first. The only time I've been pushed to have a fitness test, passed it, and then been left out'.

It was a great return for Derek, who had a tremendous game after being out for so long, because Kerry Dixon has pace and knows where the goal is, not an easy opponent. But, not taking anything away from Derek, I didn't think Kerry looked fit. There were a couple of balls played over the top which he didn't capitalise on, which made me think it wasn't the Kerry of two months ago. His sharpness wasn't there, and he was a shadow of the player who impressed me so much earlier in the season.

When I spoke to him afterwards he said he had had a groin strain, which we put down to playing at QPR. So we both had a moan about plastic pitches.

Monday 17 March
The boss wasn't at Bellefield today, and no one knew where he had gone.

Liverpool won their replay at Watford, so they are in the semis too. They were losing 1-0 and Rushy earned a penalty with four minutes left, then got the winner in extra time. I think Kenny playing again has made a big difference, because in some games Rushy has been playing by himself. Rushy works so hard it is unbelievable. He is a fabulous player, because he isn't just a great goal scorer, he puts in so much work as well, which people often don't realise. Any youngster who wants to see what a top class striker does should study him.

The other thing is they are playing 4-4-2 again, which I'm sure is their best formation. Kenny experimented with a sweeper for a time, and I think it took something away from them. It is a difficult way to play in English football. Southampton made it work for them for a time, but it doesn't seem to work usually. If the full-backs know what they are doing and push in on you in midfield, there's a chance of it working, but even then I prefer 4-4-2.

Tuesday 18 March
I started light jogging in the gym. I'm delighted, I just can't believe how quick the progress has been. I might even have had a chance of playing on Saturday if it had been anywhere else, but as it is on that stupid pitch at Luton, I don't think the boss will risk it.

There's the Super Cup match tomorrow. Apart from Nev, Sheeds and Derek, he's just throwing all the young lads in. Inchy and Paul Wilkinson will play together up front to give Sharpy and Gary a break. Sharpy and Pat are on the bench just in case we need something.

Everton 3 Tottenham 1   **Wednesday 19 March**
I went jogging in the morning. I would definitely be in with a chance of playing on Saturday if it was on a decent pitch.

Tottenham went one up, but we bounced back and won in extra time. The young lads Pete Billinge and Darren Coyle played quite well, and so did Ian Marshall, who has got back in again. Sharpy got on and got the third goal, and Pat got on for the last 15 minutes, and got booked for his first tackle, which is unusual for him! That on top of Speedie running into his elbow on Sunday as well! I didn't see that incident, of course, but from what has been said, it sounds as if he might have had the long walk, if the referee or linesman had seen it.

I was disappointed in Tottenham. They must be sick of us, but they looked like a team without any spirit. They didn't have Glenn, or Roberts or Perryman, but if you looked at their team on paper, it was much stronger than ours. Mabbutt and Gary Stevens always have a go, but it was very disjointed, people didn't look as if they knew what they were doing, and for the amount of talent out there, it was poor.

All our goals came in directly from Sheeds' free-kicks. For the third he hit this brilliant shot from over 20 yards, which Clem just didn't see. It flew out off the post and Sharpy stuck it in. It was a lethal shot.

I watched from the directors' box with Kevin Ratcliffe, Trevor Steven and Gary Lineker. We were watching the free-kicks, and at one stage Gary said, 'Everyone knows what we do at free-kicks now'. So I said tongue-in-cheek, 'Yes, we want to get me on them'. Quick as a flash, he came back with, 'We wouldn't mind just getting you on the pitch now and again'.

                                                         Thursday 20 March
The papers had a story this morning that Terry Venables is leaving Barcelona and that the boss is being lined up as his replacement. I met him with a quick burst of 'E Viva Espana' – 'I'm off to sunny Spain' – he just smiled.

The lads had the day off, so Ratters and I worked hard together. I was nearly flat out, certainly running at three-quarter pace. We both did a lot of strong running, and we both felt good, but there is no chance of us playing at Luton. The boss had a word and said he wouldn't risk us, but I shall definitely have a chance for a week on Saturday against Newcastle, which is incredible after the way I felt eight days ago.

Had another good day training. The lads weren't in until later to go down to Luton, so Ratters and I were on our own. It is going well. We started ball-work, striking it, which is the next step, and I didn't feel any reaction. Clinks said I can join in with the lads on Monday, which is good news.

The boss had to give Gary his PFA Player of the Year award today – he won it from Paul McGrath, who I voted for because of course you can't vote for your own team mates. Gary will be travelling to Russia with the England squad and won't be at the Awards dinner on Sunday.

It's a tremendous honour for him – I know just how much it means to win it from last year. He is delighted, but he certainly deserves it for all the goals he has got.

Luton 2 Everton 1   **Saturday 22 March**

Ratters and I went in and trained hard again. We were in the gym with Derek Walsh.

I didn't go to a game afterwards, I just listened to the radio. Everything was going well and then they hit us with two late goals, although from the commentary it sounded as if we were under the collar, which I'd expected. They had been beaten by Manchester United in midweek, and by all accounts hadn't given United much to worry about, but they were obviously going to be wound up for some revenge on us.

But it is disappointing to lose after being one up, because we usually keep solid. Watching it on TV we were done with dead-ball situations again. Foster got on the end of them, scored the first and knocked one down for Newell for the second. From what you could see on TV, it looked as if Derek had gone to sleep on the first one – he didn't react at all. He has done very well since he came back, but you are playing on your enthusiasm when you come back after a long absence and it looked as if he'd lost his concentration for a bit.

They got the first with a few minutes remaining, and at that stage you would settle for a point, but they were always at us, and they got the winner.

I'm philosophical about it. We lost and it is the end of a great run, but you've got to get beaten sometimes. I hate losing, I'm not a good loser, but it is a question of getting our heads back and bouncing straight back.

I'll be fit for Saturday, Ratters probably will be, and Gary Stevens, who has had the 'scope', has got a chance, so then we'll be looking at a full squad again. The only set-back was that Kevin Sheedy came off with a torn hamstring, so he'll probably be topping himself somewhere – he must feel desperate.

129

I went in and did a bit to keep ticking over. I felt quite good again and am really looking forward to training with a ball with the lads tomorrow.

There's been a lot more speculation about the boss going to Barcelona. I think there might be something in it, although he hasn't said anything, because he disappeared on Monday without anyone knowing where he was, and there were stories that he was meeting the Barcelona people.

I've been having talks about my new contract. Nothing has been concluded yet. He is meant to be coming back to me, but obviously if his future at the club is in doubt, it means things are a bit in the air at the moment.

The boss told me on Thursday that he had tried to buy Mabbutt, and Tottenham had asked for me. There have also been rumours that Bordeaux are interested. Ideally I'd love to stay at Everton if everything is right. With all respect to Arsenal and Tottenham, there would be no point in my going to them for an extra £100 or even £200 a week. It would have to be a ridiculous amount to make it worthwhile, because we are a better team and are likely to be better for a couple of years at least. We are a happy club and if it can be sorted out I shall stay. But this contract is probably my last chance to be financially secure, so it is an important one.

The lads have gone off for the internationals, apart from Kevin Sheedy, who had to pull out of the Irish squad, and Pat who has pulled out of the Wales team with a knock on his knee. I think Nev might have pulled out of the Welsh squad too, but Eddie Niedzwiecki has been injured so Nev has gone. Sharpy has gone with Scotland, and Gary Lineker, Trevor Steven and Paul Bracewell have gone with England – delighted to see Paul back in, because he has been playing brilliantly, in spite of still having a lot of pain with his ankle. You'd never know it to watch him.

There were a few comments about Irish organisation flying around, because Kevin's call up papers from the FAI arrived today – telling him to report yesterday.

The rest of us had a five-a-side on the bowling green – it's a piece of ground over in the corner at Bellefield which we stay off for as long as possible. Then at this stage in the season when the other pitches are getting rutted and bobbly, we go onto this and it is immaculate – a real pleasure to play on.

I would have been pleased anywhere though. The boss said, 'Take it easy' but I enjoyed every minute of it, getting really involved and I didn't feel a twinge or anything. It was the best I've felt for a long time, although I said that last time.

I know I will definitely play on Saturday, so it is just a question of working hard, and being prepared. I feel sharp, but that is partly enthusiasm because I haven't played many games – I've only played 7 league games up to now, and you need 14 appearances to get a medal, so I'm beginning to sweat about that a bit.

I went out to a dinner at Radcliffe tonight with Bryan Robson and Kevin Moran. Kevin has got a broken arm, and as I was sitting next to him I cut up his meat and potatoes for him. He said, 'Are you doing this for getting me sent off at Wembley or what?' and a few other people on the table picked it up and there were a few comments flying around.

Bryan said he is going to play with a harness on to protect his shoulder, which keeps popping out. He said he had been getting involved in physical situations in training to test it, and he is quite confident. I'm not sure. I hope to God it doesn't go on him, but I have a funny feeling about it. I just hope I'm proved wrong, but I think he should have had the operation. I can understand United being desperate to keep him playing, because I know they miss him when he isn't there, he is a tremendous influence on players around him, but I just hope it isn't going to rebound on England in Mexico.

I keep seeing Mark Lawrenson against Juventus after five minutes. He just went down and that was that. You can do anything in training, but however hard you try, there can't be the same sharpness as there is in a match, and that's where you get found out. And at this stage in the season every game is crucial, so you're more likely to get hurt. They are at Birmingham on Saturday and play us on Monday, and both those games will be battles. We are very good friends, but we will be enemies on Monday and there won't be any quarter given. I hope he is all right, but I'm sceptical about it, especially the way he plays, because he is so physical.

Tuesday 25 March
Another five-a-side. It's a bit quiet because of all the lads away at internationals and the reserves have got a match, so there weren't many people around. Inchy, Alan Harper and Kevin Sheedy were, so we went out for a drink in the afternoon. We don't go berserk, but it is good to have a drink occasionally with the lads. It gives you a chance to have a chat about things.

Wednesday 26 March
The England game was live on TV, so I spent the afternoon watching that. As I expected Mr Robson played 4-3-3 again, with Chris Waddle playing as a winger. We won 1-0, which is a great result in Russia, and Chris Waddle got a great goal, but there is just something which tells me that it just won't do in Mexico.

131

I think it has to be 4-4-2. Kevin Keegan was on TV saying that he would like us to play a sweeper. I can understand Kevin, having played in Europe, saying that, but I think it is a very difficult thing to do with English players, because it is not natural in our game, and it is very difficult to turn it on and off. You can't change your habits just like that, and it is a drastic change. To take just one example, Gary Stevens would have to change his game a lot, because the full-back's role is very different, and to try and implement it, even with a month in Colorado before the tournament, would be asking a lot. Bryan Robson would make a brilliant sweeper, or even a straight back-four-player, because he will win it for you and he is one who will come out and play from the back. Whether we would miss him from midfield too much is another matter. There's been so much chopping and changing it is difficult to be certain, but I think Mr Robson will play with a winger. I wouldn't. I'd play Trevor Steven on the right of midfield. Finding someone to play on the left is more difficult unless Steve Hodge comes through, but I'd want someone to work up and down the left, even if it is Chris Waddle, rather than having him as an out and out winger. I've been very disappointed in him when I've seen him play for Tottenham, but it was a terrific goal today. It just shows what he can do. He just needs to do it more often.

Overall though it was a terrific team performance. I thought Ray Wilkins had one of the best games I've seen him play for England. Being very critical, I thought Glenn looked a bit lost on the right, and I thought Mark Wright looked a bit exposed when people got at him, but it was a good team performance. We might have caught them a bit cold, because their season is only just re-starting, and I think they'll improve before the World Cup comes round, but winning there is a great achievement.

The most pleasing thing to me was that we didn't concede, and that's my main reason for thinking we've got a real chance. We don't give goals away and we can make it hard for teams, so hopefully we can get a pattern and a settled side.

Interesting watching Gary Lineker. He should have had a penalty when he was brought down in the box. The moment he began his run in the top corner of the screen leading up to that incident, I knew it was him, because I've seen him make those runs so often for us. He is, obviously, a very good finisher, but the runs he makes in the first place are brilliant.

I did wonder though whether International football will suit him. I'm sure he'll get his share of goals, but his great strength is getting the ball played over the top. For us, playing on the backs of defenders, he turns punts into dangerous through passes, but in Mexico there will be so many teams playing with a sweeper, those balls will get picked off. The passes will have to be so accurate, or his great strength will be nullified. It's something we'll have to have a chat about.

In the evening I went to the Paul Jones Testimonial dinner. Paul was a colleague of mine at Bolton. He was a player I always thought sold himself short. He should have played at a higher level than he did, because he had real pace. I saw him done for pace once, by Tony Woodcock, because he'd been a bit casual and given Tony a yard. But that was the only time. He always seemed to play well within himself though.

It was a good evening – it's always good to meet up with old friends. I went along with Frank Worthington, saw Tommy Docherty, which I always enjoy and had a good time. It was soured though by listening to the radio in the car and hearing that Neville Southall had been injured playing for Wales in Dublin. If it is a bad one it will be a terrible blow for us.

Thursday 27 March

When we went in, everyone was wanting to know about Neville. Inchy said, 'Will he need his tickets for the Manchester United game?', which is typical of footballers. Neville has got this terrible injury, but he would appreciate that more than anyone, because you've got to keep laughing.

The boss said he's got a dislocation and damage to the ligaments in his ankle. He has been put in plaster, and Sir John Moore's private jet has gone over to pick him up and bring him back. He'll be going into Lourdes, so I might pop in and see him tomorrow.

I should imagine Neville will be going mad. I'd hate to be the physio when he comes back, because he is one of those people who have to be active. When he had to take things easy with his rib injury earlier in the season, he was a nightmare around the dressing-room, throwing boots and kicking balls because he was bored. He was like a growling bear around the place, a right bundle of fun.

There was a lot of talk that it was a result of playing on a rugby pitch at Lansdowne Road, because Nev did it landing in a pot-hole. When Howard phoned Mike England however he said it was the sort of accident which could have happened anywhere, even training at Everton. The boss said, 'No, it couldn't have happened at Everton. He has Wednesdays off here', which shows that at least he's kept his sense of humour.

When I went in he was smiling. I said, 'What are you smiling at?' and he said, 'Well, you've got to keep smiling haven't you?', which is to his credit. I got injured in an international and was out for nearly five months. Now Nev is going to be out for the rest of the season after playing in an international. It's one of those things, but it is unfortunate, especially as this one was a fairly meaningless one and Nev might not have played if Eddie Niedzwiecki had been fit.

Mimmsy has been recalled from Notts County, where he'd gone on loan. I've been quite impressed with him. Alan Kelly works with our keepers and they actually work harder than anyone at our place. I think Mimmsy has benefited. He's lost a little weight since he came to us, he looks sharper now at getting down to things, he looks confident in training and I think his technique has improved. He did well in that one game at Manchester City, and I think he is the type who will respond to the excitement of the first team, so I don't think we've got any problems, although you can't lose the best keeper in the world without feeling it.

Harpo came in today and said, 'It's all your fault!' He really slaughtered me because while we were having our drink on Tuesday, Graham Turner had been trying to get him on the phone all day. The transfer dead-line is today, so it is too late now. Harpo said he's not coming out with me again.

We had another game on the bowling green. Adrian Heath, who has had a slight injury, trained, and we're looking forward to Saturday. It's a big match for us, after getting beaten last week. The Liverpudlians keep reminding me that we're looking over our shoulders at them now. It's still in our hands all the same.

The Easter period is very important. It can be won and lost then, although I think it will go to the last week. We're quite confident of getting back on the winning trail on Saturday, but Newcastle have had a great run of five wins and a draw in their last six, so it won't be easy.

Looking forward to seeing John Bailey as well. I'm sure he'll have something special up his sleeve for us – probably he'll walk in with 12 lagers just before kick off.

Friday 28 March

The boss acted quickly – he signed Fred Barber from Darlington as goalkeeping cover. He'd tried for Andy Goram of Oldham, but they wanted £350,000 which was a bit much, so he got Fred just before the dead-line.

It will be interesting to see how Mimmsy does with a run in the side. Ratters, Pat and Gary Stevens are all fit, so Neil's been left out. Richo is in for Sheeds again, and I'm back. We just had a game of head-tennis.

Then I went up to Lourdes with Brace to see Nev. He was in good spirits, although he said he has got a struggle to be fit for the start of next season. They haven't operated on the ligaments, so they must be OK, but he's got a plaster on.

I still think there is something in the air about the boss going to Barcelona. It isn't unsettling because we are good professionals and know we've got a job to do now, whatever happens later. He's not saying anything, he just smiles when he's greeted with choruses of 'Adios amigo' and that sort of thing.

It's amazing though how Barcelona can spend two million pounds on Mark Hughes when they are thinking of changing the manager. I'm sure the boss would sooner have Gary Lineker, and he got him for £1.2m less!

Nev's last comment was, 'Go and win the Title'. We've certainly got to beat Newcastle tomorrow, because it is so tight now we can't afford any slip ups. Six points over Easter would be brilliant. They are going to be two difficult games, but that's what you've got to do.

Everton 1 Newcastle United 0   **Saturday 29 March**

It was a good game, but in the end we were lucky. They battered us for the last 25 minutes. We weren't at our best. We were carrying a few injuries – Ratters and I were playing our first games back, and Pat did a rib, so Richo ended up playing left-back, but when we were under the collar, we did get down to it and battle. Even so, they missed a penalty and a couple of other good chances, and Gascoigne hit the post, so we got out of jail. When you look back on it, it is three points we didn't really deserve.

Brace kept us going. He is still suffering, but he worked hard in the middle of the park, winning the tackles. And at the end of the day we got three points, which is all that matters at this time of the season – well, at any time in the season that's all that matters.

It looks as if they've got a good little side overall though. Beardsley looked a great player, an absolutely brilliant player. I caught him with a couple of good tackles early on – they were good tackles, too – and he just got up, forgot about them and got on with his job. He looked great.

Whitehurst, who isn't the most graceful player, but puts himself about, also caused us problems. In the second half when Richo was left-back, so did Stephenson, the young winger, who was always willing to take people on and have a go at them. I was very impressed with Gascoigne, who has got good feet and isn't afraid to play. And David McCreery does a great job for them 'ratting' about in midfield. Overall they looked a good little side. The place where I thought we'd get at them was at the back. Glen Roeder is a defender who likes to play, he comes out of defence with the ball, and that tends to give you a chance. But although they took one or two chances, he and Clarke did quite well. In the end Richo popped up with our goal. He is a terror for chipping in with crucial goals when he is playing.

It was a great atmosphere – the Newcastle fans are great.

It was nice to see Bails. He knocked some good balls up to Whitehurst. The pair went off to the dogs afterwards – they'd got a dog down from Newcastle. I told him after the game that we'd battered them, and he jumped in with both feet – the language had to be heard to be believed.

135

I had the day off with my feet up. Bails' dog came in second – that's typical.

Manchester United 0 Everton 0   **Monday 31 March**

It was a game we needed to win really, but I suppose at the end of the day a point from United is not to be sneered at. They haven't been at their best, but I don't think we have either. We have had to chop and change the team with injuries, and we aren't at our sharpest. But again we battled away, and again we didn't concede. And that is what you have to do. You aren't going to play well for 42 games, you are going to have a sticky spell, and the question is can you get results during it? That's what marks a championship side. We are just keeping our heads above water and working at it, and hopefully we'll get it right and start to play.

It was very similar to the Cup Final really, where we cancelled one another out and it was going to take something exceptional to break the deadlock.

We push people and so do they, and it was a game of 20 people playing in a 22 yard strip either side of the half-way line. It was so congested in there, there wasn't time to draw breath, let alone put your foot on the ball and do anything constructive. It's hard to put your foot on it when big Norman Whiteside is around anyway. I think that was why Atkinson didn't play Olsen – he's superb going forward, but in those games it is hard for him to get a kick. He played Colin Gibson instead, and more than anything he was just filling the space Gary Stevens runs into, so it was a deadlock.

Strachan had one good chance. Sharpy had a good chance with a header which he could have put anywhere after Inchy came on and knocked one to the far post, but Higgy blocked it. In fact I thought Mark Higgins was their best player, so I was delighted to see him back and buzzing.

At the end of the day we've got to be happy with a point. Liverpool have gone back to the top on goal difference, but we've got a game in hand. West Ham are looking strong – from the televised high-lights, their performance on Saturday was one of the best I've seen from any team this season. I didn't think they would sustain it right the way through, but all credit to John Lyall. Devonshire looks on song, which makes me think he could be the left-sided midfield player we need for the World Cup. Little Wardy from Oldham does well for them on the other flank, he gets up and down the line battling away. And the front two are a great combination – they looked so good, they looked as if they were going to score on every attack on Saturday.

But Easter has certainly accounted for Chelsea. West Ham won there 4-0 on Saturday, and they lost 6-0 at QPR today. I fancied them, but they've had a few injuries and it looks as if they couldn't last the pace. I don't think their pitch helps them, because it has cut up badly, and that doesn't help players like Nevin and McAllister.

I still think that we've got to beat Liverpool to win it. That's what I've thought all along, and I haven't changed my mind. If we finish above Liverpool we will be champions.

I stayed on after the game and had a drink with Robbo – gave him a few lines about Spitting Image. They'd taken the mickey out of his injuries yesterday – shipping different bits of his body out to Mexico. Finally his head fell off.

He did all right with his harness, but he doesn't look 100 per cent. I think he is being picked because of the influence he has on other players. He calms people down, gees them up. He is there for that, because it is Ron Atkinson's last gamble really.

On the coach down I was remarking about Barbara getting so nervous at games she can't bear to watch them sometimes, and Brace told me about his Dad. They live right on the beach at Aberdovey, and his Dad can't even bear to listen to the radio. When the game is on, he goes for a walk on the beach. If we score Mrs Bracewell puts a flag up on the flagpole. If we get another, another flag goes up. I don't know what happens if they score. I've heard of being nervous, but that's the best yet. Mr Bracewell isn't going to the semi, he's going for a walk on the beach! Mind you, Barbara says she isn't going to the semi either. Last year she left five minutes into the second half. She thought we were out until she turned the radio on and heard we'd equalised sitting in the car on the M6.

Tuesday 1 April

Day off.

Wednesday 2 April

Today was officially another day off, but I went in today just to have a five-a-side. I didn't think I could afford to have two days off, having only been back for two games. Ratters, Richo and Pat were in as well.

I took my Dad and a friend, Richie Harrison, to Goodison to have their photos taken with the League Championship Trophy, Charity Shield and European Cup Winners Cup before they are sent back. I thought at the time it would have been nice if the F.A. Cup had been there too, to complete the set. The League Championship one – The Canon Trophy – is solid gold. I couldn't believe it when I found that out, because the night we won it I was throwing it around as if it was plastic. It will be a good one to win again this year, because with Canon ending their sponsorship, this year's winners get to keep it.

We're beginning to look forward to the semi-final. The main problem is tickets, particularly for me coming from Liverpool. The club have been great, letting us buy 70 ground tickets and 28 seats, which should be enough for anyone, but not me, with my extended family and all my friends in Liverpool. I keep forgetting people, and keep having to try and scrounge another ticket for them. And you always lose money on buying tickets, because you never get all the money back for the ones you've bought.

It's not a problem, because it means you are being successful, so I'll settle for the little inconveniences, but there's the possibility of an all Merseyside final, and for tickets that just doesn't bear thinking about. You can never get enough for derbies or finals. I'll certainly have to change my telephone number if it happens, just to avoid some of the hassle.

The England squad are meant to be on Wogan on Monday with our World Cup single. I think I shall have to have a sore throat, because I don't know the words or anything – at least with 'Here We Go', the Everton song, I knew the words even if I don't sing very well.

The high-lights of Gothenburg v Barcelona, the semi-final first leg of the European Cup, and then Inter-Milan v Real Madrid in the Cup Winners Cup were on TV this evening. That's when the ban from Europe really hits you. The days you really miss from last year, the nights against Bayern Munich, with their great atmosphere. They were big occasions. What was even more frustrating watching Barcelona and Gothenburg was that I thought we'd have given both of them a good game.

The other match on was Forest v West Ham. Forest won, which has done us a favour. Whatever you say about Cloughy – and personally I have a lot of time for him – his sides are always hard to beat. He has got a few good young players – Nigel Clough was brilliant today – and they always have a go. To his credit he always gets people playing. We've still got to go there, and we know it will be a really hard game.

Thursday 3 April

We did free-kicks today – basically just tidying a few things up. All on the attacking side. Sheffield Wednesday have so many giants in their side, that we are trying different things, trying to whip balls in for people to get flick-ons, rather than getting height on them.

After the free-kicks, we just had a five-a-side. We're travelling down to the midlands tomorrow afternoon. I just hope all the lads will be fit. Gary Lineker came off on Monday with a hamstring, which is still troubling him, but I think he'll be fit.

We are quite confident. We've had so many big games in the last couple of years that we think we can handle it now. But semi-finals in the F.A. Cup are very hard. There is so much tension at them. The final is a day out. You know you've got to win it, but it is different. Semi-finals are great to play in but horrible at the same time, because you know that one slip and you are out of the F.A. Cup with Wembley so close. It is so tense that it is rare that you get a good game.

I think if we do our stuff we will win, so it is up to us. It is just a question of getting down there and getting the job done. We know their style – big men at the back and getting the ball forward as quickly as possible – and we know what to expect. We've had some good performances against them. Our 5-1 win at Hillsborough was exceptional – probably our best single performance of the season. We tore them apart down the flanks, and Gary's finishing was brilliant. Otherwise the matches have all been close – the 3-1 win at Goodison in the return, which I didn't see, was evidently much closer than the score suggests – but we've won three and drawn one of the games since they came back up. I can't see us getting beaten. I never think about getting beaten in these games. I just can't contemplate it, because I think the fear of losing inhibits you. You've got to go into them with a positive attitude.

John Bailey has said he'll 'moon' in the Town Hall square in Newcastle if they beat us. I think that was a response to the game on Monday. Newcastle must have given them a real going over, but I can imagine a few teams getting done up there. It won't be like that on Saturday.

They've done well, Wednesday. I'm especially pleased for Martin Hodge, who is a terrific professional. He was only at Everton for a couple of months after I went there, but he worked so hard, and now he has proved what a good goalkeeper he is. And there are a few in the Wednesday side who have rescued their careers there, and Howard Wilkinson has got them working very effectively as a unit, so I don't think we can pay much attention to what happened at Newcastle.

Semi-finals are different anyway. It's usually one goal either way. My first semi-final, against Southampton two years ago, felt better as the game went on. But we were the underdogs, which helped us, and there were some experienced players in their team like Frank Worthington and Mick Mills, who perhaps felt it was their last chance of a Cup Final. So there was a little fear in them, whereas we were more positive.

Luton was completely different, because we had played in Munich in front of 70 000 on the Wednesday. And we came to Villa Park, which was bumpy and windy, and we were feeling flat. Luton got right into us, and it was only that reserve of determination which we had to dig into, which got us back into it. In both games, we got stronger as the game went on. In a semi-final for the first 20 minutes you don't know whether you are coming or going, and you think 'I'm not going to finish this game'. Then all of a sudden you get into it. But they are weird games, there is so much tension in them, from the spectators as well.

I don't like watching us play anyway because I get too involved, and I can imagine that watching your team in a semi-final would be too much. All the lads are coming down, but they aren't looking forward to watching it at all. I remember the bench last year, and when Sheeds got the equaliser I think they all ran round the pitch like madmen – or hooligans.

An early goal would probably help relax things a bit, it opens the game up, because you know then that you've got to go and get one. But we always want to keep it tight. We've only conceded one goal over the two previous semi-finals, and that is the way we like it.

Conditions at this time of the year don't help. It always seems to be a windy day, and the pitches are getting bobbly. In fact I think Howard is trying to get in touch with Graham Turner to get the pitch watered. I'll phone Big Andy – he'll nip along and turn the sprinklers on for us. We would like a bit of give in the pitch, so that we can at least get the ball down and try to play a bit.

If we can get Sharpy and Gary into the holes and get them the ball, I think we've got a chance. We haven't played well for the last two games, but we didn't want to get beaten, and we made sure we weren't. We have this tremendous will in the side, and even when we aren't playing well, we'll run and chase and defend if we have to, until we get it right. If you work hard enough at it, it will come right in the end.

And having had those two games over Easter I know I shall be a bit sharper, and so will Ratters. Gary Stevens is back – it's only three weeks since he had a 'scope'. Derek is just getting back, so we should all be getting back to our best now.

Sheeds will miss it. He has missed a few important games over the years, he has been so unlucky with injuries. He missed the Cup Final against Watford, so you try and win these games for people like him as much as anything.

Mind you, Richo comes in and gets important goals. He did against Newcastle, and he has done it so often it's a gift the lad has got. If he goes it will cost a few bob to replace him. But Inchy has come on and looked ever so lively around people's feet. And players like him, who are quick around defenders' feet, cause big men like Sheffield Wednesday more problems than high balls. It is difficult for them when little people like Inchy or Gary Shaw are wriggling about. I think there will be a lot of dead-ball situations. They play for corners, throw-ins and free-kicks. But although they play off side, I think with the full-backs pushed in, it gives you a chance, because there is always space. You can get at them in the holes, and you don't really have to alter things much to overcome their off side play.

In the paper this morning it said that Terry Venables is staying at Barcelona for another year after all. There have also been stories linking the boss with Juventus, but Barcelona was the strong one, so that probably means he'll stay with us, which is good.

Gary failed his fitness test, which is a blow, but the boss is keeping it quiet. Inchy knows he will play instead.

We trained at 3 o'clock, the usual head-tennis and passing in a circle, then travelled down to the Holiday Inn. It was another eventful journey. Doc Irvine, who is a practical joker, let off a stink bomb in the coach. Not the best preparation on the way to a semi-final, so the lads stripped him and threw his shirt and shoes out of the window.

Pat Jennings joined us at the hotel. He has been signed just to give us cover for cup ties, because Fred Barber is already cup tied. He is someone everyone in football respects, and it was nice to have a chat to him.

And Big Andy came round to see us. Brace, Inchy, Sharpy and I were watching TV when he arrived He said he'd be involved in a real classic match while we had this boring semi-final – a relegation battle against Oxford – but he'd be thinking of us and wished us all the best.

The boss let us have a couple of lagers with our meal, which is something he does every now and then. You know there's a big game tomorrow, and can't help having it on your mind, and I think he feels that a couple of lagers might help some of the lads to sleep. No predictions, but I've got a feeling one goal could be enough.

In the other semi, Liverpool play Southampton and I just can't see Liverpool getting beaten. So it is up to us to battle through against Wednesday and make sure it's a Merseyside final.

Everton 2 Sheffield Wednesday 1   **Saturday 5 April**

For the third time in three years, our semi-final has gone to extra time and we've won by the odd goal. I don't think that is a coincidence. At the end of the day, we wanted it enough. It was a tremendous game, they gave it their best shot, but we were that bit stronger. We have got this fierce determination. We are a physically strong side and we keep going, but I think we are mentally strong too in situations like this, and in the end it told.

Surprisingly, because there is so much said about how hard they train, we always seem to finish the stronger against them. I think they start off very quickly. In all the games I've played against them, they have been very strong and sharp at the beginning. They go like bombs at the start and for 20 minutes you are right under the collar and thinking, 'We're not going to get a kick here'. You get caught up in the speed of it. But the longer it goes on, the more chance you get to get the ball down and impose your own pattern on the game and let the ball do the work. I think it is too physically demanding for them to keep it up for 90 minutes, and eventually you get them working in areas where they don't want to work, going backwards rather than getting forward all the time.

If you can hang on in there with them, you've got a chance. And that was true this time. I felt the best in extra time – it took me an hour to get my legs going – but as a team we were stronger from half-time onwards. They were the better side in the first half, but we took over afterwards.

I've played in three semi-finals now, and we've won all three, but I can't say I've enjoyed any of them. It is just a matter of getting through it. The tension builds up all day from the moment you wake up and start reading the papers. I thought we had a chance though from the moment I picked up the *Daily Mirror*, because Ron Atkinson was tipping us to get beaten. No need for a team talk after reading that!

We had our usual 10 minute walk – round the centre of Birmingham – and then our usual pre-match meal. I had a mushroom omelette. Then we went to Villa Park, which was electric. The Wednesday fans give their team fantastic vocal support, which sparked our fans off, and even kicking in before the game the atmosphere was tremendous. The tension was incredible.

In the dressing-room beforehand, Neville came in and made a few cracks to try and lighten the tension. You notice that some people are more ashen-faced than usual, others talk a lot more. The tension of a semi-final gets to people in different ways, but we try to keep it as jokey as possible. Our crowd were right on top of the dressing-rooms, and the boss just said, 'You can hear that crowd out there, go out and win for them'.

Nev and Alan Harper and Kevin Sheedy were all in there geeing us up. Pictures of our bench are revealing – anyone involved with the club just wants to sit on the bench, because you are nearer to things, you are part of the set-up sitting there, and I think that squad feeling is part of the strength of the club.

And I thought we coped brilliantly. When you hear clubs complaining about injuries, we didn't have Neville, who is the best goalkeeper in the country in my opinion, Gary Lineker, who is the best finisher, or Kevin Sheedy, who has arguably the best left foot in the country, it says a lot for the lads who have come in. No one has had as many injuries as us.

But we overcame it. Brace, Derek Mountfield and Sharpy were our three most influential players on the day. They were the leaders, and the rest of the team came into it. Brace kept us going – the game by-passed us in midfield a bit in the first half, but he emerged very influentially afterwards. Graeme Sharp led the line brilliantly. Once we had got the ball down and started to play, he started going at people and stretched Wednesday and they were always wary of him. And Derek had a great game at the back. In the first 10–20 minutes he wasn't that dominant, but after that he was terrific against the two big men, Thompson and Chapman.

But Adrian Heath had a great game instead of Gary, and Mimmsy quickly showed us we had nothing to worry about. Wednesday started very strongly and he made a couple of tremendous saves, but the thing I noticed was the way he came for his first cross.

It was a big, high ball with Gary Thompson coming in, but he caught it as if it was a training session. I'm sure it gave him confidence, but it gave the lads confidence as well.

They were the better side in the first half. On Friday we'd talked about knocking the ball into the gullies as quickly as possible if it was bouncing to counteract their style, but I think we took the boss too literally. When we had time to bring it down and play, we were still trying to knock it into holes first time, and the game was going too fast. We were playing at their pace, instead of getting the ball down when we had a chance to and playing our way.

Colin Harvey and the manager both mentioned it at half-time. They asked me what I thought and I said that was what I thought was wrong, and in the second half we did get it down a wee bit more. We'd already lost Trevor Steven by then. He'd stretched for a ball, which would have put him through, but his groin went. It was only a strain, but you can't carry those in semi-finals and Alan Harper came on. Semi-finals must be the worst of all games to come on as sub in, and it took him until half-time to get his breath.

In the second half however he made the breakthrough. They cleared, Derek Mountfield won the header and sent it back in, and we caught them as they were coming out. I think you can do that, because they come out so quickly. So Harpo ran round the back of them and got in. Martin Hodge committed himself, giving Harpo the chance to lob him, and he did.

I thought that was it. I couldn't see them getting back. But their supporters really got behind them and they did. The ball was cleared on the edge of our box and Harpo and I went to shut down Snodin, but he turned and hooked it straight in to where they were waiting. Chapman won the header and knocked it down and Shutt got to the second ball.

Then it was just a matter of who wanted it the most. They were going great guns, but I always felt we had the edge. In the closing minutes Sharpy missed a great chance. All he had to do was keep his head, but I think he got a bit excited and missed it. So it went into extra time.

There was a funny cameo in the break. Wednesday were having glucose drinks or vitamin drinks, and Graham Smith, our youth team coach, ran out to us with a bit pot of tea. The contrast made me laugh – you are always looking for something to relieve the tension, and that did.

The boss just said, 'Keep going, keep trying to play your football and you'll win', which was the right thing to say. I don't know what Mr Wilkinson said to them, it was probably the same thing, but looking over at them they looked a tired bunch of players, and I thought we looked fresher.

Again they began strongly, and we were under pressure for the first five minutes of extra time. They had four or five corners, which was very dangerous for us, but we managed to defend well and then we went and got the goal. Again we caught them coming out. Brace hit in a great chip, Sharpy got onto the ball just ahead of Sterland and hit a great volley into the net.

This time I was sure we were through. Bobby had to make a good save near the end, but that was it.

When the whistle went I went over to Martin Hodge. I didn't know what to say because we were feeling this tremendous elation, and they were feeling gutted. Losing in the semi-final must be the worst thing in the world. In the players' room afterwards a few of the Wednesday players were in tears. I'd thought on previous occasions how horrible losing in the semi-final must be, but I noticed it more this time, because I felt a bit more for Wednesday than I had in the other two matches.

In our dressing-room of course there was this great excitement, we had champagne and a few lagers and went back to Liverpool for more celebrations. I was feeling my ankle a bit and am staying over at my Dad's, to go in for treatment in the morning. We went to our local 'The Quiet Man' with my uncle and some friends. It was buzzing obviously, because Liverpool had won their game, so it will be a historic final.

I can't put into words what it means for the City. The ticket situation is going to be absolutely chaotic. I've got cousins and uncles who are Evertonians, and ones who are Liverpudlians, and no matter how many tickets we get, there won't be enough. It will be a unique occasion. I played in the Milk Cup Final in 1984, and the atmosphere was terrific then, but this is the big one, this is the glamour day. And with us going for the title and them our main rivals it makes it even more interesting. We won't be able to get the Final out of our minds, but we've got to, because there is the League title, and that is the big prize in my opinion, and I think in the opinion of everyone at Everton – certainly the gaffer's.

Sunday 6 April

Went in for treatment. I've got a bit of trouble with the muscle on the outside of my calf – it has spasms. It stops me turning really sharply. I can play with it with a strapping on, although I'm not keen on that because they have to shave your leg.

The phone has started ringing already.

Monday 7 April

We had our Monday five-a-side to work Saturday's stiffness out. I had some more treatment. Incredibly all five England players, Brace, Links, Trevor Steven, Gary Stevens and I were all having treatment for minor injuries. I still trained as I think it is important for me.

There was a crowd round the gates at Bellefield when we came in and a larger one when we left. The chase is on for tickets. We are trying to push it to one side, but it is almost impossible. I phoned the GPO to get my home number changed, so I shall just have to wait for them to do that now.

At least my injury gave me an excuse not to go down for the Wogan show. I was glad I had after watching it, because like Bryan Robson I didn't know the words of the record – and it was obvious he didn't, because they kept panning on to him while they were singing it.

Tuesday 8 April

A normal day. We trained and had a five-a-side. Trevor and Links are fighting to get fit for Arsenal on Saturday.

Afterwards we had a meeting about the players' pool for the Cup Final. We agreed to ask Eric Hall, a London agent who has done some work for some of us in the past and handled our Cup Final record last year quite successfully, to do it for us. We don't want to get involved sorting out TV and newspaper fees – our best bet is to get on with playing football and leave all that to an agent.

Wednesday 9 April

We made our new record at a recording studio in Kirkby today. Eric had arranged it, so we talked to him about handling our pool, and everything was agreed. He is handling Liverpool as well, so it will be a double deal.

It was a good day out. There was some lager and white wine laid on at the studio – it is amazing what they do for the vocal chords, although I'm convinced that either the engineer is a miracle worker, or they dub on other voices afterwards.

Being so experienced in the pop world these days, we decided to change the sides round and have the 'B' side, 'Everybody's Cheering The Blues' as the 'A' side. A quick call to EMI and it was sorted out.

We're hoping the record is going to be a smash hit. It certainly had a smashing start, because when Gary Stevens drove out of Bellefield in his BMW on the way to the studios, he had to brake suddenly. Kevin Ratcliffe, also in a BMW, smashed into the back of him. There was a bit of stick flying around about that – someone said 'Ratters drives like he tackles'.

In the evening I watched United get done by Chelsea on TV. A draw would probably have been the best result for us, but this was still a good one. United were a bit unlucky from the excerpts on TV, but Chelsea hung in there and Kerry Dixon is certainly back with a bang. I think that was the end for United and I think Chelsea have too much to do now.

In fact, although West Ham are still in with a chance, I'm convinced it is between us and Liverpool. We've both been there before, which I'm sure makes a difference. They aren't playing too well either at the moment, but they are like us, they battle harder and get results. It has reached the stage now though, that the team that keeps its nerve will do it. There is one thing in their favour and ours – there won't be any fixture pile up for either of us, unlike West Ham.

Thursday 10 April

We had a five-a-side followed by two short shuttles to finish. Inchy is looking so sharp in training. I think he feels he has got something to prove. I don't. I'm sure that at the end of the day the boss will try and keep him and financially offer as much as any other British club. The best compliment I can pay him is that if Gary isn't fit, we will obviously miss him, but there is no better player to replace him. You can see in training when people are in good nick, the lads start looking at them, and Inchy is really buzzing around.

Links and Trevor are responding to treatment though. Kevin Sheedy is coming on well with his hamstring too. All he needs is a good week's training, because he has been coming back and getting injured again. Links and Trevor though have got a chance for Saturday at Arsenal, which is one of those grounds for us. There are grounds you go and win at, like Tottenham. And then you get grounds where whatever you do, you can't lay the bogie. Highbury is like that. I've played there twice for Everton, both times we've played ever so well, and both times we've lost. Last year we lost 1-0 to a Charlie Nicholas penalty which was never a penalty in the memory of man. It's a stadium I like, but the only time I've ever been on the winning side there, was in the semi-final against Southampton.

There is still a crowd outside the gates whenever we come and go at Bellefield. The phone there never stops ringing. The letter piles are appreciably larger. Usually I get about 50 letters a week; they've grown to about double that for all the lads. For the boss, it is probably 10 times larger. The amount of mail he gets is ridiculous.

A lot, of course are ticket requests. Some – from badly injured and sick people – really get to you, but there is nothing you can do, because you don't even get enough tickets for your family.

Friday 11 April

We were in at 1 p.m. for head-tennis as usual. I had a photo taken with the boss, Nev and Ratters with all our trophies at Goodison.

Then we went down for the Arsenal game. It is a very important one for us, because we've got to get a result, it is so tight, and it is not an easy place for us.

146

There is one thing in our favour though – we're staying at South Mimms this time. It is our lucky hotel. We've never been beaten when we stay there.

Arsenal 0 Everton 1   **Saturday 12 April**

It was a hard game. Arsenal had a lot of injuries – O'Leary, Mariner, Woodcock and Williams were all missing – but the lads who came in had a real go. I was very impressed with the two centre-backs, Keown and Adams. And it was a difficult game for Brace and me, because Robson played tucked in behind the front two and Davis played just in front of the back four, so we were almost playing against no one. Robson's position made it difficult for us to track him, so we had to just play our game.

It wasn't an easy game for us. But we stayed solid at the back, Mimmsy made good saves to keep them at bay, and I think we just about deserved it in the end, because Lukic made three great saves from Trevor, Sharpy and Kevin Richardson. Inchy came on with about 25 minutes left – Gary hadn't trained all week and he didn't look at his best, the niggling injuries were affecting him – and got the goal. A corner was flicked on and he reacted more quickly than anybody else and volleyed it in.

It was a great result for us because Liverpool got five, which increases their advantage on goal difference. West Ham won 4-1 after being a goal down, which shows they have got the bottle for it, they didn't panic when they went behind. And Chelsea drew at Forest. So its boiling up nicely now. I wouldn't be surprised if it went to the last day.

Sunday 13 April

I went in for a bit of treatment on my calf. Links and Trevor were also in. I'm sick to death of treatment, but at least I know it isn't stopping me playing.

In the afternoon there was a testimonial do for Sammy Lee at Robson's bar in Manchester, which is owned by a friend of mine, so I went along. A lot of the lads were there – I don't know anybody who doesn't like Sammy Lee.

We watched Sheffield Wednesday beat Manchester United 2-0 on TV. I was surprised because I thought that United, having held them until half-time, would just steam-roller them in the second half. Instead it went completely the other way. United just seemed to cave in. It didn't look as if they had any stomach for the fight. I felt sorry for Sivebaeck. He was pitched in against Liverpool at Anfield and this was his second game. Wednesday aren't the easiest team for someone who is not used to the pace of English football to play against, and he didn't look as if he had ever played football in his life before. I hope he gets a good pre-season next year to give him a chance to try and get to grips with it.

Robbo, John Gidman, Kevin Moran and Arthur Albiston came on to the bar after the match. I had a chat with Robbo. He was absolutely gutted, and I said to him, 'Well, the way you performed on Wogan, you can always have a job as a singer'. I won't repeat his reply, but it was two short words.

Monday 14 April

Good news. I've been called up for the match against Scotland next Wednesday. There are some games I've always wanted to play in. One is the Merseyside Derby. Another is the England–Scotland match. There's always a lot of ribbing between Scots and English in dressing-rooms, some clubs have their five-a-sides as England v Scotland, it is a big game, and I'm delighted to be in the squad. I'd love to play in the match. I don't expect to, because Ray Wilkins did well in Russia, and Robbo will be back, but I hope I will be on the bench. And it won't be a game for faint hearts, so you never know, I might get on at some stage. Aitken is a strong lad and so is Souness, and I'd really like to play against them, because you've got to want to play against the best.

The pool is hotting up. TV are wanting things, but I'm trying to keep it out of my mind and leave it to Eric to sort out. All the same I seem to be spending more time on the phone than training at the moment.

We've got Watford tomorrow, the pioneers of the long ball game, so we went in for a good five-a-side at 11.30, got a sweat on, and then travelled down to the Bell House Hotel at Beaconsfield, our Wembley hotel, 'our second home' as Brace calls Wembley. There's a story going round that Wembley and Liverpool are to become twin towns.

We normally do well against Watford. They aren't a bad side on their own midden. They have a few players who can cause you problems. John Barnes of course can cause anyone problems on his day, and Sterling can. But the way they play they do give you a chance, although I think they've tightened up a bit at the back since they signed John McClelland.

Watford 0 Everton 2 **Tuesday 15 April**

The pitch was atrocious – there was three–four inches of mud right down the middle, so it wasn't a classic but it was really exciting, full of goal mouth incidents and much closer than 2-0. So it was a great result for us. We had to dig deep again, because we were under some pressure, but that is six points from two away games, which we needed. We went one up in the first-half – Gary scored just before he went off at half-time.

148

He had been struggling, he isn't fit, and that goal was about his only kick in the half, which just proves what a tremendous striker he is. So Inchy came on, and we were under real pressure in the second half. It was just a matter of fighting. Mimmsy made a couple of good saves, Paul Bracewell kicked one off the line after a corner. That is not luck, because we always have two men on the posts at corners, and that's their job – when I see some sides who don't do that I can't believe it.

Watford are very good at dead-ball situations, but I think they've lost a wee bit, perhaps because Colin West was injured, and they had Barnes and Sterling up front. They still had the big men at the back to come up, and they are still dangerous, but I think when they had West – or George Reilly before him – to aim for, they were that bit better. In the past they were ridiculously good, one of the best teams in the country, if not the best, at whipping it in and getting someone on the end of it.

So we stuck at it. We were under real pressure for a time, but because of the way they play they always give you a chance, and I thought that if they had equalised we would have gone down and got one. And we finished strongly. We had a few chances and then in the end Trevor crossed and Sharpy, who had another very good game, got on the end of it and stuck it away.

The three points have taken us back to the top. I wonder how long we will stay there, because Liverpool are at Luton tomorrow night. Maybe it is wishful thinking, but I've a feeling with it being on the plastic pitch, that Luton might get something out of the game. We heard after the game that Chelsea had won at West Ham, which shows they've got the stomach for it and that has put them back in with a shout now. Liverpool have still got to go there on the last Saturday of the season.

We've got West Ham at Goodison on the Monday of Cup Final week. That game could prove as crucial as the European Cup Winners Cup Final was last year. But at least it is on the Monday rather than the Wednesday, so we will have five days to get over it before the final.

People say West Ham are in a good position because they have so many home games left. But I remember Arthur Albiston saying that about Tottenham last year, and I said, 'Yes, but they still have to win them'. It is all right having those games on paper, but you still have to go and do it. Last year in the end it was Tottenham's home form which let them down. And West Ham lost at home tonight. In the end the best team will win. I do believe that: the team that wins the League is the best team. The boss had a bit of a go in the press on Sunday about London journalists saying it would be good for football if West Ham won it, because of their football. The boss said that Liverpool and us have both scored 20 goals more than West Ham, which is right. You can't say that a lot of our matches haven't been entertaining with a lot of good football – the Derby match which we lost early in the season was one of the best matches I've ever seen. But you don't win the League title by scoring the most goals – unless it comes down to goal difference, which it very easily could. You win it by being the best team and winning the most matches. And the thing that strikes me about West Ham is their defensive record – they've given away the least goals of anyone. They've got a good back four nowadays, a bit more steel, and I think John Lyall has done well getting that, but you don't get that sort of record through your back four, but by defending as a team, and people like Pike, Dickens and Ward do a great job for them in that area, and Devonshire does his bit as well. They have a nice balance, and the goals they got against Chelsea which I saw on TV were great goals, but they were breaks, and one of their great strengths is counter-attacking.

Wednesday 16 April

Liverpool got a great result – they won 1-0 at Luton. That convinces me more than ever that it will go to the last game now. It is wide open, the most competitive championship race I can remember, which has to be good for football after all the blows we've had. If you go into a pub now, everyone is talking about the title race, which is good to hear.

We had the day off but I went in for treatment. The players' pool has already beaten last year's figure, so Eric Hall has paid for himself. Prudential are doing a big sponsorship, 'Merseyside Unites', and there are little deals with Smirnoff and NEC in the offing. We are trying to keep personal appearances down to a minimum. Eric's arranged something with TV which we will be available for, and we will probably do something to plug our record at a record store, but we aren't doing the shop appearance scene. It doesn't bring in very much money, and it is something we can do without, while we are going for the title. All I want to think about at the moment is beating Ipswich on Saturday, although having said that, it is sometimes nice to get out. I took Barbara and Louise out for a meal this evening just to get out of the house for a bit. I still had to phone my Dad at ten to nine to find out how Liverpool were getting on – you can't get it out of your mind.

At Sammy Lee's do on Sunday I had a chat with John Wark, who said he'd done a ligament in the last minute of their game. It turned out later that he had broken his ankle. A really sickening season for him. He had achilles problems early on like me, and now this, which has ended any chance he had of going to Mexico. It just shows how quickly a footballer's life can change – not just from one game to the next but from one minute to the next. The game is already won 5-0 and then that happens – you are trying to get a sixth in the last minute and you break your ankle.

There's been further speculation about the boss leaving at the end of the season. Of course if Juventus come in with a fabulous offer, who could blame him for going? He has his family to look after. I'm sure if Everton could match the Italian or Spanish clubs, he would definitely stay, but you have to keep an open mind about things like that. I would like to stay, but if someone comes in with a big offer I've got to think seriously about it. At the end of the day, you have a responsibility to do the best for your family.

I've a feeling the boss will stay though. He is so happy in his work, with the team, in training, everything. He has done very well putting a lot of the lads on four-year contracts. We are generally a young team, even though we've got a lot of experience, and I think we can only get better as a team, and I'm sure he is very conscious of that. People like Trevor Steven, Gary Stevens, Derek Mountfield and Brace are only 22 or 23 and will improve, Sharpy, Ratters and Links are only 25 so haven't reached their peak yet. It is a fabulous opportunity because you are looking at the side developing for another four years, maybe even longer, and the club has brought in young players like Bobby Mimms and Neil Pointon to come into the squad and improve.

It is a very professional group too, they look after themselves and are fit lads – it is very rare that we are found wanting for fitness in games. I think everything about the club is top class from top to bottom – the management, training and coaching staff all take a lot of credit – and so it would have to be a big offer to lure him away.

Thursday 17 April

My car wouldn't start, so I couldn't get in for training. I hate missing it, but I just couldn't get there.

Friday 18 April

We had our usual game of head-tennis. Links is not fit, so Inchy will play. Ipswich have a good record at Goodison, they always seem to give us problems, so although they are down there fighting against relegation, it won't be a foregone conclusion. But having said that, if we don't beat them, we don't deserve to win anything. We are in good nick, there is still a buzz around the place, and we are confident because it is in our own hands – if we win our games we will win it.

We are trying to concentrate on the League, but things keep cropping up. We had to do some sorting out on the Cup Final Banquet, which we arrange ourselves because we want friends and families to come, and it is a bit too expensive to expect the club to foot the bill for that: I want about 28 tickets myself. So we are organising it at £25 a ticket, which just covers the cost – contrary to some opinion we don't make money out of it.

151

We had a club banquet after the 1984 Milk Cup Final to which our wives were invited, which was very enjoyable, but we felt we'd like wider family and friends to be with us, so we organised our own for the Watford Cup Final and it was a tremendous night. We weren't able to have one last year because all the England squad players had to report that night, and the others had a league match on the Monday, so there was no time to do it.

Everton 1 Ipswich Town 0   **Saturday 19 April**
A really difficult game. As we feared they got everyone behind the ball and made it very hard for us to break them down. Trevor had a chance early doors with a header, which hit the post from Kevin Richardson's cross. If that had gone in, it would have been a different game. But it didn't, so it was a matter of grafting, and it was a real struggle. In the end Sharpy came up with the winner, a quality header after he got in between Butcher and Cranson for another Richo cross.

At one stage they were really frustrating us with passing back to the goalkeeper, so Inchy went in on McCall, and Cooper and Butch had a bit of a go at him. So I said to him, 'If you're going to do it, do it properly', not to be malicious, but little things like that can get people wound up and something might just break for you out of it.

Butch reacted and had a right go at me . . . 'You dirty little . . .' and I said, 'Shurrup and get on with the game, you big, stupid . . .' and we were effing and blinding at one another, all 5 ft 6 in of me and 6 ft 1 in of him, and then slowly we both started smiling. Butch is a great fellow and we had a joke in the bar afterwards. He had had to have stitches in a cut over his eye, and I said to him, 'See, that's what you get for messing with me'.

The boss pulled all the internationals into a room after the game, and had a chat to make sure we were all alright, because we are all going off tomorrow. In fact I'd been going to go down to London with Sharpy tonight, but he has pulled out of the Scottish squad – Cranson just caught him on the ankle in the last minute. So we have had to cancel our Saturday night out in London.

The boss doesn't like pulling people out of international squads, having been a player himself he knows what it means to players to go. But he wanted to be sure we were alright. Obviously I'm not 100 per cent fit, I haven't been in any game this season, but I want to go, and I said so. Pat was injured as well as Sharpy, so they both pulled out, but the rest of us were given the go-ahead.

                                           Sunday 20 April
I met Trevor and Gary Stevens at Knutsford Services and we travelled

down together to High Wycombe where we are staying. We didn't have to report until 6 p.m., but we went early so we could see the Milk Cup Final. We did it in two and a half hours, which was good time.

I'd had a sneaking feeling Oxford might win, but I didn't expect it to be so easy. QPR must be feeling really sick with themselves now, because they just didn't perform, in fact I can't remember seeing a team fail to perform like they did, for a long time. It looked as if they were scared to death, and I couldn't believe it while I was watching it.

Oxford must have thought all their birthdays had come at once. People were getting balls from throw-ins, turning and finding there was 20 yards to go into. It was unbelievable. But, to be fair to them, they looked a bit apprehensive to start with, but once they got into their stride, they played some good stuff, especially during the second half.

I had a couple of lagers with Bryan Robson and then an early night. I'm rooming with Steve Hodge. He's a good young lad, so I shall get him making my tea for me – I always had trouble persuading Brace that was part of his job. Hodgy is a good player I think. Not the strongest, but he times his runs into the box well and he is a good finisher. He is happy now he is playing in the middle at Villa, which he prefers to playing wide on the left, as he was at Forest.

Monday 21 April

We've been so busy it's unbelievable. We trained in the morning, which was quite enjoyable, although a longer session than I'm used to at Everton.

All the leisure gear for Mexico arrived from Umbro, so we tried that on.

The lads came in from Italy. There were rumours that Trevor Francis was going to play on Wednesday, but he arrived with a fractured cheek-bone. With the World Cup squad being selected that might set him back a bit. There are a few lads sweating on that. You hear little things on the grape-vine, and I think I will be going, but people like Trevor Francis, Dave Watson and Tottenham's Gary Stevens are sweating on it, so this will be an important game for some people.

I've got a feeling I won't play in this game though. With the way things have gone in the internationals which I missed in the last couple of months, I think Mr Robson is happy with Ray Wilkins and Glenn Hoddle in midfield, especially after the game in Russia. And Ray and I are so similar that I think it is either me or him for that position, and I think he'll get the nod.

Bryan Robson is not fit – he's got a slight problem with his hamstring – so Hodgy might get a game in his place.

153

We have quite a few meetings – it is a different style to Everton, where we virtually never have a meeting, never talk about the opposition, we just get on with our own game. Before a match the boss will have a chat for about five minutes and that will be it. Mr Robson though likes meetings and going into all sorts of things in depth. We've had meetings about Mexico, about the altitude, what to eat and drink there, about training there.

Seb Coe's doctor gave us a talk on eating and drinking which was fascinating. He said you should eat carbohydrates before a game – mashed potatoes, bread, all the things you would think you shouldn't eat. And he said that in Mexico we should drink as much as we want, that not drinking before a game was a fallacy. From my school-days I've always thought that if you drank cold water before a game, you'd get stomach cramps, and some of the lads asked him about water sloshing around in their stomachs. He said, 'Well, you might get that for ten minutes, but it'll soon go away'. He said as much liquid as possible as often as you can.

Last year in Mexico we had been given salt tablets, and we asked him about that, but he said they would do you more harm than good. Doc Edwards, who had prescribed them, was well pleased!

The boss took us down to the Bull at Bisham for a meal this evening. It is a lovely pub restaurant, it made a nice change and it was a smashing evening – at least until they brought us the West Ham result. I thought they were winding us up – West Ham had beaten Newcastle 8-1. Newcastle used three goalkeepers, but it was a great result for West Ham. They are coming on strong.

We were up at 9.30 trying on the blazers, slacks and suits for Mexico from Burton's, then we went off to the Hilton for a Variety Club lunch. I won a bottle of champagne in the draw, which seemed a good omen. There was a group of people from Liverpool who do a lot of work for Variety Club charities, so I sent the bottle over to their table.

We got back at 5 p.m. and trained from 5.30–7.00. The pitch was a bit heavy, so it wasn't the ideal preparation for the game tomorrow, but obviously we had certain things to fit in. In the practices Dave Watson played at the back and Hodgy was in Robbo's place, so it looks as if they will play tomorrow. Trevor Francis is struggling with his cheek-bone but he is seeing a specialist in the morning, so he will know then.

The training sessions seem to drag on a bit. I can understand why. We aren't together very often, so Mr Robson doesn't have time to work with us very much, and with players being fitted in like Dave Watson this time, we have to work on things, whereas at a club side, and especially at Everton, we know what we are doing. But still, from a personal point of view, I think they go on too long and you feel a bit leg-weary at the end. We did one exercise – a run from the 18 yard box and playing a one-two over the centre circle – which I thought would have been better cut down to half the distance, especially the day before a game. The Under-21s were watching, and Mimmsy and Wilko were in stitches watching me doing that.

Peter Beardsley and Alvin Martin, who had played on Monday night, joined us, and Mr Robson asked Peter if he wanted to train. Peter said, 'Yes, I can do with some handling practice, boss.' He had been one of Newcastle's three goalkeepers.

Wednesday 23 April a.m.
I forgot to say, there was some good news for Robbo. He is a partner in a horse, 'Taylormade Boy', and it won at Edinburgh on Monday at 7-2, so I expect he had a fiver on it.

Mr Robson announced the team. It was as I expected, except that Trevor Francis will play. Looking at it, perhaps he wants him to have a stormer and claim a place for Mexico, but it seems a bit of a gamble to me. I'm not saying that I'd deliberately hit someone in the face if I knew they had a fractured cheek-bone, but if he jumps for a high ball, you wouldn't be surprised if he got a rap in the face from an elbow.

A couple of the lads asked Bryan to ask the boss to slacken the training this morning. We usually run through our dead-ball situations, but we didn't train, we just had a chat about them, and about how we would play and how Scotland would play.

Gary Bailey is going to have a 'scope'. He rocked over on his knee in training on Monday, and the cartilage might have gone. There's speculation that he might have to miss Mexico, but if it is as successful as it was for Sheeds and Gary Stevens, he should be alright.

England 2 Scotland 1   **Wednesday 23 April p.m.**
Watching the first half from the bench, I thought the Scots played quite well for the first 20–25 minutes. They were getting the ball and trying to find Gough on the back post against Kenny Sansom all the time. There were one or two which ran loose, and a couple of crosses which went across the box, so they were doing quite well.

Then we went up and scored from a dead-ball. Hodgy headed it across and Butcher dived in and put it in. I was delighted he had scored, because he has a terrific attitude before a game, he really gets people revved up and he is a lad who wants to win badly. I've been tremendously impressed with his attitude. He is a good, solid, top class defender. It all depends how he will do in Mexico with tricky people around his

155

feet, but with his attitude I think he has got a chance. Some people are worried about him getting exposed out there, but I think he is one of the lads who will go in and won't let you down.

So that was 1-0, and then we broke and got another. Kerry Dixon hit this shot. It was difficult to see from the bench, but it looked as if Rough got there, but then it lobbed up, which meant he couldn't have been at full extension, because if he had been he would have put it round the post, or knocked it down. Instead it lobbed up and Glenn put it in.

Watching on TV later, I thought they had to be very disappointed about that one. In international football – or any football for that matter – you can't afford to give away goals like that. I know we all make mistakes, but Roughy makes a few too many for my liking. Ray Wilkins and Graeme Souness had got caught up in one or two tackles, and Ray had tweaked his knee ligaments in one of them, so I warmed up. Ray managed to last out the half, and he had treatment at the interval. It was touch and go whether he went back on, but the Doc decided to pull him out, so I was stripped and on. I don't really enjoy going on as sub, because I find it difficult to get the pace, but I was just delighted to go out and win another cap, especially against the Scots.

It is probably easier going on at half-time than when the game is in progress. I went on for the last 20 minutes against Mexico last summer, and I felt so bad after playing for only 20 minutes, I didn't think I'd ever last 90.

And I enjoyed the half enormously. It wasn't a full house, but there was a great atmosphere and the game was like a Derby. It wasn't like an International where you get plenty of room and you come from the back and you can play. It was tight. But I enjoyed it. I got a bit of the ball and got a few tackles in.

In the first half Ray had the chance to get a lot of the ball, but we didn't use him, and before I went on Mr Robson told me to go and get the ball off the back four. But they changed things in the second half, putting Gough in behind the front two, so I couldn't do that because he was in the hole. So I had to change and try and get at Souness.

Mr Robson thought afterwards that we lost it a bit in the second half as a result, but I didn't see it that way. Obviously they got a goal back, but it was from a penalty which I didn't think was one. I think Charlie Nicholas is good at that. I was standing over him and I said, 'You've done us' and he just smiled at me.

Losing that goal was a blow, but otherwise I thought we handled it quite well. Gough was getting into some useful positions, and they got a couple of long shots in, but I didn't feel we were under pressure. I thought we were more threatening than they were.

Obviously I was playing and involved, and you see things differently from the bench. When I was sitting there in the first half I thought they were the better team until we got the goal.

I went in for a tackle with Nicol, and Graeme Souness hit me with a late one. He caught me a beauty, but luckily my leg was just off the ground, so it wasn't too bad. I panicked a wee bit at first, because I thought it might be a bad one – and I also had this thought flash through my mind of what the boss would think, sitting at home and seeing it on TV.

But it was just bruising. I think you know when you get a bad injury, because you get this sickening feeling, and there wasn't anything like that. My leg was a bit stiff, it's swollen, and by the end of the game it was black and blue right down the back of my leg from the knee down, but I think it will be alright, I don't think there is any ligament damage.

I actually quite like playing against Sou-y. I've hit him once or twice with tackles and he hasn't moaned, and vice versa, and I think you'll settle for that. I had a chat with him before the game and he was talking about playing midfield in Italy. He said, 'You can play all day. You get the ball, you can turn, there's masses of room'. He was full of enthusiasm about his new job with Rangers. I think he'll do well. He is shrewd, he has a lot of experience, and I don't think he'll be afraid to take decisions – you can tell on the pitch that he is willing to take decisions. He'll be the boss.

I had a word with Glenn once. He is a terrific passer of the ball, but he tried to hit the killer-pass too often, and we were getting caught on the break. There's no way I'd want him to stop trying to find people in forward positions, because he is brilliant at it, but sometimes you've just got to keep the ball and consolidate. So I said, 'Keep it for a bit, and if anything comes, it comes', and he accepted it.

I almost forgot that there was a trophy to be handed over at the end. I was just toddling off to the dressing-room when I was called back, so I went back and got a nice gold medal.

Afterwards I just had a drink with my Mum and Dad, who had come down and were staying with my brother Gary. They were delighted I'd come on, so they had seen me playing for England. Then Trevor drove us home. I got back about 2 a.m., which wasn't too bad really.

It is terrific playing at Wembley. I always love it, and I think Internationals should always be played there – unless it is a game you really have to win, like an important World Cup qualifying game. I'd play those at Old Trafford or Goodison, where the crowd are on top of you. Spain do that in Seville. I think in imporant games you want every advantage, and if you can intimidate people a bit it helps.

I haven't been involved for long, so I'm not speaking from playing experience, but from watching the games I've seen, German and Dutch players come and play brilliantly at Wembley. Because of its history, it is the ground so many overseas players want to play at above all others, and it lifts them.

And it also is not the best place to play our way at, because of the wide open spaces. It is very hard to pressure teams there, particularly if they are good teams and especially if they like to play from the back, like a lot of the continental teams do. That will also be one of our problems in the Cup Final against Liverpool, because we like to pressure teams at the back, and we will have to work really hard to do it against them at Wembley, because people like Lawrenson, Gillespie and Hansen are quality players and they like to play from the back. Nine times out of ten Hansen will come away and make you look foolish, but the tenth time we might nick it and have something on. I'm sure we will have something up our sleeve for them, and if we can get at them a wee bit, we might get something, but it is hard to pressure people at Wembley.

Thursday 24 April
Surprise, surprise – I was in for treatment. I had ice on my leg all day. It is stiff, but there is no ligament damage.

The boss said he had nearly had a heart attack when he saw it, because he thought it might be a bad one. He said he'd nearly had another one when he saw Trevor Steven warming up – 'I was saying my prayers' – but then Trevor sat down and Tottenham's Gary Stevens was sent on to trail Gough instead and he felt better.

The club gave us our Wembley tickets. Unfortunately, contrary to popular belief, we don't get 150 each – with the size of my family I could probably get rid of them if we did.

Friday 25 April
There was a civic reception at the town hall today. Kenny turned it down, preferring his lads to rest up, which is fair enough if he thinks that is best for them.

Our boss decided we should go, so we went and had lunch, went onto the balcony to wave to the hundreds of Evertonians who had turned out, and then went back for a game of head-tennis. Then we travelled down to Nottingham.

It will be tough tomorrow. I've thought for a few weeks that this is our most difficult match. We don't usually get anything here. It's similar to Highbury – a tight game, we play well, and end up with nothing. Brian Clough has been saying that we are the best team in the country, and his youngsters have got no chance. That's just a bit of his propaganda, and we know we are in for a hell of a game. We're not accepting his compliments at face value. He does say some outrageous things at times, but I've a high regard for him, because he does get some good teams together, and they always want to play. Even this one is on a good run – I think they've gone something like ten games unbeaten.

Nottingham Forest 0 Everton 0   **Saturday 26 April**

Lourdes again! Brace said Wembley is our second home, but Lourdes is beginning to feel like mine. It seems I'm never out of the place. Ice treatment every 15 minutes, so there's not much chance of sleep, just lying thinking morbid thoughts. My ankle is badly swollen and doesn't feel too clever, and I don't feel too clever either. I just can't believe it has happened to me again.

The way I feel at the moment I don't think I've got much chance of playing at Oxford on Wednesday, and that is now a crucial game, because Liverpool won again, so they are now two points clear. I shall be sick if I have to miss it.

I don't think I have been 100 per cent fit for one game this season. I would just like to start one game feeling absolutely right. Funnily enough I felt quite good before the game. My knee was still a bit sore, but I felt fine. Then I got this whack about 10 minutes into the game. Colin Walsh caught me.

It was unfortunate really because I had nicked the ball. Sharpy made a run away, and so did Links. I saw Kevin Sheedy, who was having his first game back after injury out on the left, and I just delayed while he moved, before I put the ball out to him. And in that extra second's delay, Walshy got a tap on my ankle. Luckily I had a strap on it, but it just opened up, and it was really sore. I carried on, but I was in a bit of pain from it.

At half-time I took my boot off, and it had just blown up. So I had ice put on it and it was a matter of deciding whether I could carry on. I had a stirrup put on, a strapping to give you support and all the protection it could. The boss asked me how it was and I said, 'It's sore, but I'll give it a go', and I went out and managed to get through the game. I did alright really, but I was in a fair amount of pain, and it was a hard game. I didn't think there was any ligament damage, but it was getting more painful all the time.

I was a wee bit worried afterwards because it had come up and there was this throbbing pain. I'm always wary about pains like that in ankles. It didn't feel good at all. John Clinkard strapped me up and put me on crutches, and I went out to the coach on them.

The Mexico squad is being announced on Monday, so you can imagine how I was feeling. A few of the press lads intercepted me and asked me about it, but I just couldn't face that and said, 'I don't want to talk about it' and went and sat on the coach. I had ice all the way back to get the swelling down and the bruising out, and when we got back I was whisked straight round to Lourdes.

159

It was a hard game, a good 0-0 game. They played quite well. Clough always has a strong defence, and he gets them strong. I was very impressed with Metgod. I thought we might have got at him, but he played well. Metgod and Walker both looked very good players and we didn't get any change out of them.

The thing I like about Forest is that Cloughie always gets his wide men wide, in that hole between midfield and the back. It is difficult for the full-backs to go in there, and it is difficult for midfield players to pick them up. And that is the basis of my regard for Brian Clough – I think he has got a tremendous football brain.

Pat van den Hauwe got an injury too, and the boy Carr, who is a real quickie, got at us a wee bit and caused us a few problems, but we held out.

At the end of the day I think a draw was a fair result. They hit a post and we hit a post. Sharpy had probably the best chance of the game. I was behind him and he got there and connected, and it looked as if it was going in, but it spun and hit the post and came out. I think he will be disappointed with himself for not scoring then.

But against that they seemed to have scored late on, but the referee disallowed it because the ball went out on the way over. From where I was standing on the edge of the box, it looked a good goal. Seeing the replay on TV it also looked a good goal – you certainly couldn't see the ball cross the line. But I asked Ratters and he said it had definitely gone, so it just goes to show how different angles can deceive you. And the linesman, who was in a good position, put his flag up immediately. And if you look closely at the video Mimmsy stopped, which also suggests it had gone out. It was a hard game to go through. It was a point won really, and although Liverpool now have a two point lead, we still have a game in hand. It is still in our hands, but it just puts a bit more pressure on us. Liverpool look the team at the moment, but West Ham keep on rolling too, so if we slip up it will be crucial. But if you've got to beat Oxford away, followed by Southampton and West Ham at home to win the title, you can't ask for much more really. If I'd been offered that in August, I'd have settled for that, and we are still confident.

Pat spent the night in Lourdes too. He's got a calf injury.

Sunday 27 April

The specialist examined me and confirmed there was no ligament damage. They wanted to keep me in Lourdes today, but I think I'd have gone crackers being there all Sunday, so I made a bargain with the physio that if I was let out, I'd stay at my Mum's and just ice it all day and he agreed.

I went to my Mum's and she looked after me. I missed my Sunday afternoon pint, but you have to make some sacrifices. My brother Shaun

160

was over, so it was a nice family day really. My ankle was a bit sore, but not too bad, so I just got through the weekend by icing it all the time.

The Sunday newspapers were full of speculation that I'd miss the Cup Final and even Mexico, which was way over the top. It is a bit sore, but I can't see it being that bad. The Cup Final is two weeks away, so it is a little early to be coming out with statements like that. And the speculation about Mexico is totally unfounded. I could imagine my Mum reading that, or even friends, and being really upset without cause, so I was not too pleased.

Monday 28 April

The bruising is coming out and Clinks said I might have a chance for Wednesday. I don't think so, because it is still swollen, but it isn't too bad. I knew as soon as the specialist said there was no ligament damage that I would probably play on Saturday. Wednesday is a bit soon, although it is an important game and I want to play in it. I'm quite pleased with the progress really, and it is just a matter of intensive treatment to reduce the swelling. So it was ice all day.

Tuesday 29 April

We travelled down to the Crest at High Wycombe. I had ice all the way down trying to get my ankle right. Bobby Mimms, who had rocked over on his knee in training, was having ice too. He'll definitely be alright, and I think Pat will be OK too.

I'm more doubtful. The bruising is coming out all the time. It is feeling better virtually by the hour, and I think I will have a fitness test with a stirrup on tomorrow, but I've got a feeling Wednesday is a day too soon.

It is ironic that our fate could be decided at Oxford, because people say that is where the Everton revival began in 1984, with that Adrian Heath goal in the last couple of minutes of our Milk Cup tie.

I remember it vividly. It was an icy sort of night, and the pitch was a bit icy on top, but it was just taking a stud. We were losing 1-0 and I went to shut down Kevin Brock and forced him to knock a back pass. I turned away in disappointment, because I thought it was going into the keeper's arms. But Inchy came in, kept his feet very well and stuck it away. We were a little fortunate to get the result on the night, but since then things have gone from strength to strength.

I've played at Oxford a few times, because I played there once or twice with Bolton in the second division days. It is a hard place to come and get a result, and it is not the best place to go and play football either. The pitch has a slope on it.

They need the points to stay up, so it is going to be a hard game. I desperately want to play in it, but it is no use going out there if my ankle is not right.

I had my fitness test. I was OK running straight, but it was a wee bit sore on the turn. I'd have got away with that, but there was just too much pain when I tried a couple of block tackles with the physio. That was what failed the test, and I was absolutely sick. Kevin Richardson will play in my place.

Pat and Mimmsy will play, so Alan Harper and Fred Barber, who also came down as a precaution, are both driving back to play in the reserves. Harpo asked if he could do that, which just shows how much the lads love playing – they'd rather drive back from High Wycombe to Liverpool to play in the reserves than not get a game.

Oxford 1 Everton 0   **Wednesday 30 April p.m.**
I got bad vibes before the start. It was the worst I can ever remember feeling before a game. I just couldn't relax, I just wasn't happy. I had a funny feeling about it. I asked the boss if there was any chance of a bit of 'team spirit' – our name for whisky. You have a gulp before you go out. He gave me a Scotch and lemonade, which is very unlike me, but I was feeling so nervous about it, I just couldn't relax. I didn't feel right at all.

It seemed a wee bit quiet in the dressing-room. We all knew what we had to do, but it was a wee bit quiet.

The goals seem to have dried up at the wrong time. It's not the strikers' fault, because they've got their fair share, but last year we were getting them from the two wide midfield players and the back – Derek Mountfield got some vital ones, and Sheeds got more. But they've been missing with injury a lot – it was only Sheeds' second game back, and he had a good one. It was a tight game, and chances anyway were few and far between. But we got on top during the second half. Links had a couple of chances he would usually put away – but it was the first time he'd been properly fit for a month – so we didn't capitalise on it.

And they came back at us. Mimmsy kept us in it near the end with a great save, but then Phillips got one.

And that was that. Liverpool won 2-0 at Leicester, so it is out of our hands now. If Liverpool win on Saturday at Chelsea, they will be champions. West Ham won again too, so if Liverpool fail they are still in it.

I am bitterly disappointed. I have the feeling that the championship has gone. The game confirmed my feelings beforehand – it just didn't feel right. I hope I don't have the same feeling on F.A. Cup Final morning.

At the end of the day if you don't get points when you need them at places like Oxford, you are struggling. I've always said that the best team wins the title, and I stand by that. Luck and injuries even themselves out. And if Liverpool win it now, they are the best team – although it is very difficult for me to say it.

Not playing didn't help. I sat next to Neville, who has vowed he will never sit next to me at a match again. Some people can sit and watch a game quietly – I get caught up in it noisily.

After the game I couldn't even sign autographs to start with. A fellow in the player's lounge had a go at me about it, but I was just too fed up. When I'd settled down and got it out of my system I signed for the kids around the coach, but I needed a bit of time.

Thursday 1 May

I had a run and my ankle felt alright. There is a wee bit of pain, and I'm still having treatment all the time, but I think I've got a chance for Saturday. It will still be sore – it's one of those injuries which will hang around for a week or so.

I wouldn't say there is a funny atmosphere around the place, but we feel a bit strange. It is no longer in our hands, and personally I think Liverpool will win it now. I can't see them failing to get at least a point at Chelsea, and that will be good enough for them. It is not a nice feeling to have inside you. Funnily enough, the game at Forest was my fourteenth of the season, which qualifies you for a medal. It doesn't look as if I'm going to get one now.

It has been an in-and-out season. I think the lads have had a remarkable season getting where they have, when you think we were 17 points behind at one stage. But there is still the horrible realisation that you've slipped up.

The way Merseyside is, makes it twice as bad when the team across the park does it. It is great for the city, but not for the team who lose out. They must have had a horrible year last year, even though we were about due for something after 14 years, but they've bounced back again. All credit to them, but it is not a nice feeling.

Friday 2 May

My ankle is still a bit sore – the story of my life. I did a bit more running and will have a test tomorrow. We've just got to go out and win our games – we can't think about what is happening at Chelsea. I bet there will be a few thousand radios at Goodison, but you've just got to go out and do your thing, not worry about that.

The lads had their usual head-tennis. They seem in quite good nick, although the majority think Liverpool will win the title now. These last two days have been weird. They've dragged. It is like being in limbo – you just don't know what to do with yourself. You want a game to come up quickly so you can relieve your frustration on the pitch.

Saturday 3 May a.m.

I fancy Liverpool for the title. Chelsea have had a great season, but they had a few injuries and it has affected them. They were my outsiders, but they didn't have quite enough at the end of the day. And I've heard that Pates isn't playing today. I think he does a great job for them at the back, so I'm not too optimistic.

I passed my test. There is still some pain, but the block tackles weren't too bad, so I can get away with it even though we are playing Southampton – Jimmy Case is quite a hard lad. He goes in there and wins tackles, and he is experienced now – he knows not to go in when he's likely to get caught. He is not the ideal player to play against really when you are carrying an injury. But I don't mind hard games. And I just want to play to get the frustration out of my system. Watching the Oxford game was a nightmare – I've got grey hair now, and I think if I were the manager in a game like that, it would all fall out.

Everton 6 Southampton 1 **Saturday 3 May p.m.**

At one stage we thought Chelsea were winning, because the crowd started going mad, cheering, stamping their feet, jumping up and down. You expect rumours to fly around, but the crowd were so ecstatic that I really thought Liverpool were getting beaten. Then someone went down injured, I was over near the paddock and I saw a lad with a radio to his ear and I went over and asked him and he said Liverpool were one up. So we knew it was just a false rumour, but it had been an exciting five minutes. By then we were three up, but if Liverpool were one up you knew it was 'end of story'. So even at half-time we knew in our heart of hearts that it was all over.

So congratulations to Liverpool. You can spend all day analysing it, talking about injuries and this and that, but in the end Liverpool won it and we didn't. We gave it a good shot, but if you go to Oxford and don't win, you don't win the title.

I don't think Liverpool have played that well, but they have kept scrapping and scrapping and getting results, and they've got there in the end. All credit to them. You aren't going to play well in 42 games, and the games you don't play well in are the ones which determine your fate. If you scrap and get results you do it.

Peter Willis, who was at the centre of the controversy over the sending off of Kevin Moran in the Cup Final, was having his last game. There was more controversy, because our first goal was handled in, and he

164

could easily have sent three of us off in the second half, when Case made a ridiculous tackle on Inchy and I lost my head. We were struggling a bit trying to get the breakthrough, until Derek Mountfield threw himself at this ball to put it in. I couldn't see from where I was, but the Southampton players all went charging after the referee, I asked Links and he said, 'He handled it', but we got away with it. I think we would have won anyway, because they had a few youngsters in, but it just shows how luck can go your way, because we needed the breakthrough.

After that Links showed what a good finisher he is again – we could have done with one of the goals at Oxford – and we coasted.

I was going to come off at half-time, but Brace's ankle was bad again, so I stayed on and just tried to keep out of trouble – I tried to pass it and keep the ball moving. So Gary Stevens knocked me a couple of short ones which nearly had me in hospital again. He had tried to knock a long ball early on, Wallace intercepted it and it was nearly a goal against. His game just went to pieces from then on. It is amazing what a difference confidence or lack of it makes.

But I got away with those, and I didn't get involved in any tackling – just punching, which was ridiculous, but I lost my head. I don't even think it was frustration at losing the championship, it was just because it was Inchy, who had had this bad injury before.

Case hit him with a shocking tackle. The ball had ricocheted off the wall, and Adrian was just playing it back, and there was no way Case could have played the ball. It was a stupid tackle, Inchy went down and I went flying over there and ran into Wallace, who caught me in the face. I usually keep my head, but this time I lost it and struck out at him, which of course you should never do. It just goes to show that even at my age you can make mistakes.

There was a horrible 30 seconds when Peter Willis sent Wallace and me away while he had a word with Case. I just saw myself walking to the tunnel.

When he called us over he said I ought to know what he was like, and to count myself lucky that he wasn't sending me off, and I was. At the end of the day he was very lenient with all three of us. Case's tackle was ridiculous and that started everything, but I could easily have gone.

That incident summed it up for me really. We were all depressed. Gary Lineker left the ground with the match ball for his hat-trick and his face down to his knees. The realisation that Liverpool had won the title and Everton hadn't is not very nice. I just didn't know what to do with myself. I had a couple of drinks and went to my Mum's.

I was going to stay over because I am in for treatment tomorrow, but I was just cutting myself some lamb for a sandwich when the lights went out. Mum and Dad had gone out for a drink. I hadn't got a 50p for the meter and I was sitting on my own in the dark, so I decided to come home. I got some fish and chips, watched our game on Match of the Day – I couldn't face watching the Liverpool game – and went to bed.

Which is very unlike me. I won't play against West Ham on Monday, so I thought I'd be out into the early hours, go on a bender to get it out of my system, but I couldn't even be bothered to do that. The lights going out summed it all up.

In for treatment again! So were Brace and Derek Mountfield. We are really in limbo now. You just don't know what to do with yourself, there's no purpose any more. You are really gutted. None of us three will play tomorrow, but even that game has lost its edge now. I just can't wait for the Final. You just want to get out there and win the Cup. And I think we will win it.

Having said that, there are plans for us both to fly home on the same plane on the Sunday and do a tour of the city together. If we do get beaten I can't see myself getting on that plane. I'm not being a kill-joy or a bad loser, but if they do the double I don't think I could face travelling home on the same plane as them. I don't think I could handle it, and I won't do it. I shall stay in London or hitch a lift up the M1, but I won't be flying in that plane.

Everton 3 West Ham 1   **Monday 5 May**

After treatment I went off to a race meeting at Haydock for the afternoon. It was intended as a way of winding down, but by coincidence Sammy Lee was having a testimonial function there, so all the Liverpool lads were around. The first person I saw when I went in was Alan Hansen! I congratulated him. I had a chat with Sammy, who I have a high regard for. It looks as if this might be his last season at Liverpool. I can't see him staying if he is not getting a game. I just hope his testimonial goes well. I saw Ian Rush and John Wark, who was on crutches and must be really sick about his bad luck.

I also met an old friend of mine, the playwright Alan Bleasdale, and had a really enjoyable couple of hours chatting to him, so it was a good day out. He was the team coach when I played for Huyton Boys and we won the English Schools Championship and were beaten by Blackpool in the Lancashire Schools final. Obviously he is very successful now; I've read his books and seen his plays; but he always had that sense of excitement about him. He was always energetic, he had a tremendous liveliness about him. He loved being involved, loved the lads and he looked as if he would do well in life.

He is a great Liverpudlian and he was telling me about the time Souness and I went into a tackle at Anfield. He jumped up yelling, 'You dirty Everton . . .' and then he sat down again quickly, thinking 'Oh, God, I used to coach him when he was a kid'.

There is no avoiding the Final though. At least 20 people asked me while I was there, 'I suppose there's no chance you've got a spare ticket?' Of course there wasn't any chance, but I could understand people asking. This game is worse than last year against United, and I couldn't believe it could ever be like that. I expected this to be hectic on Merseyside, but it seems like a game everyone wants to see. It's really caught the imagination worldwide – some of the letters we've had from abroad have been incredible, not just from Europe either. We've had requests for tickets from Australia.

I got back in time to see the game. The crowds were fabulous, they gave us a great send off. West Ham had brought eight to ten thousand with them, so there was a real atmosphere and both teams had a go.

Gary Lineker's finishing was terrific again. He played up front with Paul Wilkinson – Graeme Sharp had been pulled out along with Brace, Derek and me – and Paul also had a good game again. Warren Aspinall, our young forward, was brought back from Wigan and he came on for the last 20 minutes in place of Links.

West Ham looked tired – in fact Alvin Martin looked absolutely shattered, in need of a rest. He needs to put his feet up in Colorado for a few days. So we were too strong for them.

Adrian Heath and Kevin Richardson played instead of Brace and me. Kevin looked the best player on the field playing in my position, he had a terrific game. I think he will be going, because he wants regular first-team football. Any managers who were watching must have been interested. He would do any first division team a good, steady job. He is a very good player and a good pro, and won't be easy for us to replace.

Kevin Sheedy looked in good nick as well, which is good news, because we have missed him a few times this season. The quality of his left foot to serve Links' runs is important to us. He has got tremendous attributes, and his injuries have been a real disappointment. He has played more games than I have, but I've probably finished more games than he has, because he has had to come off with injuries so many times. He is looking in good nick now though, and I think he'll be crucial in the Final. I've a feeling he just might set Wembley alight on Saturday. He missed the Watford final, he got injured in the Milk Cup Final, and he did not do himself justice in the United final, as I'm sure he would be the first to admit. It still rankles with him that he didn't do it at Liverpool. I don't know the reasons, but I think he feels he did not get a fair crack of the whip at Anfield, so I can see him feeling he has something to prove and being a match-winner on the day.

I was pleased we were so strong. It was a really packed bench – Bracewell, Sharp, Harper, me, Nev and Neil Pointon there on crutches, so there was a bit of talent on the side-lines. Nev was true to his word and refused to sit next to me.

167

Mark Ward hit this shot from 45 yards, which trickled to Mimmsy. couldn't believe he'd tried it and Ratters told me afterwards he had sai to Wardy, 'What are you trying to do?'

'Well', said Wardy, 'I know I can't outpace you and my legs ar knackered anyway, so I thought "what the hell, might as well have shot"'. Fair enough.

I think John Lyall did a brilliant piece of business in signing him. A a right-sided player getting up and getting back I don't think there ha been anyone better in the division all year. I know him from his Oldhar days, and I'm delighted for him, but I think John Lyall shocked a fev people in the game when he signed Wardy, so he deserves a lot of credit

In fact I think John Lyall deserves a lot of credit generally. He ha put a bit of steel into them and they are a well-balanced side who don give much away. People like Pike and Dickens, who work hard and d things simply, have done well, and they have got some quality players Cottee and McAvennie look very good players – so there is a good mix They finished third, which was higher than I expected, and it will b interesting to see if they can keep it going next year.

The crowd gave us a tremendous reception at the end. The result mean we finished second, which is meaningless really. You would rather finis. there than third, let alone fifteenth, but I like winning things, and ther is no consolation in coming second for me, and I think that goes for th majority of the lads.

There was one bit of cheer – I'm in the squad for Mexico, which wa announced today, so that is something to look forward to. So are Gar Stevens, Gary Lineker and Trevor Steven, which is a nice boost for us, i expected.

Tuesday 6 Ma

John Clinkard said today that it was the first time since August that or the day after a match no one had come in with an injury picked up on th previous day. He still had Derek, Brace and me in with injuries from earlie matches, but it was the first game of the sixty or so since the start of th season which hadn't produced a new face reporting an injury.

When you get a lot of injuries, people can wonder if something i wrong with the training or preparation – United for example have had lot of hamstrings. But apart from Sheeds, who has had trouble with hi hamstring, and Links, who had hamstring and pelvic injuries, our haven't been like that. Mine have all been tackling injuries, and so wa Brace's ankle. We haven't done anything different from last year, so don't think you can say it was anything we should look at. It has jus been an unfortunate year – Derek's cartilage took six months, which is ridiculously long time, but there were complications.

168

I did a bit of running – a couple of laps, nothing too strenuous – and it went quite well. It is still just a wee bit sore in the joint, but I think I will be in good nick by Saturday – certainly I shall feel as fit as for any game this season.

And it looks as if we will have a full side except for Neville. Of course that is a loss, but Bobby Mimms has done exceptionally well – the only thing I would fault him for was the goal at Oxford. Phillips struck it well, but he was done on the near post, which won't please him professionally. And having said that I couldn't believe that Hamilton got the first ball so deep in the box behind Ratters. I think Pat's position must have been off, because Hamilton was well into the 18-yard box, and the way we play he should have been off side. Ratters was looking for off side, and we shouldn't even have to think about it, Pat should take the line off him. And that set the goal up.

There is still no progress about my contract. Some lawyer in Belgium has contacted the boss about signing me and he referred him to my solicitor Zack Harazi, who is speaking to him today. I think the Belgian works for Cologne, so we'll see what comes of that. Otherwise there is nothing concrete. I've heard that Chelsea and Tottenham are interested, but there's nothing definite in the pipe-line.

I would like something settled before I go to Mexico next week, but it doesn't look as if it will be now. It is an important contract for me this time, so I am not going to rush into anything. I will take my time and do what I think is right for my family and myself. All in all, if Everton can meet what I want, I'd desperately like to stay here, but I've got to look at it financially and get some security for my family. Everton have had a reputation for not being the best payers in the past, but I think they have improved over the past couple of years – obviously they had to be competitive to get Gary Lineker and to keep Graeme Sharp. And to be fair to the club, you couldn't expect them to be top payers on the gates they were getting two years ago. Things have changed a bit now, and if you want to be successful you have to pay the going rate.

So I hope he can sort me out. That of course is assuming that he wants me for next season, and hasn't got someone in mind to take my place. There have been stories that he is interested in Ian Snodin. Only time will tell, but I expect him to call me in any time now. If I hear anything concrete from anyone else, then I'll go and see him. As I said before I'd like to stay at Everton because we are a good side. In spite of finishing second this year I think there is the basis for us to go from success to success. But without being conceited I think I do a good job for them too. My bit of experience means I can slow the game down in certain areas, I seem able to calm the lads down when they need it and get them geed up too, and the role I play helps us keep teams penned in when we've got them pushed back, so I think I have a part to play.

Mainly though I'm just looking forward to the Final now. I think they will have to fill me full of drugs on Friday night to get me to relax, because I can see I shall be frothing at the mouth by then.

Playing in an F.A. Cup Final against Liverpool will be an incredible 'high' – I wish every sports person could enjoy it. Money and contracts are all very well, but they cannot buy what the 22 or 24 players will experience out there. And I'm just thankful I've been involved with Everton. I will have played in two F.A. Cup finals and won the championship. Even this season, even though I've not played much and we haven't won the championship, it has been a good season to be involved in. It has gone to the last week of the season, which has been terrific, while other clubs have been playing nonsense games for three or four weeks. Money can't buy that satisfaction. And there's still the Final to come.

Wednesday 7 May
The build-up is really under way now. We're just ticking over in training. Still having treatment along with Brace and Derek, but I shall be alright.

Cologne does not seem very likely. Zack had a fairly unsatisfactory chat with the Belgian. There was nothing concrete at all, and the agent wanted me to sign a letter authorising him to act for me, which is not on, so I think I can forget about that one.

Watched the European Cup Final in the evening. It really brought home how much we had lost because of the Heysel disaster, because I'd have backed us to beat either of the two teams. It was a terrible game, and Barcelona couldn't even score from penalties, which is a joke.

Thursday 8 May
It is not my week. My car was stolen from outside the house, which couldn't have come at a worse time, because I had a few visits to make – last-minute ticket arrangements and things like that. Chaos.

Friday 9 May
We don't change things before a Cup Final. We had our usual Friday head-tennis, then travelled down to the Bell House at Beaconsfield, our regular Wembley hotel.

Derek Mountfield will have to have a fitness test in the morning, but otherwise we are fit and confident. We don't fear Liverpool now. It is just a matter of getting into them.

The hotel of course was hectic – filled with TV crews and fans. A lot of people know now that we stay out here, so a fair amount of fans come out. Some of the lads stay in their rooms more than usual, instead of coming down to the foyer, to avoid the hassle, but without being blasé about it, we are getting used to all the paraphenalia surrounding an F.A. Cup Final. If you can ever get used to all the press and TV attention, we are now used to it. It is just part of the build-up which you accept, and I think the lads enjoy it. In certain ways it settles them down more than anything. We've had Kevin Cosgrove with us from the BBC for two weeks now, so we've got to know him quite well.

Andy phoned and had a word with a few of the lads and wished us all the best – 'Get out there and batter them'. He's working for TV on the game.

I phoned Hi-Tec about the boots which I'd ordered for Mexico, which haven't come. It turned out there had been a misunderstanding – they'd sent me some other boots and when they arrived I hadn't seen the accompanying letter asking about my Mexico order. So I hope they can get them to me in time.

There is some press speculation that Barcelona are going to sign Gary Lineker. I don't know whether there is anything in it.

Saturday 10 May a.m.

Woke up about 8.30–9, which is quite late for me. Brace doesn't stir at that time, so I had to lie in bed and keep my mouth shut for an hour or so. I went into Sharpy and Inchy's room to rob their papers – Brace and I never get round to ordering any, so we just go and nick other people's.

The papers always provide a few laughs from reading the predictions – especially the ones which do a player-by-player analysis with marks out of 10.

Emlyn Hughes gave Brace a nice mention – he said he lacked pace and could be the weak link and marked him at six out of ten, which is very low on their scale. The lads latched onto that and gave Brace a hard time, so he wasn't too pleased about it. He has had a great season.

Everton 1 Liverpool 3   **Saturday 10 May p.m**

It was probably one of the best finals in recent years, a lot of excitement and good football, and I'm totally gutted, because we were 1-0 up and I thought we had them beaten in an hour. But you can't give Liverpool a chance and we did. And in the end we got what we deserved. It was a sickener.

That is two Cup Finals on the trot, which is not a happy thought. What really hurts is that I thought we had the game won. I am angry, because I think some of the lads bottled it. At 1-0, when we just needed to be strong in certain areas, I thought we bottled it a wee bit. It doesn't need me to name names, I think the lads know who they are. The elementary mistakes we made were scandalous. I think it was all about

171

character at the time, and we just didn't show enough as a team. And that is what wins you games.

If we had scored in the 10 or 15 minutes after half-time, when we had one or two chances, we would have won it easily. We were comfortable, and they had gone. Grobbelaar was dropping balls, he and Beglin were arguing, Kenny was shouting at him, and we were running it. But it just goes to show their strength, and their character, that they fought back.

We had battered them for an hour. We should have had a penalty – Sharpy was coming in for a cross and I didn't think Steve Nicol made any attempt to play the ball. Ironically it was the same referee, Alan Robinson, who denied us one in the 1984 Milk Cup Final when Alan Hansen hand-balled. They were two blatant decisions I thought. But we got in front. Gary Lineker made a great run and I hit a through-ball which went just where I wanted it, and he had got a yard on the defender, and although Grobbelaar saved his first shot, he put it in. A great finish.

And from then on I thought we were getting more and more on top. We troubled them with our pace every time we went forward as I had expected. And they were getting rattled.

I think that is why I feel so sick. We had the game won. And I was a bit disappointed with our back four. I know you play as a team and you defend as a team, and I don't like having a go at individuals, but I think if our back four take a good look at themselves, they'll know they made elementary mistakes.

Gary Stevens made a serious error down the right for the first goal. He knows that and he is sick about it. He had a chance to get the ball to me, and he had a chance to hit it long, but he gave it away to Ronnie Whelan, who put Molby in. And the rest is history.

We had a good chance at 1-1. We had gone back to the attack after their equaliser, and Sharpy had this header which was going in over Grobbelaar, but Grobbelaar did brilliantly to get back and turn it over. The second goal came from a ball hit over the top into space behind Gary Stevens. I thought Derek gave Rushy a chance to turn, which you just don't do to people like that, instead of being tight. It came in to Molby, who produced a little bit of magic in the box, and we were 2-1 down.

And we were so ragged then, I think because we were so sick. The boss took off Gary Stevens, who hadn't had the best of games, and brought on Adrian Heath. We had to change it somehow to get back at them, because they are a difficult team to shake when they are on top, and I would have brought Inchy on. But I always think you should try and keep your back four there. I'd have taken Trevor Steven off, because he was having a quiet game.

As it was, our shape went. We ended up with Brace at left-back

172

and me at left-half, and we were dragged all over the place. We did have a chance to equalise. I won a tackle and as I was falling, stabbed it through. Sharpy turned it on to Links, who would have been in if he had controlled it, but his first touch let him down and we lost it.

And then they got a third and that was that. I didn't see much of the goal. I'd got goal side of Rushy and someone, presumably him, clipped my ankle. I was a bit tired by that time, so I was still on the floor when I looked up and saw him sticking it in. But by that time it was like a bad dream.

At the end it was just absolute dejection. All the lads were bitterly disappointed. At times like that you just want to be by yourself, to try and get away from it all and hide.

We went on a lap though. Some of the lads just wanted to walk off, but I thought we'd given it a go and should go off with our heads high. On the lap I remember looking up at one of the gantries – press or TV – and seeing Big Andy and John Bailey gesturing their disappointment for us, which was nice. You need reassuring at times like that, and it can come from the strangest places! Seeing those two, who are good Evertonians and were absolutely gutted too, was a little boost.

Bob Wilson interviewed me on the coach and said he thought Liverpool were a little lucky. You can talk about luck, but a game is 90 minutes long, not 60, and at the end of the day the best team wins. And Liverpool won 3-1. They held the Cup up, we didn't.

A lot of people were saying afterwards that Jan Molby was the match winner. At the end he came up with the goods, and created the three goals. But he was as rattled as any of them earlier, he changed as the game changed. For me the best player was Rushy. I thought he was absolutely magnificent. People talk about world-class players, and he ranks with any of them. A fabulous, fabulous footballer. He works hard, he has got ability, and he is an absolutely brilliant finisher.

Then we went to the banquet. A loser's banquet is a strange function. Half of you doesn't want to go – you just want to go away and hide by yourself. When you are there you want to enjoy it, but there's this strange mixture of relaxing and enjoying yourself and nagging disappointment – or worse than disappointment, because we knew we should have won and had blown it, an intensely sickening feeling. So it is a funny atmosphere.

But in the end I had a good time with my family and friends. It was a bit slow to start with, and I needed a few drinks to get over my disappointment, but it got better. I got pretty drunk, and ended up having a singsong with my Mum and Dad – the Everton song – and Mr Sheedy, who has a great voice, and Inchy.

I heard at the banquet that the police have found my car. I can't say I was too interested at the time.

There were a few whispers that Gary will be going to Barcelona. It sounds as if they are definitely interested and have made moves. My contract is still unsettled, so we will both be going to Mexico with things up in the air, but I shall forget about it as soon as I get there and just concentrate on the World Cup and I'm sure he will too.

Some people were saying that we have had a successful season. I don't see it that way. I don't see any success in coming second in the League and second in the F.A. Cup. That is not good enough. If you want to come second there's no point in competing. You've got to want to win, and if you start with that aim, you aren't successful if you come second.

Sunday 11 May

I am still shattered by the result. I just can't believe we blew it – it was the first thing I thought about the moment I woke up. I didn't get the plane home and all hell broke loose as a result. Someone had obviously heard a whisper about Cologne, noticed my absence and put two and two together and put out the story that I had flown out to Cologne for talks. I was oblivious to all this, because I travelled home with Mike Morris in his car, and only discovered when I turned on the television. It was a bit of a shock to read on Ceefax that I was in Cologne.

Not getting the plane was quite useful. I wanted to spend the day with Louise, because I'm going away for six weeks or, hopefully, longer, tomorrow, and the police wanted to see me about the car. That wasn't why I did it though. It produced a lot of criticism; I was the only one who failed to catch it, and maybe I was a bit of a spoilsport at the end of the day, but I couldn't face it. The same applied to the coach tour around Merseyside afterwards – I could not handle the thought of seeing Liverpool with the F.A. Cup, which perhaps makes me a bad loser.

The boss phoned and gave me a bollocking about it. He wanted to know why I should be different. Obviously with the Cologne thing coming up it made it difficult for him, and I apologised for not phoning him and letting him know beforehand, which I should have done.

But I don't regret not being on the plane. I had a nice walk with Louise, picked up the car and packed for Colorado. I have to get the 8.45 shuttle in the morning, so it's an early night – but I still keep thinking about the way we blew it.

Monday 12 May

I caught the shuttle down at 8.45 a.m., which gave me a chance to read the papers – there was a terrible fuss about me missing the plane and the tour round Liverpool, together with the story about Cologne. When we got to Gatwick there were reporters all over the place. I suppose if you do these things you have to live with them. To be fair, I don't think any of the lads had fancied the trip beforehand, but Gary Stevens, Links and Trevor all said they had been given a tremendous reception and had enjoyed it in the end.

My boots still hadn't arrived, so I had to phone Hi-Tec. They said they had sent them, so perhaps Barbara can bring them out when she comes.

It was a long journey. We caught the 1.30 to St Louis. The TWA staff looked after us very well on the eight-hour flight, but it is still tiring. Then we had a two-hour wait at St Louis and a two-hour flight to Colorado. By the time we got to the Broadmoor Hotel up in the Rockies, it was 9 p.m. local time and 4 a.m. English time.

Some of the squad were in the foyer when we arrived, so we exchanged a few words about the Final – they were all commiserating. It was good to see them again, but I was shattered, so I went straight to bed.

Tuesday 13 May

Got up at 6 a.m. and had a bath, and I didn't feel too bad. I'm rooming with Hodgy again, which I'm pleased about. He's a good lad.

We – Gary, Gary, Trevor and I – had a chat with Mr Robson, who told us to take it easy for a few days and that we would not be going to Los Angeles for the game against Mexico on Saturday. Found out that the lads had beaten the American Air Force 11-0 yesterday.

I had a chat with Don Howe about the final.

The Broadmoor is a beautiful hotel – good rooms, a nice pool and a great golf course. The weather is in the 80s now, but the lads said it was snowing when they arrived a week ago.

We will have to be careful in the sun. Hodgy got blistered feet yesterday.

I started thinking about the World Cup. I regard being involved as a great honour, and I know that I'm not going to start if everybody is fit, but I have got to get into the team to be really satisfied. Gary Stevens is also a bit uncertain about his position. He is a terrific athlete, but he had a bad final and Viv Anderson has come in and done well, so he must be pushing him close.

Still suffering jet lag – I fell asleep at 10 o'clock.

175

Up at 7 a.m. – it's getting better. Gary Stevens rang the room at 8.15 and said we're playing golf with the lads at 8.45. It is a tremendous course. I'm not much of a golfer, but I enjoy hacking around, and what made it all the better was that we had buggies to take us around, which cut out the walking – the one thing I don't like about the game.

We were given our squad numbers today. I am No. 16, Hodgy 18. I think the team is numbered 1–11.

There was a friendly against South Korea. We won 4-1, with Kerry Dixon scoring two goals and Robbo and Mark Hateley getting the others.

The game was significant for the shortest appearance by an English substitute – 10 minutes, by S. Hodge. He got a sharp pain in his ankle and had to come off again. Gave him some terrible stick about that. Links came into our room to have a chat about this diary, and Hodgy said 'You're not putting that in, are you?' As you can see, I ignored his pleas.

I thought we (the Everton contingent) were getting until Saturday off, but Mr Robson informed us that we start training tomorrow. When we arrived, we picked up our Umbro gear, which is very nice, but there wasn't a track-suit for me. Mr Robson is lending me his, which is very good of him, until they get another flown out.

The news came through that George Graham has got the Arsenal job, and that Peter Shreeve has been sacked by Spurs. I spoke to the Tottenham lads about it and they were a bit disappointed. David Pleat is evidently favourite.

I'm still very tired. I fell asleep watching TV.

Up early again – I'm still having trouble sleeping. I had breakfast with Alvin Martin and Peter Beardsley, who are two real characters, and we had a laugh about Hodgy's appearance against South Korea. Peter is becoming known as Mr Fixit – he's into everything.

At 10.45 we all went swimming in the pool. It was good fun, but I was tired – I'm not the best swimmer in the world.

Then we went training at the American Air Force Academy, which has incredible facilities. The pitches were quite good too.

We did a lot of long shooting in training. My ankle felt a wee bit sore. I got through training with a lot of short passing.

Apart from me, Glenn Hoddle, Mark Hateley and Hodgy have slight injuries, but Gary Bailey seems to be getting better. I watched Peter Shilton and Chris Wood working very hard and they both looked very sharp.

There is a steam bath at the Academy, with the temperature 105°F. We were told at a team meeting that it might be even higher in Monterey. I couldn't believe it – you couldn't play football in that. I couldn't spend five minutes in that steam room, so I don't know what I shall be like in Monterrey. We were told that we would have a week's hard training there before winding down. Training in 105 degrees – the mind boggles. But he says we'll get used to it, so I'll take his word for it.

My weight is up to 12 st 2 lb. which is too heavy.

Friday 16 May
Still getting up early. The lads left at 12 to fly to L.A. for tomorrow's game against Mexico. There are a few injuries, so Trevor Steven got the call up and went with them.

Gary, Gary, Gary (Lineker, Stevens and Bailey) and I stayed behind and trained. I couldn't believe the weather – it snowed, it rained and it was absolutely freezing. We've gone from just a tee-shirt to track-suits, wet-suits in 24 hours. It was like England in December. I know our weather is not predictable, but the extremes here are staggering. Apart from shooting practice, which I took it easy on again, I enjoyed the training, which was taken by Mike Kelly. It was all with the ball – little, quick exercises. Then we finished with six shuttles which at 7000 feet really opened your lungs up. I found them difficult, and Links was blowing as well. We have a lot of work to do to get acclimatised.

Looking at Gary Stevens when you are struggling just destroys you, because he was not even blowing, he looked so strong.

Gary Bailey's knee has swollen up with the continual diving about, so he couldn't train.

The wives and girl friends all arrived about 9.30, absolutely shattered, with just the four of us to look after them. It is a nice gesture by the F.A. to bring them out for a week, and I think it is a good idea. We are away for six or seven weeks, and we are working hard, so it is a nice touch.

I'm not a great TV watcher, and I was just flicking through the channels when I came upon the episode of *Dallas* where Bobby comes back. I knew all the girls would be fans, so I rushed in to tell them all about it, and they were all saying, 'Don't tell us, Don't tell us'.

Barbara was shattered after the flight, so I got up and had breakfast. We trained hard at 12, just the three of us – Links, Gary Stevens and me. The doggies were even harder today. It was not a nice day anyway – the ground was water-logged.

Spent the afternoon watching the sport channel – baseball (L.A. Dodgers v New York Mets), basketball (Milwaukee Braves v Boston Celtics) and the big race, which was won by Snow Chief. We had a meal in the Sun Room of the Golf Clubhouse.

Went to bed at 11 p.m., still not knowing the score from L.A.

Alvin Martin told Barbara and me the score at breakfast. We won 3-0, which is a terrific result. Mark Hateley, who scored two, and Peter Beardsley got the goals. According to all the lads Shilts was in world-class form.

The bad news was that Robbo's shoulder came out again. Fred Street shoved it straight back into place, and no one knew. It has been kept quiet from the press, which I think is right because it would only create more pressure for him if it was known. It is a big gamble though, although he is probably the one player it is worth taking such a gamble with.

Hodgy is struggling with his ankle and is a bit worried about it. He wasn't helped when he was told of speculation in the Sunday papers back home that Stewart Robson is standing by. That just puts more pressure on him. I had a chat with him and told him to keep his chin up.

I had a quiet meal with Barbara and another early night.

A silly morning. Barbara woke at 6.30 and eventually got me up. At what I thought was 9 o'clock we went downstairs for breakfast and the only person there was Fred Street, the physio, which seemed a bit odd. I asked Fred the time, and he said '8 o'clock'. Barbara had got so bored waiting for me to wake up that she had put the radio alarm clock on an hour. I had to hold my hands up, I'd been done like a kipper.

We spent the morning sunbathing, then had a very hard training session. We worked for 45 minutes with a warm-up, possession and shooting practice, then had a game after a 10 minute break. It seems the boss was not too happy with the performance in the second half against Mexico – we were 3-0 up at half-time. We had a problem with fading in the second half in Mexico last year, but I think there are bound to be times

178

in a game when the other team gets on top – especially with international teams, because there are no mugs these days.

Robbo strained a hamstring. That is being kept quiet too.

Went out with Links, Fen, Butch, Viv Anderson and Chris Woods and their partners for a meal in an Italian restaurant; a very good evening even though we couldn't have a drink with it. They wanted to see Amanda Fenwick's ID to prove that she was old enough to have a drink, and of course she hadn't got anything with her. She is 28 with two kids!

Tuesday 20 May

Sunbathed all morning, had tea and toast and then trained. We did a 600-yard run for the Doc to check our pulse rates. It was a good run, but it was for his purposes rather than ours, and the lads weren't too happy about the distance before we did it – 600 yards looks a long way.

I felt quite strong, although I'm still feeling my ankle – I suppose it will get better eventually. I ran with Ray Wilkins in a group of four or five – I'm not sure who else was in our group because we only saw their backs getting further and further away from us!

My pulse rate went up to 160. It is taken immediately you finish and then at 15-second intervals. Mine went 160, 120, 120, 112 and then back to my normal 98, so it only took me a minute to get back, which was quite satisfactory.

In the evening we all had a meal together in the Penrose Suite, which is named after the man who built the hotel. It was excellent – shrimp cocktail, one of the best Beef Wellingtons I've ever had, and ice cream. It was a really enjoyable envening – I'm not a great lover of uniforms, but the lads looked really smart in their blazers and slacks. I had a couple of glasses of white wine – the first alcohol of the trip.

Wednesday 21 May

No training today. I had treatment along with Robbo (hamstring), Kenny (groin), and Hodgy (ankle). It is decision time for Gary Bailey. He is having a training session. If he comes through it without any reaction he stays. If the knee swells up again, he will go home, so it is a tense time for him.

I phoned Hi-Tec again. Barbara arrived without my boots. Spoke to Angela Smith, and the boots are back at Hi-Tec – the address was wrong or something. So they are sending them to Mexico, because we leave Colorado on Friday. I do need a pair of boots, so it is quite important they are there for me. Angela Smith, who is a former squash international, does their public relations. She is a nice lady, and was helpful.

179

A quiet day overall. We went into town with Gary Lineker and Michelle, and Kevin Cosgrove from the BBC, who we get on with very well. We went to a restaurant called Finns. The friendliness and good service you find in America continually amazes me. They make you feel so welcome. We had this lovely waitress and when we were ordering our starters I said, 'and for main course . . .' 'No, no. We'll talk about dinner later. You just enjoy your starters now.'

I watched the Houston Rockets beat the L.A. Lakers, which means the Rockets meet the Celtics in the final. I'm getting to learn a bit about basketball.

Thursday 22 May

Another morning by the pool. I'm getting quite used to this routine – breakfast, the pool, tea and toast and training.

Training was eventful. We were at the Academy, and we had actually finished when it turned out a mercury drum had burst and the building had to be evacuated for cleaning. Robbo was having treatment from Fred Street, when all these fellows came in in full 'moon' uniform. He thought they'd been invaded, and it was quite scary for a time seeing all the cars hurtling about around the base. We didn't know what to think.

We had to wait about an hour before we got the all-clear to go back in and pick up our gear. At one stage there was a suggestion we would have to just leave it behind – we couldn't get it tomorrow because we are flying off in the morning to Canada. Peter Beardsley wears false teeth, and he takes them out for training, and he was protesting, 'I can't go without my teeth'.

Gary Stevens and Links are in the team to play Canada on Saturday. I'm not playing, but as my ankle is not 100 per cent, that at least gives it longer to clear up.

We had our last meal together with wives. They go back to England tomorrow. There was another nice touch by Dick Wragg, the chairman of the F.A.'s international committee. He gave all the girls a doll as a going-away present.

Then we just went and packed.

Friday 23 May

It begins to feel as if the serious business is starting. We were flying out before the girls, so they saw us off. There were plenty of tears – as if we were going off to war, rather than just away for a month to play in the World Cup.

We left at 11.30 a.m. then had an hour's drive to the airport. We flew to Seattle and then on to Vancouver, which was only 20 minutes further. We arrived at 6.30 p.m. so it was another long day travelling. You don't need it. We had something to eat and then went straight to bed, because the lads are playing tomorrow. It is not the ideal preparation.

Canada 0 England 1   **Saturday 24 May**
The game kicked-off at midday, so we were up at 8 a.m. having our pre-match meal. The team talk was at 11 a.m.

All of us not playing were on the bench – they are talking of allowing all 11 reserves on the bench in the World Cup. I got on for 10 minutes – and I must say I enjoyed my little stroll. It wasn't the best of performances. If we had been up there in time to have a complete day before the game, it would have been better preparation. But it was a good work-out, because they worked hard and made it difficult for us. It was like a World Cup match for them, really; there was a good crowd in a nice little stadium and they put themselves about. The only thing was that they are more like a British side than anything else, so it wasn't that good a guide to what we can expect in Mexico. It was like a third division side against a first division team in the F.A. Cup.

Mark Hateley got the goal, and I thought once we'd got it we were quite comfortable. The good thing was that we didn't concede again, which is always important.

Until I went on it was the first time I'd watched us play in a competitive game – the game against Korea really was a friendly – and I still don't think we look balanced with three in midfield. I firmly believe, especially with the players Mr Robson has got and the way we play that he must play 4-4-2.

There was one worrying moment. Links was caught in a tackle and went down, and hurt his arm. They rushed him off to hospital straightaway and it looked really serious. He was obviously in some pain, and Glenn Hoddle said he had heard something crack, so most of us thought he had broken it, which would have been the end for him.

Later it turned out that he had only suffered a severe sprain, which is sore, but luckily means he will be able to play.

It was interesting to see Carl Valantine, once of Oldham, playing for them. He was a real favourite. And when Peter Beardsley went on there was this tremendous roar right round the stadium – they obviously remember him as a star from his Vancouver Whitecaps days.

In the warm-up match beforehand Derek Possee was playing. He hadn't changed a bit from when I played against him in the second division. I told him I had aged more than he had, he looked absolutely tremendous. Bryan Adams the rock singer played in that game as well.

Had a good night out. I must say I had a few drinks on the sly. I went out with Robbo and Butch, and I won't say they did the same, but I must admit I did. We went to the Expo and we were invited in to this Expo Club, which was fabulous, as it is entitled to be at its $10,000 membership fee.

We had a long chat about United, Everton, what it was like in the past – the three of us have been around so long now – and football in general. Interestingly they both think we should play 4-4-2 as well. And I think the majority of the lads think that.

Sunday 25 May

We were up at 5 a.m. which made me regret my night out. Another very long day travelling, which is twice in three days and will take a bit to get out of our systems.

We flew down to L.A. at 7 a.m. We left L.A. at 1.30 to fly to Monterrey. It was a nightmare flight. We ran into strong winds and had to stop to refuel. Storms in Mexico are real storms, there was thunder and lightening, the lot. Luckily I slept through most of it because I was so shattered from the night before, but I'm not the best of flyers anyway, and it was an exhausting experience. I just remember going down to land on this little desert airstrip. We had landed at Chihuahua, which is somewhere in Mexico – a town built in the desert.

We finally got to Monterrey at 7 p.m., where we had a press conference. There were cameras everywhere, bright lights. And everyone pounced on Links wanting to know if he would be fit, because he was wearing this bandage on his arm. He handled it all very well, said 'Time will tell'.

But it was nice to be there. The Mexicans are so enthusiastic and they gave us a really warm welcome, and you got a real sense of the competition for the first time.

Then we had a one and a quarter hour drive to our hotel at Saltillo up through the mountain roads. That we did it so quickly said a lot for our police escort seeing us through Monterrey so efficiently, radio-ing ahead to get the traffic lights changed for us. Security was incredible – police cars and armoured cars everywhere. We had three men with tommy guns on the coach. I sat at the back with Butch and asked one of them, Rafus, if I could look at his gun. He took the ammunition out and gave it to me and I yelled to Gary Bailey – it gave him the fright of his life when he looked round and saw it pointing at him.

I am shattered. I just need my bed.

Monday 26 May

Got up at 9.30 after a good night's sleep. Sunbathed for an hour and explored the hotel, the Camino Real, which is superb. The rooms are like a lot of little chalets spread out, so there is lots of room to walk. There is a tennis court – not that I'm likely to use that – and a pool. And the staff all seem friendly and helpful.

It was extremely hot. We went training at 1.30, which meant a trip down to Monterrey – thank God for the police escort. Robbo didn't train, just had treatment with Fred.

We were training at the Cima club – it is a beautiful club, although the pitch is not the best. When we got there we got out onto concrete, and Mr Robson said, 'We'll do the warm-up here, split into twos'. Obviously because of my ankle I wasn't keen on that and I dived in, 'You must be joking'. He was, and I had dived in head first, which I don't normally do, and which the lads loved. We trained for over an hour – 100 minutes roughly, split into two. Our pulses and temperatures were taken at the start, half-time and at the end. In the first half we had our warm-up and possession, then a game after the break. It was very hard work in the heat – even the lightest work takes a lot out of you.

We didn't get back until 7 p.m., which made it a really long day for the lads. All you can do after that is have your meal and go to bed, because you are absolutely shattered. We could really do with having morning training, but the thinking is to prepare us for the games by training at the time of day they are played.

Going to sleep presented a problem. When we got back to our room there was this music – or muzak – being piped in and we couldn't find out how to turn it off. It was driving us mad – Hodgy looked in the closet, in the bathroom, under the beds. In the end we phoned reception and there was this little nob on the bottom of the desk between the two beds – you wouldn't have found it in a month of Sundays.

Tuesday 27 May

Up at nine after a good night's sleep eventually, had breakfast and went across to the BBC hotel, where the Portuguese are staying, to use their phone, courtesy of Kevin Cosgrove. Trying to get a call out of our hotel is hopeless – you are guaranteed a wait of at least one and a half hours, but the BBC and ITV have direct lines, so they have made them available to us, which is very kind of them.

We went training at 1.15 again. The real killer is the one and a quarter hour coach journey both ways on top of the training itself. We had keep-ball, a break for vitamin drinks, and then a game. I enjoyed it but it is hard. We played keep-ball in an 18 yard square – three against three, six against three – and that is hard work in England let alone out here. Then we had a little game, nothing serious, just to get the lads passing and used to the heat.

I am not happy with my ankle though. There is a game against Monterrey tomorrow. I won't play. Hodgy is struggling as well. It is very

183

frustrating, because I haven't played now since the Cup Final, which is 16 days ago.

I'm feeling quite sharp physically, but my ankle and leg are not right. I feel it every time I hit a ball wrong. The boss is being very good about it. I had treatment from Fred Street tonight and he just advised rest. So I'm just trying to keep my spirits up – I know my chance will come and I've just got to be ready to take it.

The manager has decided to give us each our own little tip. 'The Tip of the Day'. You have to remember it so that you can tell him it, if he asks you at any time over the next month.

Peter Beardsley got his today – 'An early shout sorts it out'.

Wednesday 28 May

Dr Edwards has had a heart attack. I was sitting next to him on the bench during the game at Monterrey, and I thought he looked absolutely awful. Obviously there was something wrong and Fred Street took him out, and he was whisked off to hospital. We were told to keep it quiet until his wife had been contacted, because they didn't want her to discover it in the papers. It put a real dampener on the day, everyone was subdued.

We won the game 4-1, Kerry Dixon got two, Stevens and Barnes scored one each. It was a good result for us, because they weren't a bad little side and it was a bit dodgey for a time. We scored and they came back and equalised with their next attack, which was a bit worrying. There were about five thousand watching, and it was a good work out for us, although the pitch was a bit boggy – they had had six inches of rain in Monterrey – so you couldn't get the ball down and push it around. I still prefer 4-4-2, but I think we've all got an idea of what the team is going to be, and it will be 4-3-3.

Trevor Steven was taken ill last night, so he didn't play. I think he is suffering from heat exhaustion. I had treatment on my ankle in the morning and it felt better. It just seems that every time I train hard or have shooting practice, it flares up again.

A few of the lads are feeling knocks: Hodgy, although he played today, Robbo still isn't training, Kerry Dixon and Glenn Hoddle have knee injuries and Tottenham's Gary Stevens a strained stomach muscle, so I think we might get a day off tomorrow, or at least a slackening off in training.

At a meeting this morning, the boss said we were being limited to an hour-a-day's sunbathing. I think that is right. The sun is very hot and you have to be careful.

184

I had a telex from Hi-Tec today saying my boots are on the way.

The waiters and staff generally at the hotel are tremendous. They can't do enough for us. We've got the waiters into our slang – Bill Roffey (coffee) and Rosie Lee (tea) – and hearing them saying it is so funny.

Kenny Sansom got his tip today: 'Hand your man over, don't pass him on'.

Thursday 29 May

Up at 9 a.m. The boss told us that the news about the Doc was better – he is stable and should be out of hospital in a week. All the lads signed a 'Get well soon' card and sent little messages.

It was a cloudy day again with a bit of rain, so there wasn't much call for sunbathing. We had tea and toast as usual at 12.15 and then went training. A really great day's training: all skill and ball work, which was really enjoyable. I was working with Gary Lineker – we were split into pairs – and it was all down to touch on the ball, chipping, little skills like that. A nice relaxing day.

After training I was talking to Tony Smith of PA, and he told me that during the game yesterday a Mexican pointed at me sitting on the bench and asked, 'Did he used to be a player?' I must be looking good!

When I got back to the hotel my boots had arrived, which was very good news, because I've been struggling.

Until the Arsenal doctor comes out, we've borrowed the ITV doctor, Lesley Young, a very attractive lady. Some of the lads were thinking they might develop groin strains.

Quite a few are suffering from knocks – me, Robbo, Links, Kerry, Mark Hateley, Viv Anderson, Gary Bailey, Barnesy, Kenny and Glenn. Most of them aren't serious fortunately. And Trevor is still ill, although they've decided it is tonsilitis, not heat exhaustion.

The hotel has got an excellent video and games room set up for us. We've got about 50 videos to watch – tonight I watched a World Cup preview.

Viv's tip today was on free-kicks: 'Follow in rebounds at both ends'.

Friday 30 May

A lot more press (and Bobby Charlton) arrived today, which tells us that

185

the big day is coming nearer. So did having our pictures taken for our ID cards – you have to wear them and show them to get into games. Then we had a variation on our usual routine. We had brunch, then went training at Saltillo, about ten minutes away, instead of the trek down to Monterrey. I think that is a much better idea. I know we are playing in Monterrey, and Saltillo is about 4000 feet up, so it is different, but even though the pitch wasn't too clever, I'm sure it is better for us than that long trip, which just leaves you shattered by the time you get back to the hotel.

We worked for about 45 minutes on playing against a sweeper, but to me it was just commonsense. If you've got a good football brain you know how to deal with it.

Robbo looked really sharp in training, which was good news. And my ankle feels a bit better again, which is more good news. Glenn Hoddle, Mark Hateley, Gary Bailey and Trevor did not train. Gary Bailey's knee keeps swelling up after work, but it is too late to make changes in the 22 now. Trevor is still suffering from tonsilitis, but the other two are just little knocks.

Ray Wilkins' tip: 'Win the first knockdown. If you snooze, you lose'.

There was a reception for the teams in the Monterrey group down in Monterrey this evening. Portugal didn't turn up – they are having huge internal rows about money and there were even stories that they would refuse to play. Poland and Morocco were there however, and Ray Wilkins had a good chat with Boniek. The Portuguese management were there, and it seems as if they are a bit wary about playing Morocco which is interesting, because you would think that with Poland's record in the World Cup and us in the group as well they'd have other worries. We shall see. The Portuguese not turning up was probably bad PR, and it probably was important for public relations that we went, but there was a lot of standing around. It would have been better if the management had gone on their own from other points of view. We got back to the hotel at 10.15 and just went straight to bed, shattered.

Saturday 31 May

Today the World Cup starts. I was up at 8.30. It was cloudy again, but I really felt excited – great games every day for two weeks, which will give an added purpose to our days. The last week has dragged a bit, but now we'll have the feeling of excitement again.

We trained on Portugal's training pitch because ours was waterlogged. Peter Shilton looked brilliant in training. I've always thought Nev just edges him, and I still think that, but Shilts is so good. He looked really sharp, a brilliant shot-stopper on his line, and it is really great to think he is behind you.

The trouble was he carried it over into our match against a team of kids – orphans. We were meant to go and play them in Monterrey, but instead they came up to Saltillo. Shilts wouldn't let them score, the kids were hitting it from five yards and he was flinging himself about saving them. I've heard of keeping clean sheets, but that was ridiculous. In the end, with penalties all over the place and Ray Wilkins and Butch sent off, it ended up 5-5, which was a fair result on the day. We played ten minutes a side, the kids loved it, and it was a good public relations exercise.

I pulled out of that one – I didn't want one of the kids going over the top on me! But I'm feeling good physically, the ankle is getting better and I'm ready if needed.

Trevor had a light running session. He looks pale, but he is on the mend.

Glenn's tip: 'When in possession alright to be out of position; when not in possession, get into position'.

ITV put on drinks and a buffet for us – all the lads on Perrier water. The serious business has begun.

Peter Beardsley has become known as 'Jim'll fix it'. He has got a mind like a computer. If you want to know what video is on, you ask him. If you want to know what time training is, you ask him, etc. He is a great character, and it is like a club side – we all get on really well.

I watched Italy play Bulgaria with Robbo, Links and Hodgy with the BBC. The boss and Ray Wilkins were on the panel with Jimmy Hill and Bobby Charlton.

I was impressed with Italy, who were a bit unlucky not to win. Napoli looked a good player, and Ray said that he had just been transferred to Inter-Milan for some ridiculous fee like three and a half to four million pounds.

Sunday 1 June

Woke at 8.30 again. We had a team meeting on dead-balls from 11–12.15. Dead-balls are very important, a lot of goals come from them nowadays, but that seemed a very long team meeting on one subject.

We trained at the Tecnologico Stadium in Monterrey, where we will play our group matches. The grass is a bit long, and it is a bit bumpy, but not too bad – it could be worse. We trained behind closed doors, practising our dead-balls. Hopefully we will make them pay for us, because we have some big men in Butch and Mark Hateley, who is a good header of the ball, and Robbo and Links are also both dangerous.

From the line-up for the dead-balls, the team is as I thought. The subs won't be announced until tomorrow – they've decided after all that only five can be named, and I don't think I'll be on the bench. I think it will be Woods, Gary Stevens (Tottenham), Hodgy, Barnesy and Beardsley.

Not sure about Robbo. He's had a hamstring problem, feels his achilles a bit, and of course there's his shoulder. But it is probably worth the gamble.

We watched Brazil beat Spain 1-0 and France beat Canada by the same score. I thought Spain were a bit unlucky, they had their moments, but I can't say I was over impressed with either of them. I'd fancy us to do both of them. And I was amazed by the France–Canada game, I'd expected it to be about 4-0, but Canada gave them a good run for their money. France really didn't look too good at all. Funnily enough one or two of the lads said they thought it would be tight, but I couldn't see it.

Barnesy's tip: 'An early cross is a dangerous one'.

Monday 2 June

I was right about the bench. I'd had a few little chats with Hodgy about it, and we'd both come to the same conclusion. I'm a little disappointed, but in my heart of hearts I didn't really expect to get in for this one. But I will be very disappointed if I don't get involved soon.

We trained at 11. It was an easy session, but the lads looked sharp and confident, and after watching Poland and Morocco draw 0-0, we have every right to be. It was a dull game, Poland looked surprisingly tentative, but no one wants to lose their first match, which is probably why so many of the first games are so tight. I don't think Portugal will relish playing us tomorrow. But having said that, we still have to go and do the job.

That was what Argentina did – they beat South Korea 4-1, without doing more than they had to. It was an efficient performance. Russia looked impressive, particularly with the way they get men forward on breaks even though they are only playing with one striker. But Hungary were diabolical once they'd given away an early goal, so you couldn't read too much into Russia winning 6-0. I think Italy have impressed me the most of the teams I have seen so far, although they let it slip when they were winning, which is unusual for them.

Chris Waddle's tip: 'Get, give, go or get it and go'.

Today it starts for us. I did a bit of training with Chris Woods and Mike Kelly, then went to the team meeting. The boss told us about the hundreds of telegrams and phone messages he had received. You get a bit isolated out here, losing touch with what people at home are thinking, and that was a good reminder that everyone in England is banking on us.

I can sense a confidence and determination about the lads, and most important a belief that we can win it. I think we need a positive attitude – most of the teams out here have looked frightened to me.

England 0 Portugal 1   **3 June p.m.**

Travelling down to Monterrey we saw plenty of England fans, and the atmosphere was terrific. Sitting in the dressing-room, in a curious state, involved yet not involved, I was a wee bit envious of the lads getting changed and going through their rituals. It is interesting to watch the different types preparing in different ways, and it is something you don't notice when you are involved in preparing yourself. Shilts was doing a lot of exercises with Ray Wilkins, Robbo was doing all his stretches. Terry Fenwick, who is a very determined lad, and Butch were roaring half an hour before kick-off and geeing everyone up, while Glenn and Chris Waddle were quiet. Then the FIFA Rep comes in and checks the ID tags, and then everyone leaves the players on their own at 3.45, which is strange. Alvin Martin and I carried the big box of towels out to the bench and sat down.

It was a bad result. We went for them, we were positive and we missed one or two chances. We were the better side, and we just needed a little luck.

But having said that, I don't think we were as fluent as we should have been. It smelt bad sitting watching even before they scored. I didn't feel confident sitting on the bench, I didn't feel 'We're solid', as you do in some games when you know it is only a matter of time. I thought we looked stretched out as a team. We weren't a team, we played too far apart, units instead of one group.

Defensively the goal was diabolical. Kenny got a bad ricochet, but Butch was too far away from him on the cover, Fen did nothing and Gary Stevens left his man on the back post, so you had three defenders who did nothing. And from then on . . . they had one or two chances and I thought they were a bit unlucky not to get a penalty for one tackle by Fen.

Mr Robson brought Robbo off just when I thought Robbo was getting into the game, starting to win a few tackles. Maybe he had it in mind that Robbo was not match-fit, but I wondered about it. And having said we were the better side, I don't think we created many clear-cut chances. Links had one where he beat the keeper, but they cleared it off the line; besides that one I don't think there were many. Waddle knocked one cross in which Links stretched for, but I didn't consider that was a clear-cut chance.

We need a vast improvement if we are going to get anywhere. I wasn't impressed with Portugal, I don't think they are going to win the World Cup, they aren't the greatest of sides, and we lost to them, so where does that leave us?

There might be a silver lining in it though, because he might change the formation now to 4-4-2.

I was not happy watching it as it was. It looked disjointed. The players were working hard, but you can work hard to no avail if it is in the wrong areas. Glenn is out on the right, but that isn't his position and he doesn't stay out there so Gary Stevens ends up playing right-back, right midfield and right-wing. That gets you unbalanced, and when you are unbalanced you run in areas you shouldn't be running into, and you are working harder than ever because you are stretched out all over the place. And that was how we looked against Portugal, not a good side.

Shilts and Glenn Hoddle came out of the hat to have a drug test. Shilts couldn't manage to do the business no matter how much he drank, so he missed the coach and arrived back at the hotel about two hours later. He was a little put out, because he was not happy with the result anyway.

But no one was very happy. Everyone was a little subdued afterwards. New Balance, Robbo and Ray Wilkins' boot company, put on a reception back at the hotel, so everyone had a couple of drinks – nothing daft.

Talking about it to the lads, there were a few who agreed with me about 4-4-2. So it will be interesting to see what happens.

In the other matches Northern Ireland drew with Algeria 1-1, and Mexico beat Belgium 2-1, so all the Mexicans were delighted.

Wednesday 4 June

I'm absolutely sick. The lads who hadn't played went training, and I went over on my ankle again. I'm having it strapped up all the time and I don't know what else I can do, but it just went from under me, and it is sore again.

Obviously everyone is disappointed, but there is a strong belief in the camp that we will still qualify.

We had a long team meeting about runners from midfield and the back-four picking them up. Terry Fenwick was saying he didn't know who to go with, and there was a long discussion. But I just think the problem stems from the balance of the side being wrong. It is all very well talking about runners from midfield not being picked up by the back-four, and the back-four playing against one man. From the games I've seen there are a lot of teams playing with only one up and supporting him with runners from midfield. And we have got to learn, we have got to be able to adjust and accommodate that. But our balance is so wrong that we are doing a lot of work and not getting near anyone – the lads can't even track people because we are so stretched out.

So we had this meeting, but nothing was really sorted out. We haven't sorted out what is right for us. It was just a meeting – points were put forward but nothing concrete came out of it.

Went over to ITV and had a chat. I met Bobby Charlton – he came over to me and was quite complimentary, which was nice. He said he thought I should have been playing, which is always good to hear from someone who was a great player himself.

Watched the games – Germany drew 1-1 with Uruguay, and Denmark beat Scotland 1-0. It was a typical German performance, not the best I've ever seen by a German side, but they are always solid and well organised, they've always got people who can play from the back, they've always got great movement. I was very impressed with the right-back Berthold from Eintracht Frankfurt, who I hadn't seen much of before. They had Matthaus, who always has a go for you, and my mate Magath, who is a good solid footballer who doesn't give it away and knocks positive balls. They are not a great German side, but they are always strong and positive and they are the best I've seen in the competition so far. I don't think they'll be far away.

Denmark looked a good side too. They have plenty of ball players, plenty of ability and I thought they deserved their win, even though Elkjaer was a bit lucky with the goal. I thought Miller had got the tackle, and Elkjaer got a ricochet, but if you are being positive on the edge of the box, you are entitled to have a bit of luck.

And that has been the thing which has struck me about this World Cup already. If you get in and around the 18 yard box and can go at people you are going to get goals. Against Portugal we didn't get players in those positions.

We were so stretched out none of the strikers got the ball in a position to turn and go at people or play a one-two. We were so far apart it was difficult to get people in around the box, never mind near the goal.

Thursday 5 June
He has named the same team for tomorrow, so he has given the lads another chance. We don't know yet who the subs will be.

I managed to train. It was a wee bit sore obviously. I had a stirrup put on it – Robbo helped Fred Street put it on. Fred has been brilliant all trip as far as I'm concerned, an excellent physio. I think it is just a weakness in my ankle since the game at Forest – I haven't had time to recover, so it is just a matter of trying to get on with it as best I can.

We trained today doing dead-balls and little bits and pieces. It was the hottest it has been so far – it must have been about 110. I hope it is not like that tomorrow for our sakes – I would think Morocco will be more used to it than we are. But having said that, if we don't beat Morocco, we don't deserve to go through.

I'm quite confident. Obviously it is a desperately important game. We need to win. I don't think anything else will be good enough.

We watched a video of Doc Edwards in hospital, which was quite touching. He is a great character who has always been really popular with the players. I've known him since the Under-21 days, which goes back a long way, and we have had a few laughs in our time. I was delighted to see he looked very well – he's lost about half to one stone, and looked great.

Doc Crane, who has come out as his replacement, is fitting in really well too.

France and Russia was a good game – they looked two fine sides. The European challenge is looking quite good at the moment, because the Italians are going to be hard to beat. So are Argentina, but I thought Italy were unlucky again – their goalkeeper needed shooting.

Our waiters' English is coming on in leaps and bounds. They are saying 'Dog and bone' when the phone rings, and 'Acker Bilk' for milk.

England 0 Morocco 0   Friday 6 June
At half-time I'd have settled for the draw, and I think the lads would have done too, because everything that could go wrong did. Robbo's shoulder came out again and then Ray got sent off.

The camp was very subdued beforehand – everyone was aware that it was a vitally important game and knew we had to go and do the business. The substitutes were the same again, everything was the same – the same routine, the same pre-match meal, the same trip down to Monterrey, the same pre-match rituals in the dressing-room. The lads were really keyed up for it.

I went out and watched them warm-up. It was really hot – I was sweating just watching and wearing a tee-shirt and shorts.

The lads were confident of beating Morocco, and rightly so, but as the game got under way it was apparent that their technique was not bad. They had some good players who could control the ball. They had not got much fire-power up front, but they gave nothing away at the back, and they looked quite impressive.

And I began to get this uneasy feeling again because they were so good on the ball and had so much room. The lads couldn't get near enough to anyone to pin them down and get a tackle in. Timoumi and Bouderbala, who were good on the ball, looked to be running the show. On the bench we were shouting to people to go and get a tackle in, but there was no one near enough to a Moroccan to do so. We were getting stretched again, and just didn't look comfortable.

Then it all went wrong with a vengeance. First Robbo's shoulder came out again. Hodgy had been on the field for 30 seconds when Ray threw the ball towards the referee and got sent off. It was so unfortunate for him it was untrue. I didn't think he deserved to go.

Fortunately that was just before half-time, and the interval gave us a chance to sort it out. Obviously the dressing-room was in a bit of a turmoil. We had a lot of chat about how to play it with 10 men. I had a word with Links and said 'You just stay up there or get Mark to stay up there and you drop back, but one of you has got to play on your own now'.

But there was talk about keeping two men up front, and I said to Don Howe, 'You've got to play four in midfield with Links on his own up front, and be solid from there' and he said, 'Yes', and in the end that was what we did. The lads just all dropped back.

We have had discussions about when you press people and when you drop back. But over here you cannot play the typical English game, the way Everton play for example, shutting people down; firstly because there are top quality players at the back and secondly because it is too warm to do anything like that. If they are good players they will play through you with no problem.

And to their credit the lads did extremely well. I don't think Morocco have great fire-power and they were quite happy with the draw – they didn't go at us and try to beat us. But we got behind the ball and made it difficult for them, and we looked better balanced and more together than we'd looked in the first one and a half games. And I think that was because we had four in midfield.

Obviously, with Ray suspended, I've got a chance of playing now. In fact if I don't play now, saying I'll be disappointed wouldn't cover it – I think I will top myself.

But I just hope he plays 4-4-2. Even if I'm playing in it, I don't think the balance is right with 4-3-3. It wasn't against Romania when I played. We have got to have four in midfield, defend as a team and attack as a team. We've got to get people to come on to us, get behind the ball and start defending on the half-way line, which is what the other teams have been doing. You look at most teams and they do that.

Robbo was in a lot of pain at half-time, but his shoulder has been put back in and he says he could play again – no problem. But I don't think the boss will risk him again. That is twice it has gone now – in L.A. against Mexico and today – and the risk is too great. He has shown a lot of courage and he wants to play, but I don't think he is doing himself justice. He is not the Bryan Robson I know, who puts people under so much pressure and causes defences a lot of problems. That Bryan Robson is a world class player, but at the moment, because of injury, he doesn't look it.

We can still qualify if we beat Poland. It will be hard, but we have just got to go out and do it. We know now what we have got to do.

Shilts got caught for the drug test again. I thought that was quite funny. He didn't.

The boss didn't travel back with us to the hotel on the coach, and we didn't see him. I think he arrived back as we were finishing our meal.

Saturday 7 June

We, the people who hadn't played, travelled up the mountains to train at a monastery: a school for orphans and a place priests go to finish their training. The boss said it was 7000 feet up, the same as Mexico City, where we will be if we qualify.

There were seven of us – me, Trevor, Barnesy, Peter Beardsley, Alvin Martin, Kerry Dixon and Gary Stevens (Tottenham). Don Howe and Mike Kelly joined in and we had a little five-a-side. I quite enjoyed it, but it was hard work in the heat at that altitude. My ankle was a bit sore, but I got through without any real problem.

Then we had a discussion on how we should play, which went on for about an hour and a half. I said what I wrote down yesterday, that we have to drop off and keep compact and try to get the ball when they come forward. And I think most of us think that, but they sometimes want us to press when we have got teams pushed back, and I don't think you can do that against players of this quality. But I've put my point of view now, and we'll see what they say.

Poland beat Portugal 1-0. So now we know we have to beat them to qualify. I don't think that is anything to be scared of. I think we can beat them. Poland were a bit lucky today – I thought Portugal looked the better team. The Poles haven't looked that impressive so far, but nor have we, and they are through with three points. We basically have got to win – there are so many permutations people are getting their computers out to work it all out – but the only thing we can do is go out and win, and then we'll be through.

The boss and Robbo are having a meeting about the shoulder. Bryan

194

thinks he'll be able to play so it is a hard decision for the boss. Personally I don't think I'd risk him – and if he was fit, I'd play him in the back four anyway. But that's just a personal opinion.

Trained at Saltillo again – tunnel-ball and relay races which made a nice change. No idea what the team will be or what formation we'll play. But we heard that Ray has been given a two-match ban. I think that is very unfortunate for him, he didn't deserve to be sent off, but it obviously makes my chance of playing better. I will be very disappointed if I don't play now.

The boss is not very happy with the press – or at least with some of the Sunday papers. They had picked up on some of Robbo's comments about people not being sure when to press and when to drop off. It was said they had taken them out of context – I can't judge because I haven't read the papers, but there is a problem, and I think it comes down to the formation and balance again. We are so stretched out it is difficult to keep tight, it is difficult to get messages across and talk to people so you go in together.

We went up to the monastery for a barbecue. It is a beautiful spot, built on the top of a nice sweeping little valley – it would have been the ideal spot for a racecourse!

The only thing wrong was it rained, so we came back early. You come all the way to Mexico for it to rain. Ironically it started just as we started a game of cricket.

We watched West Germany beat the Jocks after going a goal down. They keep coming, they are looking strong. And we saw the Danes beat Uruguay – they were really flying and looked a great side.

We have been really well looked after up here. They put a canopy up for us with a couple of TVs in it, and we watched on them.

We trained at the stadium this morning – the temperature on the pitch was about 110, it was unbelievable.

From the session I think I'm in the team, and I don't think the boss is risking Robbo – the gamble did not come off. It looks as if Hodgy will play in his place and Peter Beardsley is in for Mark Hateley. But I'm still not happy about the balance – Chris Waddle turned his ankle over, so the boss played in his position, and it still was not 4-4-2. Trevor played for them and looked nippy and I would play him. But at least I'm in the team. I was given my tip of the day – 'Don't admire hustling, support it'.

Watched videos all afternoon. I was getting a bit bored, but the tension is building up now. The atmosphere is incredible – there are a lot of English fans around in Monterrey, and you can sense how important this game is: one of the most important England games in years. And not just for England but for Britain, because the Irish are struggling, the Scots are struggling and we are struggling, and you wonder what it will do to our national game, not just internationally, but the bread and butter league level as well, if we all go out in the first phase. I think it would be disastrous.

Tuesday 10 June

Still don't know the team, but there is now speculation that after Chris Waddle's knock yesterday the boss might play 4-4-2: Steven, Reid, Hoddle, Hodge. It seems a much better balance to me. I know Hodgy left Nottingham Forest because he didn't want to play on the left, but he'll play there for England and I think it is his best position. But I wouldn't play Glenn on the right because it isn't his position.

We had a good sharp training session – a quick, sharp passing game. You can feel the tension and pressure building up, but I love it, it gets the adrenalin going and that is what football is all about. It's a big game, and that is why you play, to play in the big games and test yourself against the best. If I play tomorrow it will be terrific.

Wednesday 11 June a.m.

10.30 a.m. If we play 4-4-2 we will win.

11.30 a.m. The team meeting. We are playing 4-4-2.

Hodgy and I had a note from Kevin Cosgrove – 'In the immortal words of Yeats, "Go Stuff The Bastards"'. We liked that.

England 3 Poland 0   **Wednesday 11 June p.m.**

What a good performance! We looked a well-balanced compact side; Gaz got a great hat-trick, and the lads who came in all did well. The supporters were brilliant, and it was really emotional in the stadium after the final whistle. The lads' confidence is back, and everybody is bubbling.

The atmosphere in the dressing-room is always a bit different at internationals compared to club football, but today it was really electric. When you talk about pressure games this was it and it showed. I wasn't really looking at anyone else, I was just concentrating on preparing myself, but it was a small dressing-room, and you couldn't avoid seeing how the lads were reacting.

When we went out for the warm-up it was absolutely baking. There were thousands of England fans there, and I saw a couple of lads I knew, Jimmy Coyle and Richie Harrison – Jimmy used to play football with me as an apprentice at Everton, and I was at school with Richie. Funnily enough I heard them shouting at me, and there was this big banner, 'The Quiet Man', which is the pub my father drinks in at Huyton, so I went and had a word with them. I'd spotted the banner at the Portugal game – I'll have to give them one of my shirts, it's the least I can do if they come all this way to support us.

I was confident we would win – I go into every game thinking we are going to win – but there is always this nagging fear at the back of your mind. I had a bit of a shaky start – the first two balls I hit were a wee bit short. I'm blaming the length of the grass! Then Fen let them in with a bad ball too, and they got away. Fortunately I think Boniek bottled it. I thought he should have gone for the shot but he tried to play the other boy in and with the help of Butch, Shilts made the save.

We got out of jail there, which we needed, because if they had scored then, it would have been backs to the wall and the confidence might have gone. I had a go at Fen even though I'd already dropped a couple of bricks, and to his credit he is a good character and he took it.

Then we settled and got this great goal. A move built up all the way along the left, then played in to Gary, who played Trevor in, and Trevor waited for Gary to get into position before giving it back to him. Really good football, and a quality goal. I was delighted for Gary, because he has had a bit of stick over the first two games, but he has kept on taking responsibility for scoring and he deserved it.

And then we got another good goal. Hodgy and Beardsley built it up and Hodgy's final ball in was absolutely terrific. He measured it perfectly, a great ball, and Gaz produced another good finish. A typical Gary goal, playing on people's shoulders, getting a yard on them and putting it away.

The third goal for his hat-trick was a gift, because the keeper dropped it, but Gary stuck it in, which is what he is there for, and what he is so good at.

And once we got over our sticky start, we got hold of the game and we kept hold of it, so we deserved it. At half-time we were absolutely delighted, we knew we'd won it providing we played sensibly. It was just a question of keeping it going, keeping it tight. If we nicked another goal all the better, but all we had to do was be compact and shut them out.

And we were determined to do that. At the start of the second half I was shouting, 'Come on lads, get into 'em', and Boniek, whose English is not too hot, perhaps, gestured, 'Take it easy, you're all right' and I heard this Geordie voice behind me, 'Effing kick him if he gets anywhere near you' and I cracked up. But it was a sign of our determination. Fen's a good lad.

The only thing that worried me in the second half was that I thought Glenn tried to hit too many long balls, which we didn't need. I had a go at him about it at one stage, and Hodgy did on another occasion, because we'd scrapped to get the ball and given it to him and he had given it away again, by hitting long balls which didn't come off. And at 3-0 up, we just wanted to keep it and not let them in.

I thought he played quite well, but I do think that is a fault in his game – at least as far as I'm concerned. I think he should do the Platini job, getting on the ball on the edge of the box, because he is very good at playing little balls around there to play people in, and if he goes up there, his shooting is tremendous with either foot, but he doesn't get up there and use it enough. He keeps trying to hit these 40–50 yard balls, and you don't see people getting on the end of many of that kind of ball, especially with everyone out here playing with a sweeper. We need to build up to the edge of the box, and then he can do his thing, because his strength is his passing and he has got great feet.

At the end we were really bubbling, delighted with how compact we had been. They had had one or two chances, but at least we had created some ourselves, and I thought we gave a good account of ourselves. It was staggeringly hot – I can't describe how hot it was. To give you an idea, at half-time you go in, throw your shirt off, and put a towel that's soaked in cold water over you. And I went in, and Viv Anderson threw this towel over my shoulders and I said, 'This towel's hot, that's hot water it's been in', but it was my body heat which had warmed the water up, I was so hot.

Another funny incident was when Chris Waddle came on as sub in the second half. We had these water bags to cool us down during the game, and he brought some on with him. He was laden up with them, and as the ball came towards him he dropped one, and stooped to pick it up instead of going after the ball.

I said, 'What are you doing? Get the ball!'

He said, 'What shall I do with the water?'

'Put it in the centre circle'.

So he did, and then was running round telling everyone that the water was in the centre circle.

We had a nice meal together, with a Mexican band playing, and then Umbro had a reception. Everyone was in high spirits, we felt so elated, and our confidence has come back. There was so much relief that we have qualified that the atmosphere was tremendous.

And it might have worked out for the best, because it means we now go to Mexico City to play Paraguay. They are a good team – Pele even tipped them as possible outsiders for the Cup – they really want to attack, they have two wide strikers who are real fliers, and I've been impressed with Nunez, whose hair is greyer than mine although he is quite young, and who keeps them ticking over. But I'm confident we can beat them, and playing them in Mexico City is better than playing the

Germans in Monterrey. Monterrey is too hot to be bearable – yet I am convinced that a European team will win it.

I felt sorry for Robbo. He looked absolutely gutted, and rightly so, because he is a world-class player but this must mean the end of his World Cup.

I spoke to Mum and Dad and Barbara, and it brought home to me how much our win means to the people in England, which I hadn't realised, because we are cut off out here. From the sound of their voices, you would have thought we had won the Cup, not just qualified for the second round, which we always expected to do. Obviously our early failures had really knocked everyone flat at home.

We went back to the monastery today because the Doc wanted us to have five hours at altitude as preparation for Mexico City, which is where we go tomorrow.

It is secluded, and we had a nice, relaxing day – this time we did get in a game of cricket, and the lads played cards and listened to music.

We had lunch there, then watched the Brazil–Northern Ireland game, which Brazil won fairly comfortably. They are improving, and I was quite impressed with them. The thing that strikes me about them this time, is that they aren't conceding much at the back. In the last World Cup they were a bit naive and that cost them, but this time they look solid.

Went back, packed and had an early night, because we are up at 7.30 tomorrow for our flight.

The rumours about Gary going to Barcelona are strong, and he told me that his agent, Jon Holmes, has gone to Spain for talks. It is amazing what a difference one game can make. He was getting a lot of stick and now he is the centre of attention. He is a level-headed lad and it won't affect him – he is just delighted to be playing for England, and I'm really pleased for him that he is scoring goals.

Friday 13 June

As we drove down to the airport there were people out on the streets to see us off – we got a really warm send off. We have all enjoyed Saltillo, been really well looked after, and the people in Monterrey have been tremendous.

The security was so tight again it was incredible – if anything it was even tighter than when we arrived. But we were taken care of at the airport, sent through to the plane without any hassles, and it was a smooth flight – we arrived in Mexico City at 12.30.

We got to the hotel – the Valle de Mexico – in time to see the last 20 minutes of the Scotland–Uruguay match. Scotland were struggling and some of the lads were saying, 'Get the Jocks out' and having a go at them. I wanted them to go through, both because it is good for our football, and because I wanted to see Sharpy succeed and lads like Arthur Albiston and Gordon Strachan who I know. I was delighted to see Sharpy playing at last – he has had a great season.

But they didn't. They could only draw with 10 men. As I know from the 1985 Cup Final, playing against 10 men can be difficult, but those were different circumstances. Jim Rosenthal said Uruguay had had a man sent off in the opening minutes, and although just from the 20 minutes we saw, Uruguay got away with murder with some of their tactics, particularly the time-wasting, if you are good enough you should beat 10 men in virtually a full game. Uruguay were a disgrace – you expect those tactics from some of these teams to some extent, but they went right over the top – but in the end Scotland weren't good enough.

I don't know the Scottish set up, but I cannot believe that they did not play Sharpy and McAvennie up front from the start. Both can get the ball at their feet, both are aggressive, and both score goals. I've nothing to say against Charlie Nicholas, Steve Archibald and Paul Sturrock, but I have to say I think Sharpy and McAvennie would have been better.

And how Alan Hansen was left behind is just mind-boggling. I think he would have been a real star over here, because he is quick and he can play from the back.

Saturday 14 June
I'm not fussy usually, but this hotel is built on the side of the M62. I must have got about two hours sleep – there's no double-glazing and I could hear the trucks thundering past all night. It was like trying to get to sleep in the middle of Bolton bus station at rush hour.

I got up at 6 a.m., and when I went downstairs I found that most of the lads had had similar problems. The great advantage of this hotel is that it is only 10 minutes from the Reforma Club, where we train, but that's no good if you don't get any sleep.

We went training at 11, but before we went I did a radio link-up with Alan Mullery. From his voice even he is excited about our prospects now. It was good to talk to him because I thought he had a great World Cup in 1970 out here. You do need his type of player – someone who will just get it, give it and then support – and I think we have our similarities as players.

The Reforma Club is beautiful. The pitches are the best we've had in Mexico, and training was a joy. We had a long three-quarters of an hour warm-up, getting the muscles stretched because we hadn't trained for two days, and then we had a little game – 11-a-side across the pitch. Everyone was in good nick. My ankle was still a little sore, but it is much better. The only thing wrong was that the pool had no water in it – all the lads were sick about that, because a swim was just what we needed. We had lunch there then went back to the hotel. When it rains here it really rains, and the locals say you can set your watch by it – 4–4.30 every day. A pity our kick-offs aren't 4 p.m., because that might suit us, but we are kicking-off at midday.

When we got back to the hotel we went into the video room – that's the only place you get any sanity. Going into your bedroom is like going into a prison cell – a prison cell with noise. I'd already seen the video – a Burt Reynolds film – on the Everton bus, so I was just bored and tired. Still the good news is that there are two games to watch tomorrow – Belguim v Russia and Mexico v Bulgaria.

Butch and Fen both have groin strains, so they were having treatment. Fen was booked again against Poland, his second, so there might be a place for Alvin or Gary Stevens (Tottenham) against Paraguay.

Links got a phone call from Michelle – Barcelona are offering £2.2M. He has got to go, and good luck to him. It will make him and his family secure for life.

Sunday 15 June

Footballers are known for moaning on occasion, but this time it is quite justified. The hotel is too noisy and the food is not good, but the biggest complaint I have is about the uncleanliness. Gary Bailey found a ladybird in his soup today – he did quite well to spot it because it was vegetable soup.

The hotel apart, it was another good day. Mexico won their match 2-0 and there is pandemonium. They don't have to do any more – for them reaching the quarter-finals is winning the World Cup. We watched the game at the Reforma club after training, and the atmosphere there was terrific. When Negrete scored with a sliced volley all the Mexicans went crackers.

And on the streets in the evening it was chaos. We went to see a film and we needed a police escort to get through. Traffic was bumper to bumper, people were jumping on top of the cars, dancing in the street, waving banners, all the cars were honking their horns, it was a real explosion of joy, and it was terrific to see and feel it.

Enjoyed training again. We had lunch at the Reforma club, then Robbo and I went out and had a game of head-tennis. I beat him 3-2. Even that makes you sweat heavily, and when we went back inside the lads were just about to leave for the hotel. We wanted a shower, so we decided to stay and watch the Belgium–Russia game at the club.

What a terrific advertisement for football it was. It has set the World

Cup alight – it must be the match of the tournament. I was a neutral – well, fairly neutral, I'd had a few quid on Russia – and it kept me on the edge of my seat, so what it was like for people watching it in Russia or Belgium I can't imagine, it must have been heart attack time.

I really would have bet my life on Russia, so that's another of my predictions down the drain. They are terrific athletes, a very, very good side; 7, 8 and 9 all looked brilliant, and going forward they are tremendous. But they do ball-watch at the back, it is a fault I've noticed before, and it was their undoing this time. There were a few questions about a couple of the Belgian goals being off side. You can't judge on TV, not properly, but I thought one was, the other wasn't – I thought the lad had made the run at the right time. But all credit to the Russians, because although they thought they were hard done by over those goals, there were none of the antics which the Uruguayans got up to. Their discipline was immaculate, and it was good to see.

But having said that I thought the Russians were a bit unlucky, the Belgians hung on in there. What I like about the Belgians is that they get behind but they keep coming back. There is a lot of spirit in there. Scifo did a bit, so did Ceulemans, and Gerets was magnificent. What a good player he is – he's as good as a winger going forward, yet he is a good defender.

We went back to the hotel and then 10 or 11 of us went out to see this film, 'Commando' with Arnold Swartzenegger. The less said about that the better, but anything to get out of the hotel.

Looks like Links is definitely going. Barcelona want him to sign this week, but he wants to wait until we get back. He's obviously got to go because he will be paid a fortune, but I bet he would swop that for a winner's medal.

Monday 16 June
The best decision of the trip so far – we have moved to the Holiday Inn. It's by the airport, but it has got double-glazing, it is clean, quiet, and I'm looking forward to a good night's sleep at last – I was up again at 6 a.m. this morning. It might have been a good ploy booking us in to the Valle de Mexico though – because the lads' spirits are sky high now because of the move. Everyone is walking round with smiles on their faces.

The Italians are in the hotel for a couple of nights – they go on to Pueblo if they beat France, which I fancy them to. I think they will be too strong at the back for the French.

We trained in the Aztec stadium today. It is an absolutely super stadium, but the pitch is a bit disappointing – it is bumpy. I don't think their method of replacing divots helps. They cut out a big chunk and replace it with fresh turf, so the grass isn't getting a chance to knit together properly, and it is a bit uneven.

It looks as if Alvin will play in place of Fen.

Along with Hodgy, Robbo, Butch and Trev, I did an interview with BBC – Kevin Cosgrove and Trevor Brooking – after watching Argentina beat Uruguay 1-0. We play them next if we beat Paraguay. They look a good side, but I was pleased they won rather than Uruguay. They could have won more easily, but they missed a few chances. They are another side who started slowly, but look to be improving. Again they don't give much away at the back. Uruguay tried to play Maradona man for man, and he dragged his marker all over the place, he put people under pressure and is looking really sharp. But I think we can beat them if we beat Paraguay.

Tuesday 17 June

A good night's sleep at last. The hotel is great.

We had a good training session – nice and light. Warm-up then a little game. It will be the same team except Alvin in Fen's place.

I'm getting tuned in to the game now. Did a lot of interviews – I tend to go quiet the day before a match, but strangely doing interviews helps my preparation.

France beat Italy. It looked as though the Italians didn't really want to win, they didn't do themselves justice. France looked great though – strong at the back, where I thought the Italians would have the advantage, and very dangerous going forward.

So that was another of my tips down the drain. The Bookies – Mr Sansom and Mr Hoddle – are doing quite well out of a few of the lads. They run a book on all the games, and it is a breakfast ritual to go down and ask, 'What are the odds today', and try and predict the scores.

One of the lads, whose name I won't mention, was trying to recoup his losses by betting heavily on West Germany to beat Morocco at 4-1 on. He was saved from a big pay-out to Sansom and Hoddle right at the last when Matthaus stuck one in.

Which just goes to show how difficult it is to play in Monterrey, and how difficult Morocco are to overcome. If I were ever going to put my shirt on a game, it would have been for Germany to beat Morocco. It was the worst I've ever seen a German side look physically. They seemed absolutely shattered, and when they had the lad sent off I thought they'd had it. But Morocco haven't any fire-power, and the

Germans are resilient. They hung in there and finally Matthaus put in a free-kick with a couple of minutes left. But it just shows what we were up against in the heat. Mexico City is better, in spite of the altitude, because the heat in Monterrey is killing for European teams.

There was a telex for the Everton lads from Derek Hatton and Liverpool City Council, which was a nice gesture.

We had lasagne for dinner, which was great. I love pasta and always like to have it before a game – getting in the carbohydrates like marathon runners do.

Wednesday 18 June a.m.
Up at 8 a.m. Our big day today. Hodgy and I had another missive from Kevin Cosgrove – 'In the words of Tennyson "Go dump on the bastards"' – only he didn't say dump.

I said Gary Lineker is a level-headed lad, but he is so superstitious it is ridiculous. In the Poland game he wore his lucky boots – which he had worn all season except in the Oxford game – so he now blames that for us not winning the League. He has got me at it now, I'm wearing the same clothes as I did to the Poland game – tee-shirt, shorts and a track-suit.

We've done a bit of work on the Paraguayans, because they have got these two wingers who can fly, and we needed to be aware of that. But if we play our game, get behind the ball and keep it tight, I think they are made for us really.

England 3 Paraguay 0 **Wednesday 18 June p.m.**
Once again Shilts had to make a couple of saves early on. I felt quite sharp from the start though, and I had just played a one-two with Links and knocked it in for Hodgy when I was caught right on my bad shin and ankle. That was after only about five or ten minutes. I'm not one to moan about pain, but it really hurt. He'd come in so late too. I don't know whether they knew I was struggling with my ankle, but it seemed a bit of a coincidence that I had just knocked a ball with my left and then got hit very late on my right bad one.
I struggled for the rest of the half, it was just a question of staying solid and knocking the ball, because they caused us a few problems. Butch made a bad back-pass, and luckily enough Shilts got back and then got up again to make the second save, and we were a bit shaky until we got the first goal, which settled us down. Glenn knocked it across goal, Gary went in for it but missed, but Hodgy pulled it back again and Gary was back up on his feet quicker than anyone and stuck it in.

204

At half-time I told Fred and the boss that it was sore. I'd already got a strapping on it, so Fred put the ice spray on it, and I said I'd give it a try for the first 10 minutes. I went out, and I was still struggling. Then Links was pole-axed, a straight arm right in the adam's apple as he made a run towards the box. He went off for treatment, and while he was off, we got a goal from a corner, Butch hit a good shot and Peter Beardsley turned on it and put it in. So I thought that would do for me and signalled to the bench for me to come off.

Gary Stevens (Tottenham) came on and the lads kept it tight, did the business, and Links got another, so we had won again.

I sat on the bench, icing my leg with packs of ice which all melted very quickly in the sun, and enjoyed watching. It was a tremendous feeling watching the lads in control. The Paraguayans lost their heads and tried to mix it, but the lads stayed calm and professional and it was a great win.

Hodgy, Trevor Steven and Beardsley were brilliant again. And I thought Alvin Martin came in and did a terrific job. There was a bit of pressure on him coming into a winning side, but he played ever so well. His brother has been out watching since the start, but Alvin flew his father out for the game, which I thought was a terrific touch.

I'm thinking of doing the same for my Dad for the semi-final, although I'm not sure whether he'll fly.

People say that Alvin, and Fen, lack pace, but if you are a good defender and can read it well you compensate. The best example of that was Bobby Moore, who was probably a better international player than a club player, because international football is not like the first division. It isn't blood and thunder, it's about drifting back to the edge of the box and picking things up there. In 1970 I thought Bobby Moore was the best defender in the tournament – possibly even the best player, because he used the ball so well too.

After the game I had my leg strapped up and was sent off for an X-ray. The only thing which showed up was an old break I'd got playing for Bolton against Barnsley, so I was quite pleased with that. It shows there is nothing seriously wrong – just a niggling injury. But it is very sore, and with the next game on Sunday I haven't got long.

Then I went back and watched the Spain–Denmark game. Denmark had looked so strong in earlier games that I really fancied them, and when they went one up I fancied them even more. But Spain got one back just before half-time, which Jesper Olsen won't be very pleased about, and Denmark just went to pieces. They went all over the place, didn't defend as a team, got really stretched out, and Spain ran out easy winners in the end. I'm quite impressed with them too – the goal against Northern Ireland was one of the best of the tournament so far.

It's a strange World Cup in a way, because the teams who looked so impressive to start with are falling by the wayside. Russia and Denmark looked very good but fell away when they came under a bit of pressure. I think they lacked that bit of steel, or character you need to win things – it's not just about playing nice football.

Laudrup looks an absolute dream when he is running with the ball and things are going well, but in the Spanish game you just didn't see him. And you didn't see a few of them. Lerby I've always thought, who played for Bayern Munich against us, was a tremendous fellow, but I'm not sure what he is like when there's a battle on, and Jesper the same.

Before the game Sir Stanley Matthews came into the dressing-room to see us after we'd been out for our pre-match warm-up. It was warm too. I'd met him at the Liverpool Echo dinner, so I had a few words with him – I don't shave on match days, and he said it reminded him of an old Arsenal player, Wilf Copping. I think he enjoyed coming in and being involved, and I think the lads all appreciated it because he is such a great name. Hodgy was absolutely delighted to meet him.

It is weird in the dressing-room before a match though – being left completely on our own for five or ten minutes before going out. Even the manager and coaches have to go out, there's just the lads together, and we gee one another up.

Thursday 19 June

A quiet day round the pool, just enjoying being in the last eight. I had ice on my leg all day, and was getting treatment. That was all I did, but that's all I've seemed to be doing all season, but at least this time it was round the pool. I'm not happy about my leg though, it is very tender.

We are looking forward to the game with Argentina – the quarter-finals and it should be a classic. But obviously because it is Argentina, it is being built up a lot. When I was limping up the tunnel at the end of yesterday's game, I was grabbed by a South American reporter who said, 'What about Argentina and the Malvinas?'

I said, 'We're a football team, so are Argentina, football is football and politics is politics, and the game has nothing to do with anything else. Let the best team win'.

We know it is a big game – the quarter-final of the World Cup is bound to be a big game – and they are a strong side. They have Maradona, and if you look at their record they are good defensively too. So it will be difficult.

In the evening I had a couple of white wines with the lads, and went to bed early. With an ice pack.

A big day for me – my 30th birthday. It was all happening today. Telegrams, cables and cards from home, including a telegram from my Mum and Dad, cakes from the BBC and ITV, and a card from the lads with lots of personal messages which was really moving, although some of them are unprintable.

I just had a day by the pool along with Links, who has a groin strain. There was a jacussi there too so it was another hard session for me. For Links it was just like being at Everton – he doesn't train there, he just has a bath and scores goals. I think he quite enjoys it. We were slaughtered by the lads when they went off to train. 'Have a nice day', 'That's right, Reidy, you relax', 'Don't have too many of those Perriers', all that sort of thing.

As we were still in the same positions when they came back two and a half hours later, we got it all over again.

At lunchtime there was a really nice gesture by Robbo and Ray Wilkins. They bought a few bottles of champagne, and the boss allowed us to have a glass for a toast, which was good of him considering we've been virtually alcohol-free all tour. We've had a few glasses after games, but the lads have been very responsible, as you should be in a World Cup.

Just as the toast was being made a plane went over and Hodgy shouted, 'He's a legend – he gets a fly past in Mexico now'.

If we get through the F.A. are bringing the wives out. I shall pay for Mum and Dad to come.

My ankle is easier today, so I have got a chance for Sunday. I shall have to train tomorrow and see how it goes.

Up at 8, had breakfast and then rang home to make arrangements with my Mum and Dad about them coming out. They have never flown or even been abroad, so it is a big thing for them. For their 25th wedding anniversary I organised a week in Spain for them, but they wouldn't go because it meant flying. They are going to take the plunge this time.

Then we went training at 9.15. We went to the Aztec stadium, but the FIFA officials wouldn't let us use the pitch, because there had been torrential rain last night. They said we could only use it if we wore flats, and you can't do that because it risks groin strains and all sorts of things.

So we went on to the Atlantic stadium, a club ground instead. We'd already wasted an hour at the Aztec. And when we got to the Atlantic stadium it was locked. So we were left sitting around in the coach while the police found someone to pick the lock. Then we couldn't get into the dressing-rooms, so we had to climb to the top of the stadium, come down on steps and get changed at the side of the pitch. We are playing Argentina in the World Cup quarter-final tomorrow, and it was like Fred Karno's army.

We trained for 20 minutes – we wanted to get back to see Brazil against France. I passed my fitness test. It was a strenuous one, Fred really put me through it, but I felt fit to play. If I get a whack it will be sore, but I can turn with only a little pain, so there's no problem.

We got back to the hotel in time to see the second half of Brazil and France. It finished 1-1, with France winning on penalties, which was a tragic way to finish a great game. I'd sooner play the game out and have the team who scores the first goal go through, if a match has to be settled there and then.

I was very disappointed for the Brazilians. I thought they had looked slightly the better side. They were very strong at the back, and if Zico, of all people, hadn't missed a penalty they would have won it in normal time.

Funnily enough before the game I had picked France, so I got something right, but the Brazilians were desperately unlucky. All the same France are through, and the way their luck went in this game, and the amount of good players they have got, they must have a chance now. I really like their back four, I think Amouros, Bossis, Battistan and Ayache are all tremendous, and with Giresse, Fernandez, Tigana and Platini their midfield isn't bad either.

I had a bit of dinner and then went to bed to try and get some sleep, my head buzzing. It is probably the biggest game I have ever played in – God willing there are two even bigger ones to come, but for the moment the quarter-final of the World Cup against a team like Argentina has to be my biggest ever game.

England 1 Argentina 2   **Sunday 22 June**
We gave them too much respect.

Postscript
Effectively that was the end of the diary. I was too disappointed to write any more at the time. The disappointment is still there, yet I enjoyed the World Cup. Looking back on it football is about learning, and I think I learned a lot in those weeks. Especially from the Argentina game, which I still have some vivid memories of.

Looking back on the day I have a lot of sharp pictures, particularly of the little things which will stick in my mind. 12 o'clock kick-offs are weird because you have your pre-match meal at 8 a.m., and then you are there before you have time to think about it. I had my usual breakfast of cornflakes and banana. Then I remember the trip to the stadium, with he fabulous colours everywhere, the England and Argentina fans, the colourfulness of the whole spectacle and the people, with Gary Bailey's cassette machine providing its usual great service, giving us Beatles and Stones, and the incredible security. Everything about it was terrific.

In the dressing-room just warming up, Ray Wilkins, who was on the bench, was in the warm-up room, Shilts was doing his exercises, Glenn Hoddle was sitting by the wall with ear-phones on. I asked him what he was listening to and he made a gesture like an eagle – he is a big fan of The Eagles, and that was his way of relaxing. Kenny and Butch were shouting and joking, Gary Lineker was lying on his back with his feet on a bench, relaxing his legs. By contrast Robbo was lying on a bench in a corner quietly, obviously disappointed, and I couldn't help feeling sorry for him because he is a great lad and a great player. I caught his eye for a moment.

Then we went out and were kicking in and I heard this shout 'Reidy' from behind me, and I looked around trying to see who it was and then I spotted George Courtney, the referee, and went over and had a chat with him.

Everything about it was tremendous. I remember just walking up the tunnel beside the Argentinians ready to play a game of football which a lot of people would be watching all over the world. There was a full house inside the stadium. And I remember standing for the National Anthem. Nat Lofthouse talks about that when he does after dinner speeches, and captures it very well. I'm not the greatest of patriots, but I love playing for England, and it does stir you. You feel it at Wembley, but in a World Cup on the other side of the World, you feel it even more. It sounds corny but you feel 10 feet tall and there is this tremendous pride.

The build-up was terrific, and fulfilled all my expectations. And then we got into the game. And as I said, I just thought we showed them too much respect. I thought if we had been more confident in our own ability, we could have beaten them. I thought we played it wrong. But having said that, they did not cause us any problems until Maradona 'scored'.

At half-time I went in and said, 'If that's the best they can play, we can win this game if we play anything like. Come on, let's have a go!'

I thought our back-four had just settled for doing the defensive side of their job. If we had got the full-backs round the back of them, like we did against Poland, and if we had come out playing from the back a bit more, we could have beaten them. I said to the back-four at the interval, 'Come on, let's try and get it together,' because I thought we had a great chance.

I got a kick on my leg early on. I saw the boy coming and I was able to ride it, but it did land on my ankle and shook it up a bit. I was alright though – I couldn't say it hindered me in any way. But in the excitement and that atmosphere you could play with a broken leg – which was what I virtually was doing it subsequently turned out. Adrenalin is amazing.

In the second half I just remember a ball on the edge of the box and Hodgy trying to volley it back to Shilts, when he could have hoofed it away. Initially I thought Maradona had just run in and beaten Shilts to it and headed it in, but then I saw him running away and Shilts and Terry Fenwick racing after the referee and I knew something was wrong with it. But the referee and the linesman gave it and there was nothing we could do.

Shilts was adamant that he had handled it, and of course we know from looking at it later on TV that he had. I just had the feeling that Shilts might have taken everything – the ball was there so he had the chance to take Maradona as well. And I think he will look at himself and think, 'I should have taken everything'.

But there are no complaints. If one of our lads had done it I'd have said, 'Great son'. If I'd done it I don't think I'd have gone to the referee and said, 'I handled it', especially in a World Cup quarter-final.

And the second goal was a wee bit special. I think Glenn tried something and Maradona caught it. It stuck between his legs. I was thereabouts and he turned inside me and away from Beardsley at the same time. He has got electric pace. People said afterwards that I was injured otherwise I might have caught him. There was no way I'd have caught him even with a jet up my back.

Then it was like that TV programme in which they throw a boomerang and then stop the film. It was like watching in slow motion as he went at defenders. I thought Fen was a bit unlucky, because he had already been booked so he had to watch the way he went in. You can say that Butch might have done something; that Shilts perhaps went down a fraction early. But after saying all that, he is brilliant at running with the ball. He is so quick, so strong and his control is tremendous. Sometimes you just have to hold your hand up and say it was down to the lad's brilliance, and that was one of those times. And I thought his goal in the semi-final against Belgium, when he had already gone past two on his way into the box and then went past Gerets, who is an outstanding quick defender, as if he wasn't there, just confirmed it.

After that 'No 16' was held up and I went off. I was disappointed because I felt all right – to this day I think I could have played on. But the boss wanted a change and Chris Waddle came on.

Of course it is an easy thing to say with hindsight, but I think I'd have put Barnesy on earlier. I felt Chris had already had his chances in the early games, and I thought Barnesy deserved his. I've been disappointed when he has started games, I've thought, 'Come on, do it now,' and he hasn't. I think he lacks a bit of self-confidence, especially in international football, but when he comes on as sub he looks a different player. He's brilliant then, he looks as if he wants to get at people.

As it was he went on for the last 10 minutes and put them under pressure. He whipped one in and Gary scored. Then in the last couple of minutes he whipped another in. I was on the bench and I was on my feet shouting, 'It's in', because I could see Gary coming in, and to this day I don't know how it didn't go in, but you have got to give the credit to the defender for getting in front of Gary, and getting a touch.

And at the last we had them going. You might say the substitutions made the difference, but I'd also put it down to a change in our attitude. We'd got Kenny Sansom and Gary Stevens going forward at last, Butch was looking to come up too, we had the men from the back going forward, which is what you have to do. Football is not about attackers attacking and defenders defending any more. Everyone gets back on defence now, especially in international football, and you've got to get people forward as well. I don't think we attacked as a team well enough. In international football you start attacking from the back, because that is where you get spare men. And in the end that last 10 minutes confirms my view that we should have been more positive earlier. We were unlucky, but at the end of the day, unlucky or not, we were beaten. But I think if we had got at them, it might have been different. Fortune often favours the brave, and I don't think we were brave enough.

Afterwards I think we just felt numb. I don't think it sank in until the following morning when we were going home, that we were out, when we could have been in the semi-final. In the evening we had a good night. Of course we were bitterly disappointed, but we drowned our sorrows. I certainly drank a bit, and I must have been just knocking it back, because I had an early night and I had had a few by then. I thought I learned a lot from it. I enjoyed the chance to talk to Ron Greenwood and Dave Sexton and Howard Wilkinson. And it made me think about the way we play our football. I don't go along with the idea that we have to adopt continental styles wholesale and educate our fans to accept it, because they wouldn't. And our way is successful in European competitions, we have a good League, and some of the biggest crowds in the world, who like watching the way we play. But at international level, if we are to be successful, we have got to change. We have got to be more adaptable, like the Germans, when they lost Augenthaler, they were able to change their system, use Forster, or Berthold, or Matthaus, or even Briegel, depending what they wanted. I think we were right not to man-mark Maradona, because it is foreign to the way we play, and it is very difficult to suddenly change to playing that way. But perhaps we have got to start bringing in players into the international squad who can do that, so that we have more options.

When Kenny Dalglish started using a sweeper at Anfield I could not see what he was trying to do. And I am still not sure that it is the best way for them to play, but possibly he was looking to the future and trying things out.

And we have got to have defenders who can play from the back – you have to do that at international level. Also it is difficult to pressure teams our way in internationals. It is difficult to do it at Wembley with its wide open spaces. It is impossible to do it in Mexico in the heat. So you have got to be able to change. That was what impressed me about Argentina. They had done their homework on us, and changed things a little. They sat the two lads in the holes in front of our wide midfield players and let our back-four have the ball. They were good tactically.

I'm a great believer in playing to your strengths. If we have to beat Spain in a crucial game to qualify for the next World Cup, I'd take them to Goodison, or Old Trafford, or St James' Park and steam-roller them. But if you are away to West Germany and you go and try and pressure them, they will just play through you and you won't be able to do it. And even less are you likely to do it successfully in Mexico.

Tactically we are a bit behind. And technically, at least among our back players.

In the end Argentina probably deserved it. They had Maradona, who is a great player. I still think George Best at his peak was better, I think he is the greatest player I have ever seen, but Maradona had the chance to do it on the great stage, which Best never did, and he took it. If I have any reservations it is that great player that he is, he goes down too easily sometimes, and it doesn't do him any credit. I got close to him a couple of times, but there were times when I wasn't even close to catching him and he was falling all over the place. But his power and speed and control were stunning. Argentina were more than just Maradona though. They were strong at the back. The two central defenders were solid. And they worked hard in midfield.

But it was an exciting adventure. I came home nursing my ankle and shin, which would not clear up. Eventually I had a bone-scan, which suggested a stress-fracture, probably dating back to the game at Nottingham Forest. So I had been playing with it right through the World Cup. As I said earlier, the effect of adrenalin is amazing, I played against Argentina with hardly a twinge because I was so revved up.

When I got that diagnosis I was delighted, because it was something concrete. I was told to rest it for a month. There was still no improvement, so it was put in plaster for another month, and the chance of starting this season disappeared. Finally, at the start of October I thought I was ready. I played one 'A' team match, played half a reserve Derby against Liverpool, in a fantastic atmosphere with everyone steaming in, but I was struggling again. This time, I hope, we have got to the root cause – that old break against Barnsley had calcified, the muscle had stuck to the bone trapping a nerve. I have now had an operation, and tomorrow, November 10, I start training – ready to win the championship this season instead.

INDEX